Living it Arg

Living it Arg

JAMES ARGENT

**SIMON &
SCHUSTER**

London · New York · Sydney · Toronto · New Delhi

A CBS COMPANY

For Tash, for all the lifts and all the wrestling
moves I practised on you

First published in Great Britain by Simon & Schuster UK Ltd, 2014
A CBS COMPANY

1 3 5 7 9 10 8 6 4 2

Simon & Schuster UK Ltd
1st Floor
222 Gray's Inn Road
London WC1X 8HB

www.simonandschuster.co.uk

Simon & Schuster Australia,
Sydney

Simon & Schuster India,
New Delhi

A CIP catalogue record for this book
is available from the British Library

Hardback ISBN: 978-1-47113-440-1
eBook ISBN: 978-1-47113-442-5

Typeset in the UK by M Rules
Printed in the UK by CPI Group (UK) Ltd, Croydon, CR0 4YY

CONTENTS

INTRODUCTION

It's not every day that you get to ride in the back of a chauffeur-driven Rolls-Royce. I could feel the butterflies in my stomach as I straightened my tie and settled into the deep leather seats. I was about to attend the biggest celebrity bash in the television calendar – and I was a bag of nerves.

Just a few months earlier I could never have dreamed that I'd be whisked to the red carpet in such a posh set of wheels. If the truth were known, I was still more used to going everywhere by pushbike.

The previous summer I'd been down on my luck after a disastrous stint working in Spain. When I'd arrived back in the UK, I had no job, no girlfriend and very little cash. I was just an everyday geezer from Essex struggling to make my way in life. Then everything changed after a single phone call.

'Hello, James. I'm calling you from a company called Lime Pictures and we'd like you to come in for a chat about a new television show called *The Only Way Is Essex*,' the producer told me.

That was when it all began.

Joining *TOWIE* was the start of a roller-coaster ride that would take me overnight from being somebody who couldn't hold down a job in Waitrose to starring with my best mate Mark Wright in Britain's best-loved reality show. My life was transformed, but it happened so quickly that I almost didn't have time to catch my breath.

As I sat in the back of that Roller I had good reason to pinch myself. I'd just been reunited with the love of my life, Lydia Bright, who was sitting by my side looking stunning in a strapless ball gown. I was wearing my best suit and we were on the guest list to attend the BAFTAs at the Grosvenor House Hotel, where we were due to join the likes of Trevor McDonald and David Attenborough (not to mention the casts of all the top shows such as *Downton Abbey*, *EastEnders* and *Coronation Street*).

TOWIE had stunned everybody by being nominated against all the odds for a BAFTA. I'd been biting my nails in the hope that we'd win, although I didn't rate our chances. As far as most people in the telly world were concerned, we were just a bunch of newcomers with fake tans and a few lines of slick banter. But, as the Roller approached the Grosvenor, something was about to happen that made me realise just how much my life had changed.

'Can you hear a noise in the distance?' I asked Lydia.

'It's sounds like people screaming and cheering,' she replied.

As we stepped out of the car I assumed we must have arrived at the same time as some A-list celeb, because suddenly all the camera flashguns went off at the same time and the light nearly blinded us. The paparazzi were firing off shots like mad at whoever was close by. As we walked up the red carpet I looked over my shoulder to see the cause of all the fuss. And then I realised . . . it was Lydia and me that the press were going crazy for.

'Arg! Arg! Over here,' shouted the reporters.

There were journalists everywhere and they were ignoring all the other guests, but they were desperate to speak to anyone from *TOWIE*.

That was the moment when I really knew we'd arrived. It was reem, as Joey Essex would say. Later that evening, we stuck it up the rest of the TV industry by winning our BAFTA and we celebrated long into the night.

This is the story of how I went from being an ordinary bloke to someone who's famous for being on the telly. I'm lucky enough now to earn a great income doing a job that I love more than anything in the world. It would be great to know what you think of my story, so please feel free to tweet me @realjamesargent so I can find out.

I hope you enjoy it.

1

GROWING UP IN ESSEX: FRIENDS, FAMILY ... AND MICHAEL JACKSON!

If you've ever seen me fooling around on *The Only Way Is Essex* you can probably guess that I had a happy childhood, although, like everybody else, I had my ups and downs. I've always been the sort of bloke who is game for a laugh and I reckon that's because I grew up surrounded by such a loving family. I was also lucky to have a good bunch of mates, most of whom I'm still in touch with today.

Essex during the nineties was an exciting place to grow up. I reckon that Essex is completely different from anywhere else because of the way we dress and act. We love nothing more than gelling up our hair and slipping into a pair of Gucci loafers. A lot of the people in Essex are very glamorous – they've got big houses and they drive expensive cars – but they're not posh. It's the sort of place that you could say has

1

middle-class money but has a working-class mentality, and I mean that as a compliment.

We like to spend our cash on our homes and our holidays, and, if there's a bit left over, on a nice wristwatch, too. It's not a violent place but there are a lot of tough characters. You get the odd fight outside pubs or nightclubs, but generally it's a very safe place to be. It's very rare that people get mugged or attacked.

The majority of the Essex crowd are from families who come from the East End of London and they moved out to enjoy a more comfortable lifestyle. We call the area I am from the Golden Triangle because it's a little bubble in west Essex that consists of Chigwell, Woodford and Loughton. Out here we have the best of both worlds. We're close to Epping Forest but we're only half an hour from the City of London and the West End. It's a very family-oriented place and the people here value their friendships. The bars and clubs are always packed with punters who are having a good time and there's a lot of effort spent on looking good and dressing well.

Even as a little kid, I can remember bugging my mum and dad to buy me the latest clothes. I was into sports gear by Nike, but what I really wanted when I was about ten was a shirt by Ben Sherman. I'd seen it while I was out with my two best mates from primary school, Richard and David. My mum was cooking in the kitchen one day when I approached her about it.

'Mum, if I'm good can I have some money for a new shirt, please?' I asked.

'You've got lots of shirts, James. Why do you need another one?'

'Go on, Mum, I want to buy a Ben Sherman,' I pleaded. 'Richard and David are going to get one, too. We're all going to wear different colours so we can look cool when we go out together.'

Mum liked to treat me occasionally and she agreed I could have the shirt if I promised to tidy up after myself around the house and keep my room clean. It was on my last day at primary school that I went with Richard and David to buy our prized shirts.

We went up the high street, where I chose a lemon-coloured one. We felt like the most grown-up geezers in Essex, even though we were still just boys. We wore our new tops with pride all through the summer holidays.

My mum, Patricia, and my dad, Martin, met at a nightclub called the Epping Forest Country Club, which I guess you could say back in 1984 was the Sugar Hut of its day. People would travel from miles around to go there and it was the No. 1 hotspot in Essex. It on was my mum's twenty-third birthday and she was out celebrating with friends when my dad spotted her and asked her to dance. Mum had arranged for her parents to lay on a few nibbles of food at home that night in case any of her friends wanted to come back after the club, and Dad ended up being the only person who accepted her invitation.

Dad was from just down the road in Wanstead in east London and my mum lived in Woodford Green, although her family are originally from Ireland. Mum was employed as a receptionist for a big advertising agency, and *her* mum,

3

Colette, was a nurse. My mum's father, Seamus, was a supervisor with London Transport and he had a big personality (I'll tell you a lot more about my grandparents later).

My dad is from a banking background. He was twenty-eight when he met my mum and was working in the Foreign Exchange section of Barclays. His father, Tom, was a finance manager in the City and his mum, Diane, also worked in the banking industry, as a shorthand typist.

Aside from banking, Dad's big passion in life was as a DJ. He would travel all over London to host discos at weddings and engagement parties, and he has an amazing collection of records. His disco was called Staccato Disco, which I always thought was a weird name. Dad also played rhythm guitar in a band called Tokyo Rose.

It didn't take long for Dad's music to rub off on me

It didn't take long for Dad's love of music to rub off on me. I've enjoyed listening to music for as long as I can remember, so I suppose it was natural that I would want to take up singing when I was older. Growing up, I used to follow all the usual kids' stuff in the charts, although Dad reckoned that most of what I liked was rubbish.

'You need to come and hear some proper music,' he told me one day.

'What do you mean?' I asked.

'I mean stuff by real bands who write their own songs. When you're older I'll take you to see the Rolling Stones,' he promised me.

'But I don't want to see the Rolling Stones. I don't like them,' I protested.

'Trust me – you'll love them,' he said. 'There are so many great bands out there. You just need to open your ears to them.'

It was thanks to Dad's influence that I started to appreciate lots of different types of music. Michael Jackson was my favourite, and it wasn't long before I was dreaming of being able to dance like him.

My dad's collection of records and CDs filled a whole room and everything was filed in alphabetical order. He still has it to this day and, it's like a huge maze. I would sneak in as a child and borrow Michael Jackson CDs.

Dad kept his promise to take me to see the Rolling Stones, and I also saw U2 at Wembley Stadium. Dad would somehow manage to wangle tickets in the VIP area close to the front and I would be fascinated by the fantastic stage shows and lighting effects. I also saw Michael Jackson at Wembley on his History tour, which completely blew me away.

As well as taking me to concerts, my dad would bring me along to record fairs, which were like giant boot sales devoted entirely to music. I now have a very detailed knowledge of music, whether it's classical, swing, hip-hop, garage, pop or indie. People might sometimes think I muddle my way through certain things when they see me on *TOWIE*, but music is one subject that I know well – and it's thanks to my dad.

*

The first meeting between my parents at Epping Forest Country Club was the start of a whirlwind romance for them. They got engaged after just six months and they were married the following year, 1985. My dad proposed during a weekend in Paris. He slipped an emerald ring onto my mum's finger at a small bistro in the shadow of the Moulin Rouge. The stone had a special significance for Mum, what with her family being from Ireland.

I was born on 5 December 1987 at Whipps Cross Hospital in Leytonstone, which is the hospital that David Beckham was born in. According to Mum, even then I had music in my veins, because, a few weeks before I was born, Dad had dragged Mum along to a David Bowie concert and she could feel me kicking inside her in time to the music! I arrived a week early because Mum had high blood pressure and I had to be induced. I was delivered at 2 a.m. and I weighed 7 pounds 9 ounces, so I wasn't a particularly big baby (it was only in later life that I started to pile on the weight).

My mum had a nasty health scare three weeks after I was born when she suffered a haemorrhage and had to be rushed back to hospital. She lost an enormous amount of blood and the doctors said it had been because part of the placenta was still lodged inside her tummy. Luckily, it didn't cause any long-term complications, because my little sister, Natasha, arrived twenty-one months after I was born. My earliest memory of her is of a cute little toddler whom I would play games with in the living room.

Natasha and I were like a typical brother and sister growing up. We'd occasionally have fights but we were very close. I loved watching WWF wrestling and I'd practise various moves on her that I'd seen on TV. Natasha would laugh her head off, although occasionally I'd go too far.

'James, leave your little sister alone!' Mum would tell me if ever I got too rough.

'Sorry, Mum, we're just playing WWF,' I'd explain.

For a while we lived at a house in South Woodford before moving to our family home in Woodford Green. It's a nice, comfy, detached house, nothing too flash but with plenty of room and a nice big garden.

According to Mum, I was a bit of a showman from a very early age, always dressing up in my superman outfit and diving off the sofa while pretending to be a superhero.

'You're a little show-off, James!' she would tell me. 'Whenever there's a party you always seem to be in the middle of things.'

Apparently, even as baby I used to love getting attention by doing things like splashing about in a paddling pool at a family party in my nappy.

I was a bit of a showman from a very early age

I suppose that's why I now enjoy being part of *TOWIE* so much. If there's a party to go to, I'm your man.

When I was two, something happened to me that would have a lasting affect on my health. I have no memory of it now, but I suffered a severe asthma attack and to this day I still have to carry an inhaler. It was triggered by an allergy to cats and, according to Mum, I ended up in a very serious state. It happened when a neighbour called at the house and offered to take me next door to see some kittens. My mum stayed at home but the next thing she knew was that a huge commotion had broken out.

'Pat! Pat! Call an ambulance!' the neighbour screamed to my mum. 'James's gone blue and I think he's having an asthma attack.'

They dialled 999 and I was given oxygen and rushed to hospital, where I was kept in overnight. Mum said that it caused a big scare and the doctors later diagnosed me as being an asthmatic. I was prescribed a drug called Ventolin, which made me very hyperactive as a small child.

I had a second asthma attack when I was about four. I caught a viral infection called croup, which was making me cough and wheeze. Mum treated me with steam inhalation but the condition got worse and I had to be rushed back to hospital because my airways started to close up. They kept me in overnight but thankfully I was OK.

The asthma affected me during primary school, and I would sometimes get out of breath when I did certain sports. If I tried to play football with friends I would go really red and fight to breathe. I was given a space inhaler (which is like a normal asthma inhaler but with a longer tube).

'It's important that you always carry your inhaler with you if we're going anywhere,' my mum explained to me when I was a bit older. 'Don't forget that there's always a spare one in the medical room at school if ever you need it.'

'Will I have to carry it for ever, Mum?' I asked.

'Yes, possibly, James, but lots of people have them. It's nothing to worry about. You'll get used to it and everything will be fine.'

Luckily, I didn't have any more asthma attacks – I just had to know my limits. If I get close to a cat today I lose my breath and I start wheezing. I also come out in a rash and go blotchy, which is weird because my skin is normally very clear. As for carrying an inhaler, I've now got a smaller one and it's become second nature to keep it in my pocket.

Aside from asthma, there were a couple of other medical ailments that affected me as a child, one of which was very embarrassing. The first was that my hearing was poor. Mum and Dad noticed that I always had the television turned up loud when I was watching it at home, and later on the teachers in school said that I talked very loudly. They wondered if my hearing was to blame, so I went and had some tests and the doctors said I needed grommets inserted into my ears.

Looking back, considering that I had problems with both breathing and hearing, I suppose it's amazing that I ever managed to take up singing in later life.

The other medical problem that I encountered as a child still makes me blush. I occasionally wet the bed – and it stayed with me right up until I was in the early stages of secondary school. At first, Mum just assumed that it was something that I would grow out of, but when I reached the age of seven or eight my family decided to send me for some tests.

The doctors said that I was going into such a deep sleep that I was simply failing to wake up when I got the urge to go to the loo. They tried fitting me with a special alarm that was placed into my underwear at night. A little buzzer would go off if I made a call of nature in my sleep, but, unfortunately, I just slept right through it!

It caused me quite a bit of embarrassment and, when I was approaching my early teens, it meant that I was nervous about going on sleepovers with friends in case I had an accident in the night. It made me feel like the odd one out. Thankfully, I eventually grew out of it. I suppose it was just one of those embarrassing things that affect some youngsters!

I got my love of music from my dad, but it was my grand-father, Tom, who awakened my other big passion while I was growing up: a love of theatre.

Granddad Tom lived in Brighton with my grandmother, Diane (whom I called Nanny Brighton for obvious reasons). Granddad Tom was a member of the Magic Circle and at Christmas he would keep everyone amused by putting on magic shows and performing conjuring tricks with cards and doves. His act was called Silvere the Magician. Nanny Brighton would act as his magician's assistant and together they would keep us captivated for hours on end. Granddad Tom would wear a bowtie while he entertained us, which is something I have copied from him and it's why you often see me wearing one on *TOWIE*.

When I was about six, we were staying down in Brighton when Granddad Tom revealed that he had a very special treat in store for me.

'Now listen, James. Tomorrow I'm going to take you to the Theatre Royal, where you're going to see a show called *Barnum*,' he said.

'Wow – I can't wait! I've never been to the theatre, Granddad. Will it be fun?' I asked.

'The show's all about the circus and you're going to love it,' he explained. 'There'll be actors and acrobats and lots of singing and dancing.'

It sounded fantastic. When the big event came along it was everything that I'd hoped for and more. The huge theatre was so posh and impressive, with its plush seating and grand stage. I was glued to the entire show. The performance whizzed by before my eyes, including an amazing tightrope scene, during which I was convinced the acrobat would fall off (but of course he didn't). When the curtain finally came down the applause was thunderous. From that moment I was hooked.

I remember thinking, Wow! I'd love to go on the stage one day.

I imagined being up there on the boards with all the other performers in their outfits in front of the audience. Even at that young age, I hoped that one day I would be able to appear in front of an audience.

It was around this time that my interest in Michael Jackson took off. I would practise doing his dance routine from *Moonwalker* at home for hours on end, and I even had a little black top hat and white gloves just like his. Whenever there was a party at home I'd take to the dance floor and do my Jacko routine, dancing to all the hits from his album

Bad. I thought I was so cool, although, to be honest, I probably looked like a bit of a donut!

The house where I was raised in Woodford Green was always full of children, because Mum gave up being a

> *To be honest, I probably looked like a bit of a donut!*

receptionist to work from home as a childminder. It meant that there were always lots of other kids to join in with my Michael Jackson routine. I also used to love going off on adventures on my BMX bike or playing tennis in the park with my mates. My dad is tennis mad and it rubbed off on me and my sister (who is now a professional coach for the Lawn Tennis Association).

I attended St Anthony's Roman Catholic Primary School in Woodford Green. My mum's side of the family is Catholic and I was raised in the Catholic faith. I was baptised at the age of nine months and had my holy communion at eight, which was followed by my confirmation at fifteen. As a youngster, I was brought up knowing right from wrong, and, even though I don't go around spouting religion today, I continue to believe in God.

My friends Richard and David were both really good at football, but I'm afraid that I was useless, which was partly due to my asthma.

'Come on, James, get stuck in,' I can remember one of them yelling to me during a match in the playground.

'I can't keep up, boys. I'm too out of breath. It's my asthma,' I explained.

The pair of them played for the Cubs and for Sunday sides, but I couldn't get into any of the teams.

'I'll come and cheer you on instead,' I promised.

Richard was very handsome and all the girls fancied him, but I didn't have a lot of luck in that respect, either; at least I can't remember kissing anyone behind the bike sheds. I didn't show much interest in dating until I was much older.

Even though I didn't make the football team, I used to take part in all the other activities at Cubs and Scouts. There was one occasion when we all went up to Gilwell Park in Epping Forest near Chingford, where there was a big scouting centre. One day we were paid a real honour: the Queen came to visit.

I was sitting at a computer screen when she was shown into our room and she came over to speak to me.

'Hello, young man. What are you doing today?' she asked.

'I'm playing on the computer, Your Majesty,' I explained.

I spoke to her only briefly, but the funny thing was I never told my mum and dad about it afterwards. It wasn't that I tried to keep it a secret: it was more just that I assumed it was fairly normal for royalty to drop by! It was only when my mum and dad were watching the Queen do her Christmas speech years later that I told them.

A lot of my happiest childhood memories are of our family gatherings at Christmas. It was always a grand occasion because we'd be joined by both sets of my grandparents and my aunt and uncle. My mum would always go over the top in decorating the whole house. We'd have an enormous Christmas tree with all the works, including mountains of tinsel and lots of cherubs. I used to love coming down on Christmas morning when we'd be treated to 'pigs in blankets', which are little sausages wrapped in bacon. Lunch would be a gargantuan affair, with a giant turkey that one of my best friends, Big G, would bring round from his dad's meat stall!

We'd all tuck in heartily, especially my Granddad Seamus, on my mum's side, who loved his food. He came from a tough farming background in Ireland, so he was very down to earth. He loved football and we'd always watch it together on TV on a Sunday.

Seamus was also a big darts player and was quite skilled at it, having played against the likes of Eric Bristow and Jocky Wilson. I think I get my love of food from him, although, as a younger child, I still wasn't particularly big, and it wasn't until the end of secondary school that I started to fill out.

I was very close to Granddad Seamus. He lived locally with my grandmother, Nanny Colette, and there was a big park near their house where we used to go and climb trees. I used to love listening to all his stories about his early life in Ireland.

'Life was very different back in my day,' he'd tell me. 'People used to work on the farm from morning until night. If I misbehaved I'd get the belt. You youngsters are very lucky today to be able to enjoy yourselves so much.'

'Tell me what it was like, Granddad?' I'd ask.

'We had to earn our keep. There were no fancy video games or colour television sets for us. We had to make our own fun.'

Seamus was from a small town called Carrick-on-Shannon in County Leitrim and was what you might call 'proper Irish'.

He knew all about the land and farming. His favourite time of the week was on a Sunday, when Nanny Colette would cook the most amazing roasts, which they'd share with their son, my uncle, Gerry. I'd get on my BMX and cycle up to their house so that I could get there early and join them.

Seamus was a big fan of Tottenham Hotspur, and, even though my own dad supports West Ham, I became a Spurs fan too. My granddad used to leave a 20p coin on the shelf for me during the week to go and buy a copy of the *Sun*, and then we'd read the sports pages together and discuss all the football news.

We also used to watch Muhammad Ali documentaries on video and talk about boxing. Seamus was one in a million: he could add up numbers in his head like lightning due to all the darts. He would chain-smoke one cigarette after another, pausing to share little bits of wisdom about the world.

I remember one year we bought him a George Best video. We thought he would like it because he was from Ireland, but he moaned like mad, asking why he'd want watch to the likes of George Best.

'He's a drunk and a loser,' he complained.

A few hours later he had us all in stitches because, after a few drinks while watching the video, he reckoned George Best was a hero and one of the greatest players the world had ever seen!

There were lots of opportunities to show off my Jacko impersonation when we went on holiday. The best times were always in Spain.

'We're all going to Ibiza together and your Granddad Seamus and Nanny Colette are going to be joining us,' my mum told me one day.

Wicked! Two weeks in the sunshine with Granddad Seamus to help with all the fun, I thought.

Then a bit later on I had an idea.

'Can I bring my Michael Jackson gear?' I asked.

Mum said it would fine and we packed my Jacko hat and gloves in the case. When we arrived in Ibiza, Seamus was on great form, keeping us all amused with the natural comedian in him. He used to spoil me a lot and would give me mint humbugs.

Seamus was determined to enjoy his food on holiday and he could eat loads! He would always put lots of pepper on his lunch and on one occasion I couldn't resist playing a practical joke on him. We went for something to eat together in a restaurant and, while he wasn't looking, I loosened the top of the pepper pot. When our plates of food arrived, as usual Granddad Seamus grabbed the pepper and began to shake it over his lunch. Of course, the top came flying off and a heap of pepper went all over his food.

'What the hell! Those bloody waiters must've thought they could make a mug of me by unscrewing it!' he bellowed.

I felt very guilty about it at first, but, looking back, can see that it was kind of funny. Thankfully, Seamus soon forgot about the pepper incident.

Seamus taught me a lot about life. I remember sitting on a balcony with him one evening and looking out at a gorgeous sunset. As we gazed out at the mountains and the sea,

Seamus said something to me that I will never forget. 'Picture this moment – for you will never see this night again,' he told me as we gazed at the beautiful surroundings.

It was a pearl of wisdom that I still say to myself today whenever a special moment comes along. My mate Mark Wright later nicked the sentiment off me and he said it in the jungle while he was on *I'm a Celebrity . . . Get Me Out of Here!*

One night while we were all down in the family bar on holiday, the DJ put on a Michael Jackson record. I grabbed my top hat and gloves and went onto the dance floor to do my Jacko impersonation. Then, as I danced and glided up and down, something unexpected happened.

The rest of the dance floor began to empty as the other holidaymakers stopped to wonder who this little kid was who thought he was Michael Jackson. I suppose I was showing off, but it must have had the desired effect, because afterwards everyone cheered and the bar manager came up to speak to my mum.

'I will give you ten euros tomorrow if you let him do exactly the same again,' he suggested.

At first Mum thought he was joking but he was serious, so she accepted and the next evening I performed my first paid gig! Of course, it was only a bit of fun on holiday, but it had a bit of an impact on my parents.

When we got back to Britain they sat me down for a chat.

'James, I want to suggest something to you,' said my dad. 'We think you might have a bit of a gift. The way that you love to put on a performance is very impressive.'

'What do you mean, Dad?' I replied.

'When you entertained everybody in Ibiza by being Michael Jackson it showed a lot of talent. We think it might be time for you to take things further by doing some drama classes.'

My mum was in agreement.

'You obviously love entertaining people,' she said. 'You'll have a great time and you might be able to turn it into something positive for the future. Let's see how you get on with some acting lessons.'

'OK, Mum, I'd like to give it a go,' I replied, feeling very flattered.

Looking back, I realise that it was an important conversation, because it paved the way for me to have the confidence to sing in later life.

My parents telephoned around and arranged for me to attend a drama group in Woodford called WOADS, which stood for Woodford Operatic and Amateur Dramatics Society. I was about eight when I started and I carried it on for several years, well into my teens.

While I was at primary school I also dabbled at playing instruments. I played the recorder and for a while I also practised the tenor horn during my lunchtimes. I wasn't particularly good at either, but it was all good experience. I was also in the choir.

Of course, back then I had no idea that one day I'd end up singing on telly.

2

BEATING THE BULLIES AND TREADING THE BOARDS

My time at primary school was mainly happy, but there was a horrible period when I found myself being bullied by a couple of older boys. I was popular with all the children of my own age, but these two kids were both in the year above me and for a while they tried to make my life hell.

I don't know why they singled me out. Maybe it was because they knew I spent my lunchtimes practising the tenor horn. I wasn't a goody-goody in school, but I guess that they got it into their heads that, because I played an instrument, I was somehow different from them, and it made me a target. It started off with calling me nasty names and it went on from there. One of them was big and stocky, the other slimmer, and when they were together they were a nasty pair. I can't remember exactly what names they would call me: it was just childish stuff like 'dickhead' or whatever. Then one day they grabbed hold of me in the cloakroom and pinned me up against the wall.

'You're a little prat and we're going to teach you a lesson,' the stocky one hissed at me.

'Leave me alone, I haven't done anything to you,' I protested.

I was terrified because they were older and bigger than I was and I couldn't defend myself. I stood there cornered while he put his face right up close to mine and I could smell his breath.

'You think you're special but you're a moron and if you're not careful we're going to give you a good kicking,' he threatened.

'Please! Let me go. I promise I'll keep out of your way,' I begged.

I stood there quaking in fear and I could feel tears welling up in my eyes. One of them then shoved me hard in the ribs and they gave me a few painful slaps on the side of my head.

'You're a useless wimp. You better watch yourself,' snarled the slimmer one.

When it was over I ran off in tears.

I was confused and upset because I hadn't done anything to encourage them – but, then, kids don't need an excuse to be bullies. I think they probably just saw somebody they thought they could take advantage of and decided to go for it. It was their way of having a bit of cruel fun at my expense.

I tried to stay away from them, but if they spotted me they would nick my school bag and chuck it around while I was glued to the spot like piggy in the middle. My books and all my possessions would end up scattered all over the floor.

'Ha ha, look at you now, you little idiot,' they'd gloat. 'There's plenty more where that came from.'

It made me feel worthless and small

It made me feel worthless and small.

At first I was too scared to tell anybody because I thought I'd be labelled a grass and it would only encourage them. I felt they had no right to be treating me in that way, but I didn't know what to do. I've never been one for getting into fights, but I knew that I would have to do something about it sooner or later.

The two boys in question lived close to Woodford Station, which I had to walk past in order to get to my grandparents' house, so I also had to be on my guard against them when I was outside school. If the bullies saw me in the street they would push me around or chase me away. I was very scared of them and after a while it started to really get me down.

I tried to stay alongside my friends Richard and David as much as I could, but whenever I was alone I felt threatened. It was the fear of what would happen next that I found upsetting. I thought that if I let it continue it would only get worse, but bullying robs you of your confidence to do anything to fight back. It got to a point where I was starting to become afraid of going into school and I would do anything to avoid them at all costs.

21

In the end I plucked up the courage to tell my parents.

'Mum, I'm really upset,' I confided one night after school.

'What's the matter, James?' replied my mum, full of concern.

'There are these two older kids who're picking on me and I'm frightened of them. I'm really scared, Mum.'

I could see the shock on her face. No mum likes to hear that one of her children is being bullied.

'That's terrible, James. Who are these boys and what do they do to you?'

'They call me names all the time. The other day they stole my bag off me and hid it. They take things out of my pencil case and threaten to beat me up.'

I felt relieved to be finally telling somebody about it and my mum put her arms around me and gave me a big hug.

'Have you tried standing up to them?' she asked.

'I'm too scared, Mum, they're older than me. They're rough boys and they live down by the station. They pick on me in school and they've also chased me when they've seen me out in the streets.'

'OK, you don't need to worry any more, James. We'll sort this out. I think I should go and see the headteacher.'

'No, please don't, Mum! Everyone'll think I'm a grass and it'll only make it worse.'

'But, James, it's for the best.'

'No, Mum! Please don't.'

My mum paused for a second to think things over. She may be a big softie around the home but she's also a very strong character and she wasn't about to let anyone get away with upsetting her son.

'Lots of children get picked on, James,' she said. 'It's nothing to be ashamed of. You've done nothing wrong. Sometimes the best thing to do is to learn to stand up to the bullies and make them leave you alone.'

'But how can I do that, Mum?'

'Well, your Uncle Gerry goes to a martial-arts class. Maybe he can teach you a little bit about how to defend yourself,' she said. 'All you need is some confidence. I'll be here to support you.'

My mum was like a rock.

'I'm going to speak to Uncle Gerry now,' she vowed.

My Uncle Gerry is very sporting and at the time he was a regular at a karate school in Woodford Green. I'd spent a lot of time with him round at Granddad Seamus's house and I liked the idea of his being able to help me. When he heard what had been happening he was only too happy to get involved.

'We'll soon teach you how to defend yourself. You'll enjoy coming to the martial-arts lessons – they're good fun,' he promised.

Uncle Gerry found out that there was a beginners' class due to start up soon and he agreed to enrol me. I was slightly nervous but I wanted to go along. I was a big fan of the movie *The Karate Kid*, which is about a boy called Daniel who stands up to some bullies after learning to defend himself. Maybe I could be just like Daniel-san. I also liked the film *3 Ninjas*, which is all about three young children who practised martial arts.

If they can do it, then so can I, I vowed.

I went along to the classes with Uncle Gerry and I enjoyed it. We did a mixture of fitness work and technical work, during which you would learn how to block and strike. Part of it involved the instructor trying to target you with a big stick, which you would learn to dodge. In truth, it was very basic stuff for beginners, but I was only a small primary school kid and it felt very grown up at the time.

After a while I felt my confidence begin to grow and I realised that I was capable of standing up for myself. Of course, I was still terrified when it came to defending myself in school, but I knew that I had to give it my best shot.

The showdown happened one day when I was in the playground during a game of football. It was one of those games where there are dozens of boys on each side and I was milling around with the other kids, not really taking much interest. Suddenly, the stocky bully came rushing by and barged into me.

'What are *you* doing here, you prick?' he yelled.

My heart was thumping like hell and I felt sick inside, but I knew that I had to be brave. It was now or never. When he went to grab me I dodged him and hit back with a strike move.

Bang!

My hand connected with his lip. The boy staggered backwards and I was surprised to see blood on his mouth. It wasn't a perfect karate move, but it was enough to take him by surprise.

Oh, no! I thought. I'm really in for it now!

I turned on my heels and ran away as fast as I could, with the angry bully chasing after me in a fury.

'Come back here. I'm going to kill you,' he bellowed.

He chased me across the playground. I have no idea what I would have done if he'd caught me on my own, but luckily Richard and David came to my aid. There was a scuffle but they managed to grab him and hold him back while he shouted wild threats at me.

'You're going to get it, you little idiot! I'm going to beat the hell out of you!' he screamed.

It caused quite a stir in the playground but, thankfully, a teacher came running over to break it up. I was marched down to the main office in the school and asked to give an explanation. The teacher was called Miss Saunders and at first I was worried that I was in big trouble.

'Why did you lash out in the playground like that? You've cut that poor boy's lip,' she said sternly.

I admitted that I'd hit the older boy, but I explained that he and his mate had been picking on me for some time. While I was talking I started to cry so I think Miss Saunders must have known that I was telling the truth.

'I'm sorry, miss, but I didn't start it,' I sobbed. 'They've been making my life hell and I was afraid of them. I was only sticking up for myself because he barged into me.'

Luckily, the teachers accepted my version of what happened, although I still got told off for hitting the older boy. The two bullies also got a telling-off and the school made it clear they'd be keeping an eye on all of us in future.

After that, I was still nervous whenever I saw either boy,

but the bullying stopped. They gave me some filthy looks but that was all. I continued to avoid coming face to face with them whenever I could, but at least now they were no longer on my case.

Looking back, I am glad my family encouraged me to defend myself. I managed to avoid fights for the rest of my time in school, but I had learned an important lesson in life: that sometimes you have to stand up for yourself. My advice to anybody who's being bullied today is: don't suffer in silence; make sure you tell somebody in your family; and get help. There are also lots of anti-bullying groups online these days where you can get advice.

If you're being bullied, don't suffer in silence

You don't necessarily have to take the route that I did, but it worked for me. I think I was wrong to be worried about being labelled a grass. It's not grassing if someone is picking on you and you need to put a stop to it, so don't be afraid to tell a teacher if that's the only thing you can do.

I carried on with my karate for a while, but I eventually let it lapse after a few months. I enjoyed all the martial-arts noises that accompanied the various moves, but I must admit that amateur dramatics were always more my style. I'd rather tread the boards in the theatre by playing the Karate Kid on stage than do it for real.

Away from school I began to spend more and more time doing amateur dramatics. I got my first big break on stage when the group that I'd joined decided to host a production of *Oliver Twist* by Charles Dickens. I thought I'd only get a role as a workhouse boy but I ended up being in the running for the lead role as Oliver. It wasn't a musical version, so there was no singing involved, but I still had to spend ages learning all the lines.

I'd practise for hours and hours upstairs in my bedroom until I thought I had everything perfect. If I am honest, I probably put a lot more effort into learning that script than I ever did for my work at school. Drama was something that felt natural and fun, whereas school work could be a bit of a chore.

My audition went well and, when a phone call later came through from the theatre group, my mum answered it.

'Congratulations, James! You've got the part. I'm so proud of you,' she told me, giving me a great big hug.

I couldn't wait to tell all my mates and I even got my picture in the local paper. It was only a tiny little production but I felt like a huge celebrity.

Arg had finally arrived!

When the big occasion of the first night arrived, all my family came to see me, including Granddad Seamus, who was pleased as punch for me. My headmistress from my primary school was also in the audience, so I was a bag of nerves. I was terrified that I'd forget my lines, but thankfully all that hard work learning the script paid off.

The first night went well, although there was one part of the show that caused a bit of a ruffle with Seamus. There was a scene where I had to be manhandled in a very rough way by one of the actors. It was only make-believe, but of course everyone wanted it to look as real as possible, so the actor had to be quite forceful with me as he pushed me around the stage.

Unfortunately, Seamus thought that my colleague was a bit too rough. In fact my granddad was furious because he reckoned my treatment was completely OTT. Seamus was all in favour of running up onto the stage to sort the geezer out on my behalf! Thankfully, Mum persuaded him not to do it, but that was Seamus all over: no grandson of his was going to be roughed up on stage, even if it *was* in the script.

The production was a big success and I later went on to land the role of the Artful Dodger in the musical version of the story, *Oliver!*. Of course, this involved singing the famous song 'Consider Yourself', so it was a new skill I had to master. I'd always wanted to play the Artful Dodger because he was a cheeky chappie, just like me. I felt as if I had won the lottery when I got the part.

I was twelve by this stage and, thankfully, my asthma didn't interfere with the singing and dancing. I just relaxed and let myself get into the natural rhythm of things. It was a very well-directed show. All the mums and dads who came to see it reckoned that the production was good enough to have been put on in the West End.

By now I was attending secondary school, having left St Anthony's to attend the Trinity Catholic High School in Woodford Green. On my first day I was terrified. As I walked to school I was worried that I'd meet more bullies.

Oh, my God! I thought. Am I going to get picked on again, or are people going to want to start fights with me?

Richard, David and I all hoped that we would be in the same class, but it turned out that Richard was sent off to another one, leaving David and me together. We got a bit tearful about it and we tried to persuade the teachers to change things, but they refused. I needn't have worried, because I still managed to stay friends with Richard and we're still mates today.

I didn't have any more problems with bullies, either – although I did experience a nasty incident on my fourteenth birthday. There was a custom in our school called 'birthday beats', whereby if it was your birthday anybody was entitled to come up and punch you hard on the arm or elsewhere, reigning down one blow for every year of your age. A fourteenth birthday meant fourteen punches. If you were clever about it, you would keep your birthday a secret in order to escape a bit of a battering. You would be petrified. Unfortunately, in my case, it went around the school like wildfire that my birthday was coming up.

There seemed to be scores of kids all screaming: 'Arg's fourteen tomorrow. Let's give him the birthday beats!'

It meant I was in line for a real pasting: fourteen punches over and over again, all day long. I was so scared that I nearly bunked off school that morning, but I went in, feeling sick with fear. It started straightaway.

'Arg! It's your *birrthdaaayyy*!' *Whack!*

'Happy fourteenth!' *Whack!*

'Hello, birthday boy!' *Whack!*

One kid punched me full pelt with all his strength on my upper arm and I remember just standing there and having to take the pain. Afterwards, I went into the toilets and started crying and by lunchtime I was a wreck. I started to get out of breath due to the stress and my asthma began to play up, so I had to take my inhaler to calm myself down.

I kept thinking, Oh, my God! I've got bruises all over my arm and everyone's going to beat me up.

Thankfully, a kid I knew in the year above me called Chris took pity on me. He must have seen how upset I was because he ordered all the other kids to lay off me. I was grateful, because without him I'd have got a right pasting. I'd survived the birthday beats.

I fell into a crowd of popular kids at Trinity. There were eleven of us and we called ourselves The Famous Eleven. I wasn't the boy who got all the girls or the one who was the best at football, but I think my mates regarded me as a bit of a 'cool geek', if that makes sense.

Pretty soon, everyone knew who I was, so I suppose they must have liked my personality. Everybody called me Arg, rather than James, and the nickname stuck with me for the rest of my life. As I say, I was a bit of a donut at times but I just tried to be a lovable character – which was my way of keeping out of confrontations.

Trinity was a good school and I generally liked all the teachers, although I loved messing about and occasionally got told off for it. I would wait until the teacher turned around to write something on the board and then I'd chuck a big pencil rubber at one of my mates. I also used to do silly things such as shout something out at random in class in order to get attention, or I would throw paper aeroplanes. My mates and

I would play this silly game in which I'd have to try to walk around the classroom in circles. The idea was to do as many circuits as possible without the teacher noticing. It didn't always work.

'Argent! What the hell are you playing at?' the teacher would bellow.

I was also always being told off for talking too much to my mates in the classroom. I loved all the banter of school life but it got to the point where I started to get letters sent home for bad behaviour or for not doing my homework.

I was always being told off for talking too much

I was petrified that my dad would tell me off, so I used to get up every morning and run down to check the post. If there was anything addressed to 'Mr & Mrs Argent' I knew that, nine times out of ten, it would be a letter from the school. I'd quickly open it to check the contents before ripping it up.

Sometimes, the odd letter would sneak through and I'd get a telling-off from my dad. I could get away with murder with Mum because she's a big softie, but Dad would put me in my place. He was always very fair, but, like all good dads, he knew where to draw the line.

Throughout most of my time in school I stayed passionate about the theatre. After playing the Artful Dodger, I went on to land a number of other really good roles, many of which were performed at the Kenneth More Theatre in Ilford. I played Edmund in *The Lion, the Witch and the Wardrobe*; I was the lead in *David Copperfield*; Miles in *The Turn of The Screw*; and Enjolras in *Les Misérables*. I had a fantastic time in amateur dramatics and got on really well with all the older people I met. There were also lots of great girls my age to talk to. If anybody reading this thinks they've got it in them to do the same I strongly urge them to give it a go. It's never too late to start, and if an ordinary down-to-earth bloke like me can make a good go of it I am sure you can too.

If you've watched *The Only Way Is Essex*, you'll probably know that there's a funny story connected to my time at the Kenneth More Theatre. Every year they hold a big event known locally as the 'Kennys'. This is the Essex answer to the Oscars and everyone dresses up in a black-tie outfit to celebrate all the productions that have been staged over that year. The Kenny Awards are then given out to the best performers.

I was delighted when I was nominated for Best Supporting Actor for the Artful Dodger and secretly I was convinced I would win. But, when the awards ceremony came along, the Kenny went to somebody else.

Bloody Kennys! I thought. I'm not going to come along to *them* again!

But of course I did go again, because by now I was mad about the theatre. I was sitting at the awards a couple of years later when the theatre owner came on stage to present a special award, which was known as the Judy Walker Award for Young Performer of the Year. I wasn't nominated for anything as far as I knew. I was just there to enjoy the awards ceremony.

'The winner of the special award this year is a young boy who has been performing shows here for a number of years,' the theatre boss told the audience. I wondered who it might be. 'He has played Oliver Twist'

Oh, *I* played him, too, I thought.

'And he has played the Artful Dodger'

I've played the Artful Dodger too; that's mad.

'And he's played David Copperfield.'

Only when I heard him say that did I clock that I was the one he was talking about. I was shaking and full of adrenaline when I went up to receive my Kenny. It was the very best feeling, and it sounds silly but I treasured that award as if it were a real Oscar!

When I started to appear in *TOWIE* I was still very proud of it, so much so that I took it around to show Gemma Collins, whom I was dating at the time. I ended up leaving it at her flat. After Gemma and I split up I was desperate to get it back, but Gemma kept stalling, so some of the boys and I launched Operation Save Kenny. Joey Essex volunteered to go round to Gemma's for a drink and then he simply grabbed my Kenny Award and legged it outside.

Thankfully, I got it back.

It was during the later years of secondary school that I started to put on a bit of weight. My mum says that I comfort-eat, and she is probably right. I'm someone who really enjoys his food. I love a big fried breakfast with egg, bacon, sausage and all the trimmings, and I can follow it up by eating a big lunch and dinner. I suppose it was my love of food that made me take food technology as a GCSE subject – although I preferred to call it 'cooking and eating'. I wasn't huge by this stage – the real weight gain came after I left school – but I was definitely beginning to grow.

It was while I was at Trinity that I had my first experiences with alcohol. My mates and I would take part in a practice we called 'street ratting', which would involve gathering together outside to drink bottles of WKD or whatever else we could get our hands on. We were too young to drink in pubs or bars, so we'd rely on somebody who looked old enough to buy us booze. We'd go out on a Friday and drink it in the streets. I liked the effect that it had on me, but I never went over the top. We'd just run up and down making a noise, but it was all fairly harmless.

I didn't do too badly at school academically. I took nine GCSEs and got four Bs (in English language and literature, food technology and drama) plus three Cs and a D. Altogether, it was enough of a tally for me to take my A-levels, but trying for a place at university wasn't something I was interested in.

I found A-levels extremely difficult. I took media, film, English and drama. Even though I had done well in my GCSEs and I was obviously not an idiot, I found A-levels too hard – they were out of my comfort zone. The one subject I thought I would have excelled at was drama, but the A-level course turned out to be a disaster. The performance side of my drama was flying, but I had difficulty keeping up with the coursework. The teacher always used to give me a hard time and I wondered whether he didn't like the fact that I'd done a lot of amateur dramatics outside of school.

Eventually, he called me in for a chat.

'I am sorry, James, but I'm going to have to drop you from the course,' he told me.

'But why?' I protested – but I knew the answer: it was the lack of coursework that had let me down.

The teacher tried to soften the blow by explaining that other people who had been asked to leave in the past had gone on to do well, but I was devastated. I couldn't understand why I could flop when I'd made such a success of amateur dramatics outside of school.

I took art instead, but I could barely draw a stick man. I just messed around for the rest of my A-levels, and, even though I stayed on for the full two years, in the end things just fizzled out and I didn't even turn up for all the exams.

It was while I was in my teens that my family received two very severe blows, and we were thrown into deep shock. The first blow to hit us was that my Granddad Tom became very ill. When it happened, my mum sat me down with Natasha to break the news.

In my teens my family received two severe blows

'Something very serious has happened to your Granddad Tom,' she explained. 'He's suffered an aneurism, which means he's going to be very poorly for some time.'

It was unexpected, because Granddad Tom was always so

full of life and we were so used to seeing him perform his magic act.

'Can we go and visit him to cheer him up?' I asked.

'No, James, he's too unwell. But Nanny Brighton's there with him and they send you all their love.'

Much as Natasha and I wanted to see Granddad Tom, I think my family did the right thing by shielding us from visiting because he was actually gravely ill. I think it would have distressed us a great deal to see him like that. We prayed he'd pull through, but, sadly, his health continued to decline. When my dad sat us down again it was bad news.

'I know you love your Granddad Tom very much, so this is going to be very hard. I'm afraid he's passed away,' my dad told us, his voice charged with emotion.

As anyone who has lost a much-loved grandparent will know, it's a heart-wrenching experience. Granddad Tom was a lovely, kind man and his death brought back memories of all those Christmas parties and summer fêtes when he used to entertain us. It was the first time I had experienced the death of somebody I loved, and the grief was very painful.

I cried a great deal.

When my family began to make the arrangements for the funeral I wanted to pay my own tribute to Granddad Tom.

'I'd like to do something at the funeral. Can I read a verse from the Bible for Granddad?' I asked.

My parents agreed but on the day of the funeral I was too choked up to speak. It was very hard because we'd never had a chance to say goodbye to him, and when I saw his coffin at the funeral I was overwhelmed. At dark times like this you learn to pull together as a family and that's exactly what we did. We grieved together and we said our last farewell to Granddad Tom.

Fate can sometimes deal you some very tough cards because there was a second shock on the way, although it didn't come until a couple of years later, when I learned that Granddad Seamus was also very ill. I was almost seventeen at the time. Seamus just didn't seem like his old self and he seemed to be getting slower every time I saw him.

Eventually, he confided in my mum that there was some-thing very wrong. I'd noticed a lot of hushed conversations in the house, so I could tell that something wasn't right. When my mum sat down with me to explain what was happening, I could see she was very upset.

'Granddad Seamus has cancer of the prostate,' she explained. 'It means that things are going to be very hard for him, but we all have to hope for the best.'

That horrible word 'cancer' seemed so final.

Looking back, I think we all feared what was coming next, but I just didn't want to accept it. I went to visit him all the time while he was ill. Seamus was a very proud and strong man, so I hoped he would make it. He was very dig-nified about it and I think he wanted to spare me the worst details, so we didn't discuss his illness in any detail. I just wanted him to get well. He had Sky Sports put in at home and we'd while away the hours together watching boxing or football.

As his illness progressed, the doctors put him on very strong medication and he was tired all the time. It was heartbreaking to see him getting weaker and weaker. When my mum sat me down for another chat she gave me some devastating news.

'I'm afraid the cancer's spread,' she said. 'Your granddad's a strong man but we all need to pray for him. He's a fighter.'

Even at this point, Seamus was still incredibly dignified.

'My luck's out' was how he told my mum that the cancer had spread.

Seamus found it very difficult to get around his home towards the end. It got to the point where he couldn't walk and he was moved to Whipps Cross Hospital. My parents warned me as much as they could in order to try to prepare me for what was going to happen next, but I never believed that we would lose him. I just imagined that he would be OK and that he would get through it. I just couldn't take it in. Seamus was one of my best friends. We'd spent so much time together that I just assumed he would always be there.

Surely he can't die, I thought, so soon after we've lost Granddad Tom.

When Seamus finally lost his battle with the cancer I was distraught. I cried my eyes out and blubbered like a small child. I thought of all those wonderful times we had shared, playing football in the park or climbing trees or discussing his beloved Spurs.

It was a very dark moment.

We had a big funeral for him at St Thomas's Church next to my old primary school. All of his side of the family came over from Ireland and it was a very sad occasion while every-body said their final goodbyes to him.

The grief I felt was extremely painful and the death of my two grandfathers was without doubt the hardest thing I had to deal with while I was growing up. I still miss them very much today. If I close my eyes I can see Granddad Tom doing his magic tricks, and Granddad Seamus is always in my thoughts. I often remember his pearls of wisdom, like those special words he said to me while we on the balcony together as we watched the sunset on holiday in Ibiza: 'Picture this moment – for you will never see this night again.'

3

MY LATE TEENS: WELCOME TO THE ESSEX PARTY SCENE

One of the great things about life with the Essex crowd during my late teens and early twenties was the fantastic party scene. There was always somewhere to go and let rip. It was in the sixth form at Trinity that I started to go out regularly on the town with my mates. Sometimes I'd head down to a nightclub in Walthamstow called Charlie Chan's, where occasionally I'd manage to bluff my way in despite being too young. We'd also try to sneak into bars and pubs in South Woodford for a few drinks. The most famous club in the area was called Faces. My friends and I were always desperate to get into there, but I never could sneak in at this stage because of my age, as most nights were for over-twenty-ones.

Of course, all this partying required a bit of cash. My first part-time job, which I got while I was still at Trinity, was at Waitrose, where I worked Saturdays on the patisserie counter. It brought in a nice bit of money, but, to tell you the truth, I hated it. I had to serve customers and help out with the cleaning, which I was happy to do, but I wasn't a great success. I was constantly warned for standing about talking to my workmates or for getting up to mischief.

Things came to a head when I decided to play a stupid prank in a lift. They had a food elevator in the store that was used to transport goods up and down between levels, but people were strictly banned from travelling inside it for health-and-safety reasons. We'd load it up with a batch of food and then press the button to send it all to another floor, where it would be unpacked by somebody else. I loved mucking around at work, so, when somebody dared me to take a ride in the forbidden lift, I was game for a laugh. Holding my breath, I got in there and hid behind a load of boxes and decided to take a ride down to the basement. Unfortunately, when it got to the bottom of the shaft, the door opened and the general manager was standing there! I'd been caught with no means of escape.

'James, can you come up to the office please? We need to have a word with you,' he said, sternly.

I'd had so many warnings by now that I knew what was coming next.

'We think it might be better for everyone if you agreed to leave us,' he explained diplomatically.

I wasn't officially sacked. I think they still liked me as a person, but they'd had enough of my constant messing about and my poor time-keeping. It had been a good little Saturday job and it had been handy to have some of my own money coming in, which I knew I would miss. My mum and dad weren't very impressed when I told them I'd been bumped out.

Right, I thought, I've got to get another job.

I decided to apply to Faces nightclub to see if they needed a pot boy (whose job it was to go around collecting all the empty glasses while the club was open). Ironically, I wasn't old enough to get into the nightclub as a customer, but they hired me and I absolutely loved it. I was like a little kid in a sweetshop, having landed my dream job at the best club in Essex. I was working in a nightclub environment two or three nights a week and it suited me down to the ground. One of my best friends, Milno, who was one of The Famous Eleven, also worked there. I had to collect all the glasses and wash them before putting them back on the shelves, and go around the club to make sure everything was clean and tidy and sweep up any broken glasses. If any arguments broke out between customers, I had to call security – in fact, there was always loads of different stuff to do. The staff at Faces were all really friendly and, even though I was just a humble pot boy, I felt really cool: here I was, listening to music while watching all these beautiful women dancing. I was getting paid to mix with people who were getting drunk and having a good time, and this was in the very club all my mates were desperate to get into! While I was sweeping up I would do a little dance routine, which the customers loved, and people would laugh and smile at me. Now that I'm in *TOWIE*, when I go to

Faces I am lucky enough to be ushered into the VIP area, but back in those days even as a pot boy I felt like a king!

Despite all the gorgeous girls who came into the club, I was still very shy when it came to dating women. I had lots of friends who happened to be girls and I was a popular guy, but I'd never actually had a proper girlfriend. I'd kissed a few girls at parties while I was at school, but that was about it. The first time was on the dance floor at an under-eighteens night at a club; I must have been about fifteen. But I can't remember her name. I had no trouble being friendly and talking with women but when it came to be intimate, never mind being sexual, I was not very confident at all. I would start to get nervous and would literally shake and tremble. I don't know why. I guess I was just a late starter, whereas some of my friends were already going out and getting lots of sexual experience.

I was still very shy when it came to dating women

When I was about seventeen, my friends started to take the piss out of me for it and they'd call me a virgin for a laugh. It got worse when a film came out called *The 40-Year-Old Virgin*, which starred Steve Carell, whose character in the movie looked the spitting image of me! So I became known as the 'Forty-Year-Old Virgin of Essex'. All the banter had the effect of making my lack of success with girls into a much bigger thing in my mind. By the time I was eighteen, despite working in Faces, I had never pulled a girl. Eighteen is quite old to be a virgin in Essex (trust me) and all the ribbing from my mates meant it began to play on my mind.

Meanwhile, I needed to find a full-time job after leaving Trinity. My work at Faces was great but it was only a few nights a week and Mum and Dad were keen that I go into something that would keep me occupied. They were concerned about me and we had one or two conversations about what they thought I should be doing with my life. At one point it seemed as if I was out partying every night and then sleeping during the day, so I can understand why they were a bit worried.

'Don't you think it's about time you got a permanent job?' my dad said to me.

I was still interested in theatre and entertainment, but during the sixth form I'd eased off a bit from all the amateur dramatics, so I wasn't sure what to do next. When I heard from a friend that there was an admin job going at a local solicitor's office I decided to apply. It would be steady nine-to-five work and I suspected Mum and Dad thought it would keep me on the straight and narrow, so they were pleased when my application was successful. It was my first full-time job but I had zero interest in it, and it lasted only about six or seven months. I was frequently late and I would also get caught using Myspace or Facebook to talk to my mates during office hours. The bosses in the office would sneak by my computer to peek at whatever was on my screen, so I'd have to quickly click onto something else. In the end they agreed it would be best for me to leave. I'd flunked it, just as I had at Waitrose.

*

I was unsure what to do next, but I still fancied myself as a bit of a performer, so after the job at the solicitor's office ended I tried to find acting work as an extra in movies and on TV. I went and had my photo taken and registered with a theatrical agency. A few weeks later I got a phone call asking me if I'd like to be an extra in *Harry Potter and the Goblet of Fire*.

'Of course I would,' I replied eagerly.

I was offered the chance to be in a crowd scene during the Quidditch World Cup, which was due to be filmed at Warner Brothers' studios at Leavesdon, near Watford. I was really excited and on the day I caught a coach up there with all the other extras in the morning. The set was amazing, with all these huge tents decked out in bright colours. At one point I was standing quite close to Daniel Radcliffe (who played Harry Potter) and Emma Watson (Hermione Granger) and I remember thinking how much I would love to be doing what they were doing. When the film was finished you couldn't spot me in the crowd – but it was still great fun. I also had a small role as an extra sitting in a hallway in a scene in *The Golden Compass* with Daniel Craig and Nicole Kidman. When Nicole walked past me I couldn't help but notice how beautiful she was, and I again sat there thinking about how much I would like to work in the entertainment industry. It reminded me of all the amateur dramatics I'd done and I hoped that one day I'd be able to put them to use on stage or on television.

The movie-extra work was fine but it didn't really provide me with a proper income, so I still needed a full-time job. I was forever sending off letters and CVs to firms in the City, but I would never get anything back. Then, out of the blue, I got a lucky break when the chance came up of a job in the retail industry. My best friend at the time was a boy called James Kane, whose family owned a chain of jewellery shops with five branches around Essex and east London.

James had a word with his dad and he begged him to give me some work. When he said yes I was over the moon and for once it seemed that I'd found a stable job that I could do reasonably well. I didn't have much passion for jewellery and I had no interest in learning about gold, but I was working with a good friend and I was grateful for the money.

My links with James were to open up a whole new group of friends. It was through him that I would later meet Mark Wright for the first time. James was a friend of Mark's younger brother, Josh, who was a promising young footballer. I had finished working at Faces by now but I left the club on good terms and they were always happy to see me. They'd give me the odd drink voucher whenever I visited the club, which was nice. I didn't know it at the time, but my old job at Faces was about to open up some new doors for me. Now that I was a bit older I would go to Faces often for nights out with my mates and everyone was always amazed by how many people I knew there. I seemed to be on first-name terms with everyone in the whole nightclub. I would spend the night chatting away to various different groups of boys and girls, not just those who had been to our school but also to people who came from different areas. Of course, I wasn't famous for being on the telly back then – I was just a normal boy from down the road – but I was good at socialising and people seemed to enjoy my company. Friends told me that I was bubbly and popular, but, as far as I was concerned, I was just being plain old Arg. Then an idea struck me.

Why not try to make some money out of the fact that I know so many people on the club scene? I thought.

After all, plenty of other people seemed to be doing it. When I'd worked at Faces as a pot boy there was a great DJ there called George D. He was also a nightclub promoter who would put on all the best parties in Essex and London. Any event that he hosted was always jam-packed and he would ensure that all the most beautiful women were there. George was similar to me physically, in that he was a bit chubby. I'd piled on a bit of weight during my late teens, so I used to think of him as an older version of me. I could see from his nice clothes and expensive watches that he was earning good money. Maybe I could be the new George D. George and I used to talk a little bit about the various tunes that he played and I remember on one occasion he put a proposition to me.

'I'm hosting a big party on New Year's Eve. I've got hundreds of tickets and I'd like you to help me to sell them,' he explained.

'George, I'd love to have a go at that,' I replied.

I think he must have seen how popular I was around the club and he reckoned I'd be able to shift a few. He was right, because by the time the big event came along I'd sold about a hundred tickets and he was delighted. It stuck in my mind, and, now that I was no longer a pot boy, I had a new idea: I'll put on a party and charge for the tickets, I thought.

First, I needed a venue. There was a place down the road

called the Karma Bar, which was owned by the same management as Faces. It was a smallish place that could hold about 250 to 300 people, so I decided I'd approach them with my new proposition. They knew me from my time at Faces and they were pleased to see me.

'Look, will you give me one night that's normally dead?' I asked. 'I want to see if I can put on a party and make some money on the door from the ticket sales.'

'Yeah, why not? Let's give it a go,' replied the manager.

We agreed that I'd try it on a Friday night, which was normally a quiet time for them because there was so much going on at other venues on the same evening. On average they'd get only about ten or twenty people in there. But I was going to do my best to change that. I enlisted the help of a couple of friends, Harry and Ellis, whose families had connections with the nightclub scene in the West End. We hired a DJ to play house music and we busily set about selling as many tickets as we could. At this stage I wasn't sure it would be a success; in fact I was nervous it might be a washout. So I went on Facebook and invited as many people as I could to come along, and I also texted everybody that I knew.

Oh, my God! I remember thinking. I hope everyone turns up.

I needn't have worried. About 350 people attended on the first night and the owners of the bar were amazed. All the staff said they had never seen it so busy on a Friday. The management of Faces even came down to see what all the fuss was about and they patted me on the back for all the new business I'd brought in. I was delighted.

49

This is what I'm going to do, I told myself. I'm a nightclub promoter!

It was an impressive turnout and even George D himself got to hear about how good our party had been. He got in touch and asked me if I'd like to co-promote some events with him in the West End, to which I readily agreed. Our party night was called Liaison and we hosted big evenings at Faces, as well as in other venues like Club Warehouse and Pacha London. I was the same ordinary bloke I'd always been, but I felt very cool and all of a sudden people started to show me a little respect. My mates liked the fact that I could help them to skip the queue, and of course we gave out the odd free ticket here and there.

It was around this time that I first met Mark Wright

I felt I'd finally found a moneymaking venture that I was good at, but I continued working at the jewellery shops during the day. My friend James, who'd got me the job through his dad, used to come to the party events that I organised and it was around this time that I met Mark Wright for the first time through James, which was to open up a whole new world.

4

MARK WRIGHT, A HOLIDAY IN MARBELLA AND AN EXPLODING TV

The first time I met Mark Wright it was a painful experience. We did go on to become best buddies but that was only after Mark had nearly knocked out one of my teeth with a beer bottle! Of course it was an accident, but it was a strange beginning to what was to become a lasting friendship. In many ways Mark and I are opposites. He was the flashily dressed man about town who could charm the birds from the trees, whereas I became his slightly overweight pal who was much quieter and very shy when it came to pulling girls.

I got to know Mark's younger brother Josh first, whom I'd met at a party I'd hosted with George D in the West End. Josh was a footballer on the books of Charlton Athletic at the time, and he and I immediately hit it off after being introduced by James Kane. Even though Josh was slightly younger than me, I looked up to him a little, because his football career had brought him quite a lot of money at a young age. Josh and his pal, called Eren, would ring me up all the time to see if I'd heard any gossip about any girls who were worth chasing. I think they regarded me as a fountain of information because I knew everyone on the club scene in Essex. They would come to my house for a drink and to ask me if the girls they fancied had been up to any mischief in the clubs. We soon formed a genuine friendship. Being a footballer, Josh would bulk up on his calories on a Friday before playing on a Saturday. He would take me out on a 'carb night', during which we would have a huge meal together. His football career was going really well and, when he was picked for the England under-nineteens, I went along to watch him.

The first time I met Mark was at a huge party that his family had thrown for his sister Jessica. Mark was very into football at the time. He'd previously played for Tottenham Hotspur's youth team, and he was currently playing for Bishop's Stortford, one of the big non-League sides in Hertfordshire. There's always some amazing banter among people connected to football, and Mark's mates were no exception. I was used to larking about with my own pals, but Mark's crowd took the piss out of one another on a whole new level. They were constantly pulling pranks. If you were asked to pose for a photo, you could always expect a slap around the back of the head to distract you. Mark was very much the leader of the group and I could see straightaway he was a boy's boy.

'Who the hell is this Arg kid?' I heard him ask Josh, a bit dismissively at the party.

'He's cool, Mark. He's a nightclub promoter,' Josh reassured him.

Little did Mark know that I was actually a virgin from up the road who worked by day in a jewellery shop! When it came to posing for a group photo at the party it was my turn to fall victim to a prank – or to be 'bantered', as they called it. All the boys lined up next to me for the camera and we smiled our best cheesy grins. As I sipped on a bottle of beer I noticed a few of the others laughing, when, suddenly, *whack*!

Mark slapped me hard around the back of the head. It took me by surprise and made me jump so much that I knocked my front teeth on the bottle that I was holding. The blow was so hard that it took a small chip off the side of a tooth. I took quite a knock and I was probably lucky not to have lost it. I was surprised to say the least, but the rest of the group thought it was hilarious and they all fell about laughing. I could see the funny side, too, and it was from that strange start that my long friendship with Mark Wright began. He hadn't meant me any harm: it was just one of those things, and I'd been holding the bottle so closely at the time.

Mark loved to be the organiser of everything and his constant banter was hilarious. He could talk anyone into anything and he always managed to do it with a smile on his face. I think everyone in the group looked up to him. He's a good-looking boy and he always had girls throwing themselves at him. He was dating Lauren Goodger in an on-and-off way at the time, but that didn't stop other women trying to chase him. He was tall and handsome and good at football, and he drove a Mercedes. He had all the chat and it was easy to see why he was making good money from his job as a nightclub promoter.

We soon became very good friends. Through Mark, I also got to know Jack Tweed, who was going out with Jade Goody from *Big Brother*. Jade realised that I wasn't much of a hit with the ladies, so she liked me to be around Jack because she knew that I wouldn't lead him astray!

Years later, when people saw Mark and me together on *TOWIE*, it was as if we were joined at the hip. Some people who saw Mark on *TOWIE* say that he can be very selfish, but underneath he has a heart of gold. He adores his mates. They mean the world to him and he will always do anything to help out one of the boys. I quickly became part of his circle and we all enjoyed going clubbing together.

While we were out and about we always acted like big kids, making a lot of noise and drawing attention to ourselves. I was very happy to be part of this new crowd, who all seemed like fun people who were going places. We were a boisterous group, and all the attention we created often meant other groups of boys could become jealous of us, which led to the odd argument here and there, although, thankfully, nothing serious. We were just young and intent on having fun. At this point it was only Mark, Jack and Josh who were earning decent

I was very happy to be part of this new crowd

money, and they were very generous towards the rest of us and funded a lot of our great times together. They paid for our dinners and would often look after us, which we all much appreciated because not many people who were that young had good incomes. Sometimes we'd go for an all-day party at Nu Bar in Loughton and then get a minibus to Faces for the evening. We would mainly go out clubbing at weekends but we would also get up to mischief midweek.

One regular prank involved getting a load of tissues and using them to completely smother a victim's car in shaving foam, eggs and baked beans, along with anything else gooey that we could get our hands on. We called ourselves the Tissue Bandits and would strike at night so that the next morning the target would find their car completely covered in mess. The majority of the time we would do it only among our group of friends, but sometimes we would target random people in the area whom we didn't get on with!

We became the Essex in-crowd, but it meant that all the other groups of boys in the area disliked us. I still got on with everybody fine, but I think people were envious of us, not least because we were collectively very popular with all the girls in the area.

One of the great Essex traditions that I soon became involved with was the annual boys' holiday. Marbella was always the place to go and we would save up all year to be able to afford it. The thing that attracted us about Marbella was the sheer glamour and glitz that it oozed, with its beautiful port and luxury yachts and its posh nightclubs. Gangsters from the

East End of London and Essex would go there frequently to show off their perma-tanned muscles and flaunt their wealth in front of all the beautiful women. Anybody who was anybody wanted to be seen there – and for boys like us it was a chance to party like wild. For the short space of time we could afford to be there, we'd spray champagne everywhere and we'd blow a month's wages on pretending to lead a millionaire's lifestyle (even though we'd be skint when we got back home).

Another popular holiday haunt was Cancún in Mexico. After I became friends with Mark he invited me to join the lads on a holiday there. I remember thinking that I would love to join my new best mates but, unfortunately, at the time I didn't have the cash. To be blunt, I was skint, but, thankfully, Mark had a plan.

'Don't worry, Arg. I'll pay for your holiday and you can pay me back whenever you can,' he offered.

'No, Mark, I can't let you do that,' I replied, but Mark had made up his mind.

'Arg, I want you to be there,' he insisted. 'And I want you to have a good time. I'm *loaning* you the money. I'm not giving you it. But I want you to come on this holiday.'

That settled it. I didn't need to be asked again. I went on the Cancún holiday and I loved every second of it. The night before we left we all went to a local nightclub in Essex called 195 for a group bonding session. One of the boys, George Andretti, brought his passport to the club to use for ID purposes. Unfortunately, when we arrived at the airport by cab the next morning, Andretti realised he'd lost his passport in the club and ended up missing the flight and the holiday. We were all gutted because we wanted him to come, but there were still about eight or nine of us who went. We all had terrible hangovers on the plane but, during the holiday itself, the boys had me laughing from the moment I woke up until I went to sleep at night. One minute we'd be playing pranks and the next we'd be drunkenly crying about how much we loved one another! It was a huge laugh. We went out there with visions that all the American girls would be throwing themselves at us.

'We're English and American girls love English boys!' was our motto.

We were convinced that all the women would be charmed by our accents and that we'd go with a different girl every night. But, unfortunately, when we got to Cancún the opposite happened and it was like being on *The Inbetweeners*. We dressed ourselves up in tight shirts and long trousers with smart shoes, yet all the American guys were wearing baggy shorts with huge T-shirts and baseball caps. We stood out like sore thumbs and we soon discovered which style of dress the American girls preferred – and it wasn't ours! But, despite our lack of success with women, we still had plenty of laughs, and we went to a famous bar called Coco Bongo's. Whenever we were together in a group, we sang a song called 'Low' by Flo Rida and T-Pain, which was a huge hit in the charts at the time (it was a song that we would all later perform together at Jack and Jade's wedding). All in all, we had a sick time in Cancún (sick meaning good, in case you're wondering). I had one of the best holidays of my life and I was very grateful to Mark for paying for me to go along.

If Cancún had been wild, nothing could have prepared me for the chaos of the annual get-together in Marbella. When we arrived we went seriously off the leash, acting all flash. We were up for anything. We thought we were the top dogs, although, looking back, I realise that at times we behaved like dickheads (you are only young once). Marbella has always attracted rich people who use it as a playground and we wanted a slice even though we weren't rich. Our lack of serious cash meant we had to stay every year at the same cheap hotel, which was called the PYR and it had four beds in every room. When we arrived I could imagine how the poor manager would shake his head, thinking, Oh, God! Not this lot again!

Nothing could have prepared me for the chaos of Marbella

We always chose the same hotel because (a) it was cheap and (b) we could have the run of the place.

There was no security there to stop you from taking back girls, and we could do as we pleased. We acted like rock stars. Jack had become a minor celebrity through his relationship with Jade, and, of course, Josh played for Charlton – so in our minds we were the bee's knees.

It was on my first holiday in Marbella with the boys that banter went to wild extremes. The hotel had long marble corridors that linked all our rooms. One of the first things we did when we arrived was turn the corridor into a massive water slide. We all went into our rooms and got buckets of water that we threw onto the floor until the place resembled a giant swimming pool. Then we grabbed tons of shampoo and shower gel and we chucked it onto the floor to make it super-slippery.

Slip-'n'-slide time!

We all stripped off and took it in turns to sprint full pelt down the corridor and dive onto the soapy mess to see who could slide the furthest. It was very immature, but it was amazing fun! God knows what all the other guests must have thought. All you could hear was this hysterical laugher followed by swishing sounds and occasional bang as somebody collided with something. One of the guys hit the end of the corridor so hard that it broke a reinforced glass panel, which caused us all to run off and hide for a while in case the manager came to investigate. It's fair to say that we created a right mess and I'm not quite sure how we managed to get away with it.

Our nights would be spent touring the local bars and clubs in search of beautiful girls and the banter between us would go on from morning until night. There were hordes of people out there who were from Essex, including Sam and Billie Faiers, whom I knew through my mate Lewis Bloor before we all appeared on *TOWIE* together. Sam and Billie were there on a girls' holiday at the same time as we were there, and occasionally we would bump into each other. I'd known Sam for quite a while. We got on like brother and sister and I remember that Sam would dance with me during my nights out at Faces. She's a lovely bubbly girl and I like her a lot.

One thing I'd been warned about before I went on the holiday was that I should pack plenty of spare toothbrushes.

'Why should I do that?' I asked.

'You'll find out when we get there,' advised Mark.

Basically, there was a custom that, if anyone left their tooth-brush unattended, it was fair game for a bit of bantering. This would usually involve somebody using it to clean the toilet, or, worse, putting it somewhere very impolite. I came back from the pool one day to discover I'd fallen victim.

'Aarrgh! Who's being sticking my toothbrush up their arse?' I screamed.

There was also a custom whereby, if anybody left an item of clothing lying around while we were out, it was fair game to be used in a tug-of-war event. Some of the pranks were a bit near the knuckle but it was all good natured. I went out on the balcony one evening to discover the boys were play-ing a game of Frisbee – using china plates! Some of the boys were standing three or four floors up and flicking the plates off the balcony as if they were made of plastic. Every time one smashed below, a large cheer would go up (thankfully, somebody had checked that nobody was on the ground below).

Days would be spent on Plaza Beach, which was packed with gorgeous women showing off their bodies in bikinis. All the guys seemed to have very athletic bodies with rippled stomachs, which made me very conscious about my weight. Mark, Josh and Jack were all very slim and muscular, so I felt the odd one out. At first I refused to take off my T-shirt because I was embarrassed.

All the guys seemed to have very athletic bodies

Wearing a T-shirt all day made me stand out. I soon paid the price when I fell asleep while sunbathing. Josh spotted that I had dozed off and went to the bar to fetch a huge bucket of iced water. I guess he'd decided that, if I wasn't going to take off my T-shirt on my own, I needed a bit of help. The beach was packed and everybody watched as Josh crept up on me and let rip with the bucket ...

Splash!

I woke up with a huge start as the icy water completely took my breath away. It seemed to attract the attention of everyone on Plaza Beach and I went bright red amid all the laughter. Of course, I had no choice but to take off my T-shirt now that it was dripping wet. Everybody cheered after I removed it and in a way it did me a favour because after that I didn't worry any more about showing my body!

It was a tradition that on the last night of the holiday we'd hold our own awards ceremony to give out special mentions to whoever had pulled off the wildest stunts. We'd go to an Indian restaurant called Khan's in Puerto Banús, where the awards would be handed out in different categories such as Biggest Banterer for the best prankster, Most Bangs for the biggest Romeo, and Best Newcomer for anyone who was making their debut in Marbella.

Mark always won Best Organiser, and I think I won Best Room Mate because I'd always be first to arrange the food. The ceremony would be hilarious because people would be offended if they hadn't won certain awards, and there would be heated discussions about who deserved to win. The prospect of the awards meant that everybody spent the whole holiday trying to outdo the others by behaving in the most outrageous way or trying to pull off the best prank. Newcomers to the group would always be the biggest target, which meant I had to take my fair share of stick on that first holiday.

On one occasion, a pair of expensive sunglasses that belonged to one of the boys got smashed up while he was in the pool, which led to a heated argument. Sometimes, it would get out of control. If one of us got lucky with a girl and stayed away from the hotel, then the chances were that somebody would take a leak in their bed. They would come back to find their bed soaked and would have to change the sheets and dry out the mattress.

On another occasion someone found a turd strategically placed outside the door to their room! It all sounds disgusting now, but I can't help but laugh. We were all in our late teens and early twenties and it was our way of letting off steam.

The *pièce de résistance* of the bad behaviour came courtesy of a boy called Andretti (the one who'd missed out on the holiday in Cancún). He nearly got us all arrested by chucking a full-sized television set from the top of a balcony. When it happened I couldn't believe my eyes. I turned around to see Andretti struggling to lift up the giant telly. Then, as he shuffled towards the balcony with it in his arms, I had to do a double take. Surely not?

'Andretti, no – don't do it,' one of us screamed, as he slowly moved towards the balcony with the intention of hurling it over.

A few us tried to stop him, but it was too late, and, to be honest, most of us were crying with laughter by now. I watched as Andretti made his way to the edge and let go of the giant TV. There was a split second of silence before . . .

Boom!

There was a deep, rumbling explosion that sounded like an earthquake. Surely, this would bring the manager running up to us! We all scattered back to our respective rooms and decided to lie low for a while. We hoped we would get away with it, but soon all hell broke loose. The manager charged up to our floor and threatened to call the police. Until now we'd managed to explain away any damage that we had caused as being accidental. Either that or we would blame it on someone else. But there was no way out of this one because it was a TV set from one of our own bedrooms.

We pleaded with the manager not to call the cops and in the end he relented on condition that we pay a big fine to cover the cost of the TV. It must have been an expensive TV set because we were charged around €2,000. Andretti had initially been regarded as a bit of a hero for doing something so outrageous, but we were now cursing him, since he didn't have enough cash to pay. It was decided that the damages would have to be split between us, so we all chipped in what amounted to around a couple of hundred euros each. It was an expensive prank.

When the last day of the holiday arrived, it felt as if I'd been in a war zone, although of course secretly I loved every minute.

'What are you planning to do today, Arg?' one of the boys asked me.

I decided that I wanted to spend the last day chilling out and topping up my tan.

'I'm just going to relax by the pool,' I answered.

'OK, that's cool.'

Little did I know that the banter and pranks traditionally increased to frenzy levels on the last day. As I lay by the pool relaxing in the sunshine, nursing a light hangover, I noticed that a lot of the other boys kept popping back to the hotel.

Maybe they need a bit of shade after all the partying, I thought.

By the end of the afternoon, they'd all come back and I noticed one of two of them giggling and laughing. When I went back to the room that night I realised what they'd been up to. My room was like a complete bombsite! My clothes were everywhere. There were boxer shorts stuffed in the freezer and garments scattered everywhere that had been covered in shaving foam.

I went to the balcony and looked across the courtyard. There, at the top of a palm tree, was my suitcase. How they managed to get it there I had no idea, but I had to go and knock it down with a stick. When I finally got it back inside, there was one last nasty little surprise inside it. By now the other boys were crying with laughter, so I should have known there was more to come. As I opened the bag the smell hit me. Inside there was a plastic bag that contained a brown gooey mess. I'll leave it to your imagination as to what it was, but let's just say it wasn't leftover tapas! The boys all thought that it was hysterical and I had just become the first victim of what officially became known as the Phantom Shitter. To this day I have no idea who did it – nobody was going to own up to it in a hurry. In subsequent holidays it became a great talking point, with everybody living in fear of falling victim to the Phantom!

That first holiday in Marbella had been a wild experience, and, despite having fallen victim to a fair bit of practical joking, I'd enjoyed every moment. Everyone dished it out and everyone had to take it, so it wasn't as if I was alone. As I flew back to England, the only small disappointment was that I still hadn't managed to pull a girl. Of course, most of the boys around me had enjoyed plenty of action in this respect over the course of the holiday. Chasing girls was one of the chief activities in Marbella, but, as usual, I'd scored a duck.

While the boys were out pulling, nearly every night I would end up in either the pizza or kebab shop at 3 a.m. I'd get a takeaway and end up eating in quietly in my room while the other lads were pairing off with the girls. Sometimes there would be somebody getting passionate in the room at the time, which made things a bit awkward, to say the least.

While the boys were out pulling, I would end up in the kebab shop

I needn't have worried, because, although I didn't know it at the time, my luck with girls was about to change when I arrived back in Essex.

5

A Haircut from Hell and a Crazy Girl with Perfume in Her Mouth

It was the summer of 2008 and I was about to meet a girl who would change my life. I was twenty at the time and, as my mates helpfully kept reminding me, I was still a virgin. The fact that I'd never slept with anyone was beginning to play on my mind due to all the leg pulling that I went through from mates who seemed to be enjoying the company of plenty of women. I felt like the odd one out and the longer it went on the more nervous I became around the opposite sex. It was two and a half years before the launch of *The Only Way Is Essex* and I looked like a very different person back then. For a start, I had a skinhead haircut, which didn't suit me at all. In fact, it made me look dreadful. The reason I'd had it done was that Mark Wright and Jack Tweed had a little tradition that they'd get their hair cropped short

67

into a skinhead every year, at the start of the summer. It looked cool and they'd let it grow out for the rest of the year. They were good-looking boys, so it was a style that suited them both. I decided I'd join them: after all, we were mates and I thought it'd be fun. As soon as I saw my reflection in the mirror, I realised it was a mistake. I've got huge ears that stuck out like bat's wings and a big nose, so a skinhead made me look awkward and strange. At this point in my life I weighed 18 stone and, worse still, my head was covered with moles.

'I don't think I look too great,' I told Mark, who I suspected probably had a good laugh at my new look.

I had my haircut from hell shortly before we were all getting ready to go to one of the biggest events in the Essex social calendar: the Duke of Essex Polo Trophy. It was an annual event held at Gaynes Park in Epping, and it always drew huge crowds. The highlight was a big polo match between England and Argentina, which would be attended by various celebrities and VIPs, some of whom would arrive by helicopter. At night-time it turns into a massive party with DJs and music. People look forward to it all year round because everyone gets suited and booted and all the beautiful women turn out in their finest dresses. It is a bit like Essex's answer to Royal Ascot, and I remember that the boys and I were really up for it. I wore a black suit with a white shirt and tried to look my best, despite the skinhead hairdo.

The event itself was fantastic. Jade Goody was there with Jack and she wore a stunning black-and-white dress and matching black hat. Other celebs who arrived early included the models Caprice and Danielle Lloyd and the singer Simon Webbe. As usual, Mark, Jack and I were out to have some fun. The sun was shining and we eagerly tucked into the champagne, and by the time the evening came along I was a little bit tipsy. There was a great disco and the boys and I were all dancing and really going for it. While we were partying, I looked across the dance floor and spotted a girl I knew. Her name was Robyn and she was somebody whom I'd always got on with quite well as a friend. Secretly, I quite fancied her, and with the drinks flowing I wondered if now might be a good time to approach her. I paused for a moment wondering what to do – after all I'd hardly been a big hit with the girls so far. While I was thinking about things, I noticed a pretty blonde girl dancing by the side of Robyn. The pair of them were in a group of girls who were all friends and every time I glanced over I noticed that the blonde girl seemed to be having a laugh and a joke with Robyn. They were obviously very close. It was then that I had an idea. Maybe I could find out from the blonde girl if Robyn fancied me too? It was a crazy plan, but after a few drinks it appealed to me because I was too shy to speak directly to Robyn.

While they were dancing I sidled over and managed to get the blonde girl's attention. As I looked at her properly for the first time I could see that she had beautiful long hair and piercing blue eyes. She wore lots of makeup and was very stylishly turned out, but she was also very tipsy!

'Hello, are you all right? What's your name?' I asked, smiling.

'My name's Lydia.' She smiled back at me.

And that was how it happened. That was how I first met Lydia Bright, who became the great love of my life, as seen by millions of viewers on the first few series of *The Only Way Is Essex*. It all began because I'd fancied her mate, although, if the truth be known, I had started to become captivated by Lydia herself from the moment we spoke. She was seventeen when we met. But, for the time being, I continued to stumble on with my crazy plan to get fixed up with Robyn.

'You're called Arg, aren't you? I know who you are,' she said.

'Could you do me a favour, Lydia?' I asked. 'Don't tell her this, but I fancy your mate Robyn. Is there any chance you could get me in there, or find out whether she likes me?'

Lydia seemed to find my unusual approach hilarious.

'Ha-ha! Yes, I'll see what I can do,' she replied.

We parted and went our separate ways around the dance floor. I carried on having a laugh with the boys but a little bit later my path crossed Lydia's again.

'I think Robyn just likes you as a friend,' she said, as if trying to let me down a little bit gently.

I laughed it off and had a little joke with Lydia, who seemed quite drunk herself by now. I was disappointed by Robyn's reaction, but I found my eyes increasingly drawn to Lydia every time I glanced over at her. She was always smiling and seemed so bubbly and full of life. She was dancing in a very alluring way, really throwing herself into it and bumping and grinding with all the right moves. I watched her and then, as my eyes panned around the room, I saw Robyn. She was with another boy and they were kissing.

Oh, bloody hell! I thought. Robyn's found someone else.

Then, while I was watching Robyn and her new bloke, I noticed that Lydia had clocked me. We seemed to share a little smile about the humour of the situation with Robyn, and, from that moment on, I started to pay a lot more attention to Lydia on the dance floor. She really was a fantastic mover, while most of the girls around her couldn't manage to string together more than two steps. After a while, I plucked up courage to go over to Lydia and we started dancing and having a bit of a conversation. I can't remember exactly what we spoke about but I remember feeling comfortable in her company, and we were laughing and giggling a lot. The fact that I had tried to use her as a way of chatting up her friend seemed to have broken the ice between us in way that I hadn't expected. We carried on dancing and I had this big smile on my face because he she kept making me laugh with all her funny little dance moves.

Never mind Robyn, I thought. I think I'm in with Lydia here!

The music was pounding and the drink was going to my head. I could see that Lydia was feeling the effects of all the drink, too. By now we were dancing much more closely. I remember thinking how attractive she looked as we moved towards each other. Then, before I knew what was happening, suddenly we were sharing this long, passionate kiss. We pulled away from each other and I was slightly surprised at what had happened. I felt quite happy with myself that this funny girl obviously liked me, and all my thoughts of Robyn were gone.

Then, a few moments later, Lydia did something that I

thought was very strange. She grabbed her handbag and went inside it to pull out a bottle of perfume. I assumed that she was going to spray her body with it, but instead she opened up her mouth and squirted in the perfume! I don't know whether she'd muddled up the perfume with a breath freshener or not, but it seemed very odd.

What the hell are you doing? I thought.

I don't think she quite knew why she had done it, because by now she'd had a lot to drink, but it added to the mystery that I sensed about this unusual girl. She had agreed to find out about her mate's feelings for me and she had then capti-vated my attention herself with her sexy dancing. She obviously had a fun sense of humour. By now I was caught in the moment and we carried on kissing, even though I could taste the perfume in her mouth. After a while we parted.

'I'm going to find my friends now – but I'll see you a bit later,' I said awkwardly, wondering now where Mark and Jack were.

I didn't see Lydia for the rest of the night but I kept giggling to myself about what had happened. I don't know if she went home or what, but it was the last we

I didn't know it then, but I was about to fall in love

saw of each other that evening. I left the polo event that night with the boys and went home feeling happy with myself, even though I wasn't really expecting anything more to come of it. I didn't know it then, but I was about to fall in love with the crazy girl with the perfume in her mouth.

*

A few days later I was on Facebook when a new message popped up. It was from Lydia.

It said something along the lines of, 'Did I get with you last week?'

I giggled to myself. I was pretty sure that Lydia knew full well that we had kissed (she hadn't been *that* drunk). The message was just an excuse to get in touch and I felt quite pleased to hear from her. I sent back a funny message confirming that we'd kissed but I didn't pursue it much further. It wasn't that I was playing it cool: it was just that I didn't expect anything else to come out of it. Looking back, I realise she was sending me a clear message that she liked me, but I wasn't very good at reading signals from girls at the time, which might help explain why I was still a virgin. We had a brief correspondence on Facebook but that was all.

It wasn't until I was at Faces a few days later that the next thing happened between us. Thursdays were always good at the club because it was an over-eighteens night (as opposed to over-twenty-ones), so all of our younger crowd could easily get in. I was there one Thursday when I spotted Lydia on the dance floor with her friends. She was doing her sexy routine again and for the first time I realised just how much I really liked her.

Ah, you know what? I thought. I do fancy this girl.

I went over to talk to her and we were soon dancing together again. Inside Faces there was a main dance room, where they played house music, and there was also a little side area called Room 2, where they played R&B and hip-hop. As midnight arrived I found myself with Lydia in Room 2 and we were soon bumping and grinding sexily with each other. We had another little kiss and we agreed to exchange telephone numbers. After that, our secret liaisons in the hip-hop room became a regular thing. We'd text each other during the week along the lines of, 'Meet you in the hip-hop room at midnight on Thursday!'

It became our funny little custom to meet for a dance and a kiss together at midnight where nobody could see us, before going off again into the main room with our respective friends. Whenever my phone pinged to tell me a text had arrived I found myself hoping that it was from Lydia. I had never kissed the same girl continually over a period of time, so this was new to me and I remember thinking how much I was starting to enjoy our secret meetings. I never attempted to take her home or invite her on a date. It was just our special time at midnight, and I wasn't sure what to do next.

I think it was just natural shyness on my part. I didn't know whether Lydia would turn out to be just a girl I kissed occasionally in a club, rather than a relationship. I didn't want to spoil things by making the wrong move. What I did realise was that I was starting to look forward to Thursdays more and more. I always made sure I went on to Faces on that night, and I did my utmost to try to link up with her. Even if there was an evening when she couldn't make it I'd want to go there on the off chance, just in case she changed her plans and turned up.

After a few weeks, our meetings were interrupted, because Lydia had a holiday planned in Marbella with some girlfriends, and, for a week or two, I really missed seeing her. I was hoping I'd meet her when she got back but then something happened that caused a bit of a cloud in my mind. I was waiting for a train when I bumped into a friend of both me and Lydia and we got chatting. My heart sank as she told me that Lydia had kissed a boy while she was out in Marbella. (It's impossible for somebody in our Essex crowd to keep a secret for long, and this was no exception.)

Of course, Lydia and I hadn't even been on a proper date at this stage, so I had no real cause to feel aggrieved, but for some reason the news that she had kissed somebody else upset me a little. I was starting to hope that what we shared might lead somewhere, but, if she had kissed someone else, then maybe it wasn't so special after all. I was disappointed. Maybe, I shouldn't bother trying to take things further, I thought. Perhaps my initial feeling that it was nothing more than a few kisses with me in a nightclub had been correct. I think the girl who told me about Lydia's holiday in Marbella must have realised that she'd inadvertently put her foot in it, because I then received a phone call from Lydia, who knew that I was upset.

'Look, it was just a kiss on a girls' holiday; it was nothing,' she explained. 'I didn't realise that there was a chance that we might be able to see each other. I'd like to see you,' she added.

I could understand Lydia's point of view. We weren't exactly going out with each other and, since I'd not made any moves in that respect, she must have doubted whether I wanted to make a go of it. Maybe this was the time for me to seize the moment.

'I would really like to see you. Can I take you out?' I asked.

Lydia agreed and, with that, we arranged a date. When she gave me her address I had a bit of a surprise, because it turned out that she lived near the top of my road, five minutes' walk away. I wondered how this girl could have lived so close to me all these years and yet our paths had never crossed before now. This was getting more mental by the moment. The rest of the conversation flew by in a blur. This was going to be my big chance: we were finally going to meet to go out together on a proper date.

When the big day arrived I didn't have a lot of cash to take us out, but I was determined to make a good impression. I had a new pair of trainers that I decided to wear and I had a nice pair of jeans, but I wasn't sure what else to wear. I looked in the wardrobe and the only thing I could find was a big banana-coloured hoody. It looked a bit odd, but it was clean and bright, so I decided to give it a go. During my final years at school I had put on a lot of weight and I had continued to pile it on when I started working, so my wardrobe was a bit limited for choice at this stage. I toyed with the idea of trying to slim down, but I had a problem: I just loved my food too much. As I stared at my clothes I remembered that I was due to go on holiday to Florida the next day, and most of the new stuff I had bought recently was meant for the beach, so yellow hoody it was.

I had an idea that Lydia and I might go to the cinema, but it was a warm summer's evening, so I decided to walk to Lydia's house rather than arrive in a minicab. I thought we could call one later, as I hadn't even started taking driving lessons by this point. As I strolled up to the top of my road in my hoody I couldn't help but feel nervous: here I was finally going on a date with a girl I liked. When I knocked at her door she came outside immediately, smiling at me. The cinema was quite a distance but it was a lovely evening, and the area where we live is surrounded by greenery and trees, so I thought it would be nice to take a stroll together.

'Lydia, would you like to go for a walk with me?' I asked.

She agreed, and we walked together all the way from her house to the cinema in South Woodford. All the time we were chatting about shared friends and telling different stories. It felt as though we had known each other for ages. Our hands slipped together and we walked along like that, hand in hand. We spent the whole journey of about three miles laughing and joking with each other. Lydia looked stunning and she didn't even pass any comment about my bright yellow top, which now seems a strange choice of clothing for a first date. When we arrived at the cinema, *Mamma Mia!*, the musical film about Abba, was showing and I suggested we see it. I don't know what sort of film Lydia expected to see but I was still a big fan of music and theatre, so it was a natural choice for me and I bought us two tickets. Inside, we got loads of popcorn and sweets and settled down together. I knew every word to the songs in *Mamma Mia!* – and when the film had started I sang along to all the great Abba numbers. I was fixated by the film, while Lydia laughed her head off and loved every minute of it. Every time I turned to her she was laughing and giggling, and I suppose I must have made quite a sight. There can't have been many 18-stone skinheads in Essex who knew every word of Abba! But, thankfully, Lydia found it funny. I think I enjoyed the film more than she did but she was probably quite touched to have found somebody who liked music and theatre.

When the film ended and the lights came up, I felt the date was going like a dream: I was with a girl I was starting to adore and I got the impression that the feeling was mutual. Just as we were getting out of our seats Lydia spotted one of her mum's best friends sitting among the audience. As I stood up something happened that made my world come crashing down. Lydia waved to her family friend. The woman did a double take at me in my bright-yellow hoody before shouting at the top of her voice across the whole cinema.

'Oi, Lydia! how come you've gone on a date with Banana Man?' she bellowed.

I was so embarrassed and I immediately went bright red. I suppose I did look a bit like a giant banana in my yellow top with my white scalp showing through my skinhead, but it was the last thing I wanted to hear.

Oh, my God! I recall thinking. I wish the ground could swallow me.

But Lydia laughed along with it bravely, despite my blushes.

'Just ignore her, it doesn't matter,' she told me kindly.

When we got outside, I asked Lydia what she wanted to do next.

'Do you want me to take you home now?' I said.

'No, come on, let's go out for a couple of drinks,' she

replied eagerly, clearly not worried about being spotted in a local pub with Banana Man.

So we went for a drink in The George in South Woodford and we continued to get on really well, constantly laughing at each other's little jokes and enjoying each other's company. I sat there looking at her. There had been many times when I was younger that I had looked at a girl, but I'd never received any attention back like this. Not only was she a girl who was attractive and witty, but I was getting vibes from her that she was feeling the same way about me. I could tell that she was really enjoying herself. As the evening drew to a close, I knew it would soon be time to go.

'Right, Lydia, come on, let's get a taxi and I'll drop you home,' I said.

But Lydia had other ideas: 'No, we can walk home.'

'What? You want to walk another three miles home? Are you sure you're not tired?'

'Yes, I'm sure. I don't want us to get a taxi. I want us to walk home.'

It was as if Lydia didn't want the night to end, and I was more than happy to oblige by walking her back. We made our way back to Woodford Green holding hands and talking all the way. I hadn't tried to kiss her all night, not in the cinema or the pub, and I was beginning to wonder what to do next. I kept thinking, Right, I really want to kiss her. I don't know if I'll get a chance or not, but I really want to.

As we got closer to her house I asked her if she'd mind taking a detour via the local garage so that I could get a milkshake and some crisps (this was something of a traditional late-night treat of mine, which may help to explain why I'd gained so much weight). Lydia agreed, and I asked if she wanted anything, but she was fine. Then we sat down on a little bench near the garage next to some greenery. I looked at her and said, 'Lydia, do you know what? I've really enjoyed tonight and I'd love to do it again.'

Lydia replied by telling me that she'd enjoyed it, too, and agreed that she wanted to see more of me.

Should I kiss her, or should I ask her first?

I now had a bit of a dilemma. Should I move towards her and kiss her, or should I ask her first? It didn't seem to matter that I'd kissed her before many times in the club, because this was different: we were alone and on a date. I was starting to feel a bit shaky with nerves in case I messed things up.

'Lydia?'

'Yes?'

'Would it be all right if I kissed you?'

'Yes, of course.'

And then we had a really nice passionate kiss as we sat there on the bench. I pulled away and thought about how amazing it felt. Then I remembered that I was due to go on holiday to Florida the next day and suddenly I wished I weren't going.

'I'm going to really miss you,' I said.

Lydia said that she would miss me, too, so we agreed that we would try to speak on the phone every day until I got back.

'I want to take you out a lot more,' I said, and we kissed again.

After that, I walked her to her front door and we said goodnight. It had been a brilliant date and I was so pleased that I ran and skipped all the way home. I was the man! That evening, after I got home, Lydia sent me a long text message telling me that, even though she had not that long ago met me, she couldn't believe how much she liked me. It made me very happy.

I ran and skipped all the way home

I'd done pretty well that night for a geezer who looked like a giant banana!

6

LOSING MY VIRGINITY AND A BAD EXPERIENCE WITH A BURGLAR ALARM

It felt weird as I flew to Florida because I had so many mixed emotions after my first proper date with Lydia. On the one hand, I was looking forward to three weeks of hot baking sunshine, but at the same time I didn't want to go because I was so excited about the great new girl I had just found. Secretly, I wanted to be with her and I wished I that were back in Essex. I was travelling to Miami with James Kane, my friend from the jeweller's, and his family. We were joined by Ferne McCann, who later appeared on *TOWIE*. During the flight I told them all about Lydia, and they were pleased for me. It turned out that James's dad, Jimmy, had been a childhood friend of Lydia's mum, Debbie. They told me that Debbie was a crazy character with lots of frizzy blonde hair and a real zest for life, which was something that I would soon find out for myself.

During the holiday I enjoyed soaking up the sun, but I seemed to spend most of my time reminiscing about my date with Lydia and wondering how things would develop between us. We spoke to each other on the telephone every day at a prearranged time in order to keep up to date with chitchat about what we'd been doing while we were apart. I wanted to buy her a nice present but I wasn't sure what to get, so I asked James's sisters, who were triplets, and their mum, Jackie. I told them that I didn't want to get something that was so over the top that it looked weird, because we'd been on only one date, but at the same time I wanted to let Lydia know how much I cared about her. The triplets told me that there was a new perfume by Juicy Couture that was then available only in the States. It sounded like the ideal gift. I bought Lydia a big bottle and, as we all flew back, I decided that I'd go straight round to her house as soon as I arrived in the UK.

When I finally got to meet Lydia's family it was a crazy baptism. I was nervous about seeing her parents for the first time, because I'd been told Debbie could be very outspoken, and I'd heard that her father, Dave, was a tough bloke who came from south London. When I arrived at the house it was obvious that Lydia had told them a lot about me, because the entire family were lined up in the kitchen to greet me. There were nine people there in all. Lydia has an older sister, Georgia, a younger sister called Roma and a brother called Freddie; and there were three children whom Debbie was fostering at the time. I felt as if I were being paraded for inspection! I needn't have worried about how Debbie and Dave would greet me because they were very friendly towards me from the beginning.

I was dressed pretty casually and very tanned, but my skinhead still hadn't quite grown out. Lydia had shown her mum some photos of me that were taken when my hair was still very short, and I think my haircut must have become a bit of a topic of conversation between them while I was away. While we shared a cup of tea and exchanged pleasantries in the kitchen, Debbie suddenly said something that made me laugh, but at the same time made me feel very embarrassed.

'James, I must admit, I've seen pictures of you and you look like Shrek!' she said, looking at me straight in the eye.

And with that the family all had a good laugh. It was an unusual thing to say at a first meeting, but, then, that was Debbie all over. She is a lovely, bubbly character who wears her heart on her sleeve and she will always say what's on her mind, even if it sounds a bit too honest. Lydia was mortified.

'Mum, you can't say things like that!' she exclaimed.

I promised everyone I would grow my hair and, once all the laughter had died down, I gave Lydia her perfume. She was delighted with it. But there was another awkward moment to come. Just as I was wondering what would happen next, Lydia invited me to go up to her bedroom. I felt a bit uncomfortable going upstairs while Debbie and Dave were there, but Lydia regarded it as completely normal. I suppose it was just an innocent way of getting some privacy, and her parents didn't seem to mind. It was the start of a great friendship that I was to enjoy with Lydia's family.

It was the start of a great friendship with Lydia's family

Debbie is now well known to viewers of *The Only Way Is Essex*, but Dave prefers to keep out of the telly limelight. He's a very friendly man who had a tough upbringing in Lewisham, where people tend to fend for themselves from an early age. Dave was a tiler who'd grafted his way up to running his own business, and he worked hard to provide his family with a nice lifestyle. He was a good-looking man with shoulder-length hair and loved popping into his local pub, the Three Colts, for a quiet drink. I got on well with Dave, and I also became close to his best friends, who were called Elaine and Paulie. I still go to Spurs with Paulie today. Debbie and Dave had met when they were the same age as Lydia and I were. Debbie would sometimes moan at him if she thought he'd been spending too much time there. Much as Dave will probably tell me off for saying it, it's Debbie who wears the trousers in their household, but, on the whole, I was pleased that Lydia had a nice family and that they all welcomed me so warmly, even if they *did* think I looked like Shrek!

My relationship with Lydia continued to develop really well, but I wasn't always very good at choosing great things for us to do. In fact, I'd sometimes get it disastrously wrong and I would take her on a date from hell. One such occasion was when Josh was due to make his first-team debut for Charlton Athletic and Mark, Jack and I all wanted to go along and show our support.

I know, I thought, without pausing to consider the fact that Lydia had absolutely no interest in football: I'll invite her to come too.

Mark and Jack came to pick us up and it was a funny combination of people to choose to go on a date with. Mark and Jack kept farting in the car on the way there, which I found hilarious, but at the same time I was worried that Lydia would think we were a bunch of donuts. At one point the car stopped next to a huge poster at a bus stop of a fat man, and Mark chirped up, 'Arg, what are you doing on that poster?'

It gave the boys a laugh, but I am not sure what Lydia made of it all.

It was an evening match and by now the nights were getting cooler, so, by the time we got in the stands, it was freezing cold. Poor Lydia had to put up with three blokes all cheering on their mate loudly while she sat there bored and shivering. Looking back, I realise it was a very poor choice of date, but I felt so comfortable around Lydia that it seemed natural to want to do ordinary things with her such as going to a football match.

I felt I could do anything with Lydia, although early in our relationship I was a bit worried about eating in front of her. I know it must sound a bit strange, because everyone knows that I love my food and that I can eat for England. But all the quips about my appearance were starting to make me feel uncomfortable and I was very conscious of my weight issue when I was around Lydia. She had a beautiful slender figure and here I was weighing 18 stone. I must have looked huge alongside her.

The first time we went for a meal together was at a restaurant called Zizzi's in Loughton. I think we ordered pasta and I felt very shy eating in front of her. I cared about what she thought of me, so I didn't want to sit there shovelling food in case she thought I was a slob. Mind you, we got on so well that it was only matter of time before we'd go for a meal and I'd eat my starter and main course and then help her to finish off hers, too. We would always order a sticky-toffee pudding with ice cream to share for dessert and I would eat most of it. Occasionally, I'd go too far. One of the first rows we ever had was when we'd ordered a portion of dough balls to share in Pizza Express. I was happily munching away at them and popping one into my mouth in between conversations. Suddenly, I realised there was only one left for Lydia, who hadn't had a single one so far. She understandably got quite irate and accused me of being greedy.

I knew within a few weeks of flying back from Miami that I had fallen in love with Lydia and I hoped that she felt the same way. I was out one day when I bumped into a friend of hers who confided a secret to me.

'You do know that Lydia loves you, don't you?' she said.

I wasn't sure if she was joking, so I pressed her for more.

'What? You reckon she's in love with me?'

'I *know* she is, because she's told me.'

And with that short sentence I had the best feeling in the world. Nobody outside of my family had ever told me that they loved me and it gave me special warm sensation inside. A few days later I was at Lydia's house reading a magazine in her bedroom while she lay on the bed.

'James, come here, I've got something to tell you.'

I went and snuggled up bedside her.

'I love you,' she said.

I told Lydia that I felt the same way and we kissed and cuddled for a bit. And then Lydia put on some music, 'Flying Without Wings' by Westlife, and we slow-danced in her room, looking into each other's eyes. I laugh now at how cringey it was, but at the time it was a very special moment. Debbie and Dave were now used to our spending time in her room together and didn't mind, although there was one rule: Dave made it clear from the beginning that I could come around any time and stay as late as I liked, but I was strictly forbidden from spending the night there.

I had not made love to Lydia yet, but I knew that sooner or later she might be expecting it. In fact, it wasn't until close to my twenty-first birthday, after we'd been dating for nearly four months, that it happened. My fear of having sex was starting to worry me. What had begun a few years ago with gentle ribbing from my mates over being a virgin had now turned into a big issue for me. To be honest, I was scared. I think blokes can have a lot of pressure put on them to perform 'like a man' from an early age, but some people

I had visions of my twenty-first birthday arriving and still being a virgin

develop more slowly in that respect. I guess I was just one of those people. If anyone reading this finds themselves in the same position my advice is not to stress about it, because that only makes it worse. It will develop naturally in time when you are ready, and that's what happened with Lydia and me.

My mates were starting to ask questions about whether

we'd done it and I'd shrug them off, although I confided to a few close friends that I was very nervous about it.

'Arg, you still haven't done it with her yet. She's probably thinking, What's wrong with you?' one of them said to me.

Looking back, there was no real reason to worry other than the fact that it had been built up to such a big thing in my mind.

Am I going to be terrible in bed? I'd ask myself. Do I even know what I'm doing? Is she going to hate it and will it put her off me?

I was aware that I would be twenty-one soon and I seemed to be leaving it later and later. I had visions of my twenty-first birthday arriving and still being a virgin. By now Lydia and I were often kissing passionately on the bed and our hands would be all over each other. I could tell that she wanted to take things further, and so did I, but I just didn't know how. We would be in full flow and then I'd suddenly have to stop because I would be literally shaking with nerves. After a while, Lydia worked out what the problem was.

'James, I know,' she said, obviously referring to the fact that I was a virgin.

'What do you mean, you know? I'm not a virgin,' I fibbed.

'It doesn't matter. I know. It's fine.' Lydia was really kind and understanding. 'Let's just take our time. We can do things slowly,' she said.

I was really grateful to her for taking the pressure off me like that and I respected her for being so nice about it. A few weeks later it finally happened. I'm not going to go into too much detail about it out of respect to Lydia, but let's just say that I got drunk and Lydia made a man of me. We'd had a drunken night in Faces and we went back to Lydia's house, where we kissed passionately. Then we finally made love. It didn't last very long, but, to be honest, I felt as if a giant weight had been lifted from around my neck. I was relieved that all the worrying would now be over and we could get on with our lives. It may seem silly that it had been built up into such a big thing for me, but that was the way it was.

The next day I felt as if I were walking on air and I asked her if it had been good for her. She replied in her usual warm but very frank way.

'To be honest with you, it was terrible, but I'm sure it'll get better,' she laughed.

Lydia always hit the nail on the head and, even though I was a bit embarrassed by her response, it showed how close we were that she could be that honest. I just laughed it off – I knew now that everything would be fine. I confided to some of my friends, who were delighted for me and offered to go for a celebration drink. I don't think Lydia minded my telling them. After all, we were adults and we were in a relationship. After that, we had a very normal and healthy sex life. In fact, Lydia even used to have a little nickname for my intimate part. For some reason she used to call it 'Marmen', although to this day I don't know why. I assumed it must have been some sort of private joke with her mates. Girls in Essex always chat with their friends about sex, and

I assume Lydia was no different. She was a very affectionate person.

Lydia had a fantastic way of turning me on, whereby she would do a sexy dance routine at the end of the bed, bumping and grinding the way she used to dance in Faces, but more intimately. It would always have the desired effect on Marmen!

Lydia had nothing but good qualities as far as I was concerned. She did a lot for me: she would drive me around and would treat me to nice little gifts; she knew I was a fan of Will Young and when his new album came out she bought me a copy and wrapped it up. It was the first present she ever bought me. One little secret that she kept from me early in our relationship, however, was that she had a part-time job in Woolworth's, which she kept quiet about while she was studying for her A-levels. I think she was embarrassed about my seeing her on the checkout in her uniform, but I soon found out about it. I went down there to see her one day with Josh and she went bright red when we saw her, but she didn't mind too much.

Our first Christmas together was very special. Lydia and I had taken to performing little songs together to entertain her family. We'd do numbers from *West Side Story* together while Debbie and the kids all sat on the sofa and watched. When Christmas came we spent the whole day at Debbie and Dave's house and I sang lots of numbers by Frank Sinatra and Dean Martin. Then Lydia and I went round to see my parents for a while before returning to her home. This was the one time of year when Dave relaxed his rule about no sleepovers. Dave said I could stay the night because it was Christmas. Secretly, I had already slept over a few times before, creeping out of the house in the morning. Lydia was very much the goody-two-shoes little princess of the family but she also had a wonderful sense of mischief and would encourage me to stay overnight. I was too scared at first but we'd tiptoe up the stairs together and I would creep in for the night. On one occasion, I'd made the mistake of leaving my shoes downstairs and, when I woke up the next morning, I could hear shouting in the house. I crept downstairs to find that my shoes had been moved. One was on its side in the corner and the other was dumped on the other side of the room. Apparently, Dave had been so angry at learning that I'd broken the no-sleepover rule that he'd kicked them in a fury.

'Oh, he's booted your shoes,' Debbie quipped when she saw me looking at them.

Dave would understandably always have a right hump after something like that happened, so I'd have to watch myself for a few days. I'd normally try to buy him a takeaway curry to make amends and he'd soon forgive me. I suspect he used to think that I took the piss a bit too much and that I'd had things very easy in life, but he always treated me very well and I respected him immensely.

Unfortunately, the next time I broke the no-sleepover rule it was to have catastrophic consequences. One night, I had crept upstairs with Lydia and we lay on the bed watching a film. Before I knew it, I was fast asleep. I woke up in the middle of the night and my first thought was, Shit! I've got to get out of here.

Lydia was fast asleep and I had trouble waking her, so I decided to creep out without saying goodbye. I walked out of the room and quietly closed the door before tiptoeing slowly down the stairs, being careful not to wake Dave or Debbie. Then I heard a noise that made me freeze and sent shivers down my spine.

Beep! Beep! Beep!

It was the burglar alarm and I realised I must have set it off. I didn't know whether to run back to Lydia's room and hide or go and wake up Debbie and Dave and tell them. In the end I panicked and decided to sprint full pelt for the front door. By the time I got to the bottom, the loudest alarm I had ever heard had gone off.

Screech! Screech! Screech!

I reckoned that the whole of Woodford must have been able to hear it. It was so loud that the whole house immediately woke up and I could hear Dave shouting.

'What's going on, what's going on?' he bellowed.

I didn't have the guts to go back and apologise. I was far too embarrassed and scared. I sprinted out of the house while this crazy racket was going on and ran all the way home. Because I lived so close to Lydia, I could still hear the alarm faintly from within my house. I decided to keep my head down and hope for the best.

The next day when I went up to Lydia's house Dave seemed to be a strange mood.

'Is there anything you want to tell me?' he asked.

'What do you mean, Dave?' I said, trying to bluff it out.

'Well, is there *anything* you want to tell me?' he repeated.

'Er . . . no,' I stammered.

'Well, that's very interesting because last night the burglar alarm went off and I looked outside my window and all I saw was your fat arse running off down the street.'

I had no answer to that one!

It was while Lydia and I were falling in love that my good friend Jack Tweed learned that his partner Jade Goody had cancer. When the news came it hit every-body like a hammer blow, and Jack understandably took it very badly. It couldn't have happened at a worse time because Jack had rec-ently been accused of assaulting a teenager and he was facing a prison sentence. I didn't con-done what he'd done but I also knew Jack had been through a lot after being thrust into the public eye at such a young age, and I was determined to stand by him.

It was at this time that Jack learned that Jade Goody had cancer

When I first met Jack we used to call him 'Lamppost' because he was so skinny. Lydia adored Jack because he always acted like a gentleman around her and could be a real charmer. Jack was normally very placid, despite the fact that people would shout things at him all the time because he was famous for being with Jade. I hated the idea of such a good friend being in prison. Before he went off to jail Jack had asked me if I would do him a favour. He had two beautiful watches, a Cartier and a Rolex, that Jade had bought him.

'Will you look after my watches for me while I'm gone?' he asked.

I agreed. I also tried to keep in touch with him the best as I could. I'd ring Jade to see how she was and to ask about Jack. I was always amazed how brave she was. She would answer the phone in a cheery fashion and always took the time to ask after me. I went to visit Jack a couple of times in Pentonville Prison, which was a horrible place. I had to be searched and go through all the elaborate security checks. Jack tried to put on a brave face, but I had never seen him looking so pale and pasty.

Jack and Jade were married after he was released and both Lydia and I went to the wedding. Even though we all knew that Jade was going to die very soon, we all wanted to give her and Jack a really fun day. Lydia and I had just been away on a holiday together to Gran Canaria, and Lydia had also recently celebrated her eighteenth birthday. The wedding service was very emotional and many of us in the congregation were openly weeping.

In the evening we all went outside for a fantastic firework display. It was a very memorable day but it was bitter-sweet: I knew that the next time we would all be gathered together would be for Jade's funeral. She died exactly four weeks later on Mother's Day. It was one of the saddest situations that I have ever encountered and it made me realise how fragile life is.

As I looked at Jade's coffin at the funeral I remembered her dancing away and smiling just a few weeks before. Jack did his best to hold things together but at the end of the service he collapsed to his knees and started crying. I hated seeing such a close friend going through so much grief. In the weeks that followed I visited Jade's grave several times with Jack, where he'd say a little prayer. It was a tough time for him and I respected him for the way he handled it.

7

THE SINGING BUG AND
AN ITALIAN NIGHTMARE

Singing has always been one of my greatest passions. Give me
a microphone and a song sheet and I will happily get up on
stage and croon the night away. My friends and family say
that I come alive when I am performing on stage. As a young
schoolboy I often sang in choirs and during my teens a lot of
the amateur-dramatics roles that I had involved singing. It's
something that I enjoy and my family told me that I had a
good voice from a young age. But by the time I reached my
early twenties I had neglected that side of my life, and for a
few years I didn't perform in public. I guess there were just too
many other distractions. After I left school I had to concentrate
on trying to find a job, and singing on stage was no longer at
the front of my mind. I still sang behind closed doors, particularly when I was at Lydia's house, where she and I would
perform together to the rest of the family and her little brother
Freddie would join in. He used to sing 'You're Beautiful' by

James Blunt. It was hilarious, he was like an *X Factor* contestant (but I don't think he'd have made it to the final!). It was only when all my job options ran out – which was about to happen – that I turned to singing as a possible profession.

I was still working in the jewellery shops by day, while trying to supplement my earnings through nightclub promoting. Lydia was supposed to be concentrating on her A-levels but in reality she was spending her every spare moment with me. Our relationship had continued to blossom and we were very much in love. The holiday we had shared in Gran Canaria had brought us even closer. We had spent the days lazing by the pool and the nights making love. Each evening we had snuggled up in our room to watch a film from the hotel's DVD collection called *Tropic Thunder*, a comedy starring Ben Stiller, but we'd never actually finished watching it because we'd either fallen asleep or got distracted by our lovemaking. When we got back to the UK I'd bought our own copy on DVD so we could finally watch it to the end. All the time we spent together came at a price, because Lydia started to fall behind with her A-level coursework. Debbie and Dave were under no illusions about where the blame lay: it was my fault. I felt they were being a bit unfair because in my mind we were both equally to blame.

Lydia had previously been placed in a class for gifted kids at school. She was very much a golden child and had done extremely well at her GCSEs at the age of sixteen, having passed in twelve subjects (including several at A grade). When it came to A-levels, the subjects she opted to study included further maths, for which you need to be a real brain box. She was expected to get three straight As. I was the first to admit that she was far brighter than I was. But, instead of studying at home and revising for exams, as our relationship developed Lydia spent more and more time with me. When she started missing the odd class, Dave and Debbie told me bluntly, 'You're going to ruin her A-levels.'

It was around this time that a bit of friction started to develop between Lydia and Mark. He's a natural wind-up merchant and he would gently rib Lydia about things that we'd got up to on boys' nights out. Mark is smooth-tongued and has the gift of the gab, which he gets from his dad, Big Mark.

He would tease Lydia by saying things like, 'Arg gets a lot of attention from the girls while we're out.'

He didn't mean any harm by it but I think it began to grate on Lydia's nerves and she could be quite harsh on Mark as a result. I think part of the reason for the friction between them was that Mark and I were so close as mates. We spent a lot of time just chilling out together and we would do things such as watch films together in his flat. I suspect that Lydia saw Mark as a bit of a negative influence on me and later in our relationship it would become a bit of a problem. It was quite funny to see because whenever I did anything wrong, such as come home late or fail to reply to an important text, Mark would always get the blame. I would use him as an excuse, even when he was entirely innocent.

'I'm sorry I never called, but Mark kept me busy all night,' I would tell Lydia, even when poor old Mark had nothing to do it.

Ironically, Jack was more likely to be the one to lead me astray, but in Lydia's eye's he could do no wrong. In the end, Mark became quite conscious of the fact that Lydia gave him a hard time.

'I've tried being friendly and doing my best, but she just doesn't like me!' Mark would complain, looking all hurt with innocent eyes.

Meanwhile, Lydia's studies continued to suffer and, when her results came through, they were nowhere near as good as expected. She still did well enough to win a place to study teacher training, but she didn't quite get three As. Lydia's family had previously hoped that she would be able to go to a top university, so overall her grades were a disappointment. Debbie and Dave were very unhappy and they felt I'd had a direct impact on her performance. They insisted that Lydia take some time out to decide what she wanted to do next.

In Debbie's eyes that meant taking a break from me.

Looking back, I suspect that Debbie thought Lydia and I had fallen head over heels for each other far too quickly. Debbie thought her daughter was still a young girl and she wanted Lydia to see a bit of the world before she got serious with a boyfriend. I don't think Debbie necessarily wanted to split us up: she just wanted to apply the brakes a little bit so that we could take things at a slower pace. In the end, Debbie came up with a plan that both Lydia and I hated. Debbie had some close family who lived in Italy. It was arranged that Lydia would go and stay with them for a few months while she got her head straight. Lydia made no secret of the fact that she didn't want to go and I was against it, too. But Debbie insisted that Lydia go and stay for a couple of months in Porto Recanati in Ancona in central Italy. When the day to say goodbye arrived I went round to Lydia's house. I had a sick feeling in my stomach because, for the year that we had been together, we had hardly been apart. Now, as I stood outside her house ready to say goodbye, I could feel the emotions beginning to well up within me. What would I do with myself without Lydia? We had a kiss and a cuddle and I told her I was going to miss her.

As I walked down the road I lost control. I broke down and started to cry uncontrollably. Then, at the worst possible moment, Debbie drove by in her car on the way to the airport with Lydia in the back. As they went past I saw Lydia turn her head and our eyes met. She could see I was crying and her face crumpled. Later that night Debbie called me and said that Lydia had cried hysterically at the airport.

I hated being apart from Lydia. For the two months that she was away I tried to put on a brave face in front of the boys, but they could see that I was inconsolable. I had visions of good-looking Italian boys all queuing to try to chat up Lydia. They dress slick and well out there and they have a reputation for being very amorous. Surely, they'd be all over a blonde girl like a rash. I assumed that they'd all have amazing bodies because they look after themselves so well, which made me feel worse. I kept wondering what would happen if an Italian hunk with a well-oiled six pack were to

While Lydia was away I was inconsolable

sidle up to Lydia and start to flirt with her. The thought made me feel sick inside.

Lydia and I kept in touch by phone, but it was a very gloomy time for me. On a couple of occasions I was tearful during my lunch breaks at the jeweller's. I'd walk off down the road alone thinking about her and get all upset. I couldn't believe that one person could have such a big effect on me. I even considered flying out there to be with her but in the end I decided against it, because I knew I had to respect her family's wishes. I was so lonely that I would go to Debbie's house just to hear little bits of gossip about how Lydia was getting on. Debbie was very kind and made me feel welcome when I popped around, but occasionally she'd make a joke about how Lydia was bound to bump into lots of good-looking Italian footballers. There was one boy who lived locally who apparently played for one of their top clubs, which made me feel all the more worried. I don't think Debbie was trying to be cruel (she doesn't have it in her to be like that) but she felt that Lydia needed some breathing space and that it would do her some good to spend time in another country. It was something that Debbie herself had done when she was younger.

Lydia told me on the phone that she'd been going to a local nightclub called Bubaloo, or something similar. I was pleased that she was starting to have a good time, but it also made me worry all the more about those imaginary Italian hunks. Her sister Georgia went to stay with her, and I knew Georgia could be a bit of a party animal. In the end, I needn't have worried, because Lydia came back in one piece. On the day Lydia flew back to the UK, Debbie agreed to drive me up to

Stansted Airport. I had to beg to get the day off from the jeweller's but eventually they agreed to let me go. Lydia had no idea that I was going to be there and, as I saw her emerge from Customs, my heart raced. She had bright-red cheeks due to all the sun she'd been exposed to and her hair had gone slightly curly. I threw my arms around her and we kissed. That night we made love, and it was as if she had never been away.

Lydia decided to take a gap year rather than go into teacher training, and she found a job as a receptionist, first with a company near Heathrow and then at a firm in Camden. It meant a lot of travelling and, although Camden was a great area for nightlife, it wasn't the best destination to commute to from Essex. At this point in our relationship we hardly ever argued – although we did have the odd spectacular tiff. On one crazy occasion she got so angry that she threw me out of the house.

It all started when we were innocently teasingly each other. Lydia used to take the piss out of me for my not being able to drive, while she had a full licence. Dave had brought her a brand-new Fiat 500, which was her pride and joy. I'd try to respond to her banter by making a witty remark, and one of the things I would tease her about was her forehead. If you look at photos of Lydia very closely you will see that her hairline is a bit higher than you might expect. Debbie shares that characteristic. It's nothing too out of the ordinary, but for some reason it made Lydia very conscious about the shape of her forehead. If I mentioned it she would become very touchy and take it to heart. It was the one thing that was guaranteed to drive her mad. So, whenever she did something to piss me off, I would tease her by calling her 'Forehead'. One day, while we were having a minor argument in her bedroom, I pushed things too far.

'Forehead! Forehead!' I teased.

I could see the red mist starting to rise, but I carried on. With that, I think she whacked me a couple of times. It was all very childish but, before I knew it, Lydia was in a fury. Georgia came into the room to see what all the fuss was about.

'Get out of the house!' they screamed at me.

I made a hasty retreat downstairs and went outside, assuming that Lydia would let me back in when she'd had time to cool off. But after five minutes she appeared at the window.

'How do you feel now, James?' she gloated.

I begged to be let back in but, to my amazement, Lydia responded by trying to throw a glass of water over me through the window. As I wondered what to do next, my eyes came to rest on her gleaming new Fiat 500.

'If you don't let me in I'm going to let down your tyres,' I shouted back. I had no intention of doing any such thing, but Lydia didn't know that.

'Don't you dare touch my car,' she screamed.

I bent down and unscrewed a dust cap on one of the tyres.

'Piss off! Don't touch my car! Don't touch my car!' she yelled.

I picked up a small stone and used it to let out a tiny hiss of air from the valve. It was such a small amount that it wouldn't have made any difference, but it sent Lydia into a wild fury. I was feeling quite clever with myself, but then I saw something that made me freeze. Lydia and Georgia had their mobile phones and were using them to film me.

'I'm telling my dad!' Lydia screamed, before closing the window.

A few moments later my phone rang. It was Dave, who was out with Debbie and the kids.

'You've let her tyres down, you prick!' he said (in fact he may have been less polite than that). 'You better make sure that by the time I get home the air's back those tyres.'

I made myself scarce for a couple of days – before buying Dave yet another curry to make amends!

Despite the odd fiery bust-up, Lydia and I were blissfully happy together. We were always having fun, and one of the things we used to do for a laugh was practise WWF wrestling moves together. Lydia used to make me laugh because there was a famous move called a Frog Splash – but she used to call it a Frog Spawn!

We loved going to a curry house in Wanstead called 62 Spice, or to Prezzo in South Woodford. Lydia also had an appetite for chewy sweets, which I would buy for her. Whenever she had a drink, she was also partial to a chicken and mushroom Pukka Pie with chips, and she would refuse to go home without it!

Trying to sing professionally still didn't figure in my mind

We'd also spend time visiting her grandmother, Maureen, who we are both very close to, and we'd make a regular thing of going to the cinema on a Wednesday night when there was a special promotion for tickets. We'd always go to the same cinema that we went to on our first date.

It was a fun time, but the only cloud was that we were both in dead-end jobs. It seemed as if Lydia were working miles and miles away, and all the commuting was starting to get her down because it took her ages to get home. Meanwhile, I knew that working at the jeweller's wasn't what I wanted to do for the rest of my life. Lydia wanted me to try to better myself – or at least find something that I enjoyed. At this point, trying to sing professionally still didn't figure in my mind. A lot of our friends in Essex had gone to work in the City as stockbrokers and bankers. When Lydia suggested that I should do the same, it got me thinking. I was very good at talking and socialising, so surely I'd also be good at selling stocks and shares.

'You know what? You're right, Lydia. I'm going to get a job in the City,' I vowed.

I asked around and heard that a broker I knew had a job going as a land broker near Liverpool Street. I applied and I was delighted when he gave me the job. Lydia said she was really proud of me – it seemed as if we were finally going places. I gave in my notice at the jeweller's and I thanked the Kane family for all they had done for me. Next, I needed to give my wardrobe a boost. The fashion in the City at the time was for dark suits with a nice crisp white shirt and a bright tie, usually red. The established brokers wore matching ties and belts from Hermès, but I suspected it would be a while before I could afford those. I was very excited as I rode the

Central Line up to Liverpool Street. I began full of enthusiasm but I am afraid to say that I turned out to be a right flop!

I loved the social side of working in the City, because there was a big drinking culture. I was great company in the bars and restaurants, but unfortunately I didn't manage to close a single deal. Within a couple of months my new employers called me in for a chat.

'Thanks for being here, Arg – but it's not working out.'

What a disaster! They were letting me go. The first thing I thought was, Shit! How am I going to tell Lydia?

I was so embarrassed: sacked after such a short space of time! On the Tube home that night I was full of fear and anxiety. I was so scared that Lydia would think badly of me. Surely she would think that I was a loser who wasn't going anywhere in life.

Then I had this crazy idea.

I'll keep it a secret while I look for another job, I thought. And then everything will be fine.

It was a stupid plan but at the time it made perfect sense. So the next morning I put on my suit and tie at 8 a.m. and left my house as normal so that nobody would suspect anything. I knew that it was wrong: Lydia was my best friend and I hated lying to her in this way. But that was exactly what I did. I'd go out in the mornings and come back in the evenings and pretend that I had done a day's work in between. What I actually did was go round to a mate's house and spend the day there. The trouble was that, once I had started to lie, it became impossible to stop. I was frightened of how Lydia would react, so I spent two long months in limbo, getting up every day and faking going to work. In the end it all became too much and I confessed to Lydia and Debbie that I'd lost my job, although I made out that it had only just happened. To this day they probably won't know about my period of faking it until they read this. It's not something that I am proud of, and I hope they'll forgive me.

Debbie has a saying about life that goes along the lines of, 'What's meant to be will be.' I think that's what happened with my being such a flop in the City: it just wasn't meant to be. I had finally used up all my options and it was now that my mind turned back to singing. My mum and dad had always encouraged me to think about performing, but sometimes I think you need to hear things from somebody outside your immediate family. When I told Debbie that it hadn't worked out in the City she sat me down for a chat.

'Your passion in life's always been theatre and singing to audiences,' she said. 'You love getting up in front of everyone. It seems like something you want to do. Why don't you sing for a living?'

At first I wasn't convinced. 'I don't know, Debbie. I can't just start singing on stage again now: I haven't done it properly for years.'

But she was adamant. 'I'm going to get you a local singing gig,' she insisted.

Debbie used to joke that the only way I could get Lydia into bed was when I sang to her (which was partly true!). Despite Debbie's initial concerns that Lydia and I were too close, I think she'd now come to regard me as something of a son of her own. She would cook for me almost every day. She could make a wicked portion of poached eggs on crumpets. As viewers of *TOWIE* would later see, Debbie, Lydia and I would sometimes all relax by sitting up in bed together to share a cup of tea, we were that close. I could talk to Debbie about anything and I was grateful for her advice about my singing. On one occasion, she had even forgiven me after catching me naked while I was with Lydia in the bedroom (Debbie just let out a scream and slammed the door closed after accidentally walking in on us!). Luckily, Dave didn't get to hear about it.

Debbie threw herself into helping with my new singing project. She had a good friend called Nicola who ran a restaurant called Rosso in Woodford. Nicola agreed to give me my first gig. I downloaded loads of backing tracks to prepare with, and I would hold a hairbrush as if it were a microphone and practise singing in front of Lydia and Debbie. (I also used to practise on my own in front of the mirror, but we won't go there.) Rosso was an ideal venue for a first gig because it was small and intimate and I knew that all my family and friends would be in the audience. The Kanes and the Wrights came along to wish me luck and it went really well. I mainly sang numbers by Frank Sinatra, Dean Martin and Bobby Darin – and it went like a dream! The restaurant was packed and everybody gave me a warm reception.

I must have caused quite a stir, because the next thing that happened was that a friend of mine called Adam Brooks contacted me. Adam was the boss of Nu Bar in Loughton, which is where all the Essex in-crowd flock to be seen. Adam had heard about my packing out Rosso and invited me to come and sing. I was very apprehensive to begin with because this would take things to a whole new level. It was a bar that was frequented by every trendy young person of my age in the area and I was aware that if I messed things up I would have the piss taken out of me big time. Adam persuaded me that it would be fine and he booked me to sing on a Friday night. Nu Bar would always be packed from 10 p.m. until the early hours, but it was relatively quiet during the early evenings. Adam suggested that I sing at around 7 p.m. or 8 p.m., which would bring more people into the bar early on and it would give me a chance to generate some regular income. Debbie agreed to drive me there on the big night, and, as usual, I was a bag of nerves. I spent so long getting ready that we were running late, which Debbie told me off about.

'Hello, Arg. I didn't think you were going to show up,' Adam said when I finally arrived.

When I went behind the microphone the bar was jam-packed; you couldn't move in there. I think a lot of people who knew me from my work as a nightclub promoter had come along just out of curiosity, not actually believing that I would sing. Mark and Josh were there to wish me luck, as was Jack, who was on a Home Office tag at the time after another tussle with the law. He was allowed to attend because it was during the early evening. As I opened my mouth to sing the crowd gave me such a warm welcome that all the nervousness began to evaporate. Soon the whole bar were joining in by singing and waving their arms in time to the tunes as I performed lots of big-band numbers. It was a great night and I enjoyed every moment of it. Adam was delighted and afterwards he invited me back to perform again in a couple of weeks. After that it became a regular thing and I sang at Nu Bar on a Friday every other week. We would go back to Jack's house afterwards and we would let rip on the karaoke machine.

Word about my singing started to spread and I began to look for other gigs in the area: I wanted to be the No. 1 local singer for weddings and parties. Debbie would drive me around in her car and I popped into every restaurant and bar that we could find so that I could leave my singing details and a card. As the summer approached I was starting to get regular work, although it wasn't quite enough to provide me with a full-time income. I needed something else to supplement it and Mark had an idea. His cousin Elliott (who runs a restaurant called Eduardo's in Spain, and who is now in *TOWIE*) had just returned to the UK. He was setting up a waste-disposal business. It was a rubbish job (quite literally). I had to go around collecting refuse from people's houses and putting it into a skip. It got me some spare cash but I felt like a real pauper. There had to be a better way of boosting my singing career than doing this. I was beginning to wonder just where my life was going. I needed something really gritty to get my teeth into. Maybe I should consider going abroad to work.

Then I had a big idea.

When the annual boys' holiday to Marbella came around, it got me thinking: why not spend the rest of the season singing in Spain? I'd flown out there with my mates and I

Word about my singing began to spread

was looking forward to all the usual fun and chaos (although, hopefully, minus any exploding TVs this time around). This year Lydia was in Marbella at the same time with all her girl-friends. We'd timed things like that so the two groups could meet up and party together. During our respective holidays, Lydia and I saw each other every day and she spent most nights at my apartment, often trying to look away while the likes of Josh wandered around naked.

It was while Lydia and I were chatting by the pool out there that we first discussed the idea of moving to Spain.

'James, I love it out here,' Lydia told me.

'So do I,' I replied. 'In fact, what have we got at home for us? You're unhappy in a dead-end job. My singing's doing OK, but I could be doing a lot more. Why don't we do a summer together out here?'

It all made perfect sense. Marbella was somewhere we both adored and we felt it would be a joy to live and work there. I knew lots of the bar and restaurant owners, so I was confident that we could both find work, I as a singer and Lydia as a waitress or promotions girl.

'We might as well do it while we're both young and we don't have any ties,' I added.

Lydia loved the idea and we made up our minds there and then. We planned that we would fly back from holiday with our mates before returning on our own for the rest of the summer.

It was settled: we would start a new life in sunny Spain.

8

A Stolen Kiss and Heartbreak in Marbella

Lydia and I flew to Spain together convinced that we were about to live the dream. We booked one-way tickets to Málaga and we eagerly packed our bags in the hope that our new life in the Mediterranean would be crammed with fun. After all, we'd both spent many happy holidays in Marbella. We knew the area well and we had lots of friends and contacts who could help us to settle in while we were finding our feet. We were deeply in love and we were starting a new life in the party capital of Europe. What could possibly go wrong?

Unfortunately, things turned out to be very different from what we expected. It was while we were living in Marbella that the first cracks began to appear in our relationship, and, amid a backdrop

The first cracks began to appear when we were in Marbella

of sun, sand and champagne, it was to have explosive consequences. Little did we know as we arrived in Málaga, but our Spanish jaunt would eventually lead to our temporarily breaking up.

It all began so well. Debbie had a close family friend called Melissa, who owned a huge villa in the hills above Mijas, near Fuengirola. It was a bit of a drive from Marbella itself, but Melissa agreed that Lydia and I could stay there while we looked for a place of our own. Melissa had been like an aunt to Lydia while she was growing up, so Lydia and I would call her 'Aunty Melissa'. She lived with her husband Peter and their three kids, and she was a wonderful host and treated us to lots of nice dinners. The villa was beautifully decorated. It had a big swimming pool, a large barbecue area and several bedrooms arranged over three floors. Lydia and I were very comfortable. The only drawback was the distance to Marbella, which was where we needed to be in order to find work. The bus journey took well over an hour and we had to change en route, so we were faced with nearly three hours' travelling in the boiling heat every day. It was a long, meandering route and there was no air conditioning on board, so it was very hot and stuffy. We would sit there sweating and dehydrated for what seemed like an eternity. Catching a taxi was out of the question because it cost around €100 each way. I had gone to Marbella with a small amount of savings but I didn't have enough to cover that sort of outlay. So, even though we were extremely comfortable at Aunty Melissa's villa, our first priority was to find our own place to live near the centre of town, ideally close to the main party strip in Puerto Banús.

This turned out to be much harder than we anticipated, because everywhere was so expensive. We found ourselves making the exhausting journey backwards and forwards to Mijas while we searched all the local lettings agencies and estate agents.

On one balmy afternoon, our travels nearly got us into serious trouble. We decided to get off the bus a few blocks early and walk the rest of the way back to Aunty Melissa's villa with the hot sunshine blazing down upon us. I was convinced that I knew the way but, after a few streets, Lydia and I discovered that we were well and truly lost. Worse still, we seemed to be drawing the attention of all the local guard dogs. Every villa that we passed had a huge beast tethered in the yard for security, and as we walked by every one of them would go into a ferocious frenzy.

Bark! Bark! Bark!

Pedestrians were not welcome in these parts and the dogs all went absolutely wild, making a deafening racket as they tried to jump up at the flimsy-looking fences to get at us. Meanwhile, we spent ages walking round in circles to try to find our bearings. All the time there was not a soul in sight – just the incessant snarling of guard dogs. After a while we became terrified that one of the dogs would escape and savage us. Finally, Lydia snapped.

'They're going to kill us! What are we going to do?' she screamed, tears welling up in her eyes.

The only time I'd ever seen her that afraid was during a trip to Winter Wonderland at Christmas, when we were at the top of a scary ride.

It sounds crazy, but we genuinely feared we'd be savaged. Here we were starting our new dream life, and we thought we were about to be eaten alive by the slavering beasts of Mijas. In the end, we had to phone Aunty Melissa, who came out in her car with Peter to find us and bring us home safely. It felt as if Lydia and I had literally gone to the dogs!

Within a couple of weeks we felt under huge pressure to find our own place, but our search proved to be fruitless until one day, by chance, Lydia got talking to an old lady in a hair salon. The woman said she had a second-floor apartment to let near the Bull Ring in Puerto Banús for €1,000 a month. It wasn't a particularly modern building, but it was clean and large, and it was in the right area, so we agreed to move in. There was enough room for a third person, so we hit upon the idea of sharing it with a friend called Danielle, who was also in the area looking for somewhere to live. Danielle was dating a friend of mine back in England called Fabian. I also knew her uncle, who was called Jamie and lived up the coast at Estepona. Lydia and I liked the thought of her staying with us because it meant we could share the costs. With hindsight, we realised it was a mistake, because I think Lydia and I would have benefited from our own space without a third person. It was going to be enough of a test for us to live together for the first time as a couple. Having somebody else on the scene just complicated matters. I'd always been told that a relationship can seem perfect when you are living apart, but once you share the same roof it can change things. It's when a relationship can come under stress, and that was what happened with

Lydia and me. We found that living together and working in Marbella were very different from going on holiday there.

Thankfully, Lydia soon found a job working as a waitress in a cocktail bar (just like in the song). It was at a place called the Lounge, which was next to Linekers Bar on the main strip. The money was OK and she earned a lot in tips, but the hours were extremely long. She would start at six or seven in the evening and work right through, sometimes until four or five in the morning. It was very tiring and I don't think either of us had thought about the effect that the long hours would have on our relationship. Lydia rarely got a night off, and during the days she would be tired and often needed to catch up on her sleep. After a while, it began to get her down and she became very tired and irritable. We would go shopping and visit sights in what little spare time we had together, but Lydia mainly settled into a pattern of constant working.

Life in the apartment felt very crowded with Danielle around, and at first she and Lydia would clash over petty things, although, as time went on, they seemed to form a solid friendship. Meanwhile, I had some success at finding singing work. A friend booked me to perform at a birthday party for his mum and I also found work in several bars and restaurants, including a karaoke pub called Comfort and Joys. I was pulling in reasonable money – about €150 a night – so I could earn in two or three nights as much as Lydia was making in an entire week. It also meant that I had plenty of time on my hands, especially during the day, when I could do whatever I wanted. It was while we were in Marbella that Spain won the World Cup, and Lydia and I joined a huge street party to celebrate. Meanwhile, poor Lydia was stuck working long shifts and I felt that she was starting to resent my having such an easy time while she was grafting so hard. We began to have a lot of petty arguments, which made things awkward when Danielle was there to get in the way. A lot of our rows were because I wanted to spend more quality time with Lydia,

I should have seen the warning signs much earlier

but, to be fair, she was exhausted during the daytime, so I would go off and do my own thing. When we argued, Lydia started to turn to Danielle for support and I would feel isolated and alone. Looking back, I suppose I should have seen the warning signs much earlier, but I genuinely didn't realise how unhappy Lydia was. We still loved each other, but the arrangement in the apartment and with our respective jobs just wasn't working out.

Things came to a head when I landed a big singing gig at Nikki Beach in one of the trendiest parts of town. I was delighted because it was exactly the sort of place I had dreamed of performing at while I was in Spain. It was at one of the most beautiful venues in Marbella, with a big stage and an open-air restaurant, all set amid perfect scenery. Mark and Jack happened to be in Marbella at the time and they booked a table for dinner at the venue so that they could come and see me. I was really excited and I wanted Lydia to come too. Whenever I sang at a big event I would look for Lydia in the audience and I could always tell from her eyes that she was really proud of me. I naturally assumed she would come along but, on the eve of the Nikki Beach gig, Lydia and I had a petty argument. It was over nothing in particular, but suddenly it meant there was a question mark over whether or not she would come along. I still hoped she would be able to wangle time off from work, so, before I went to the gig, I left her a note pleading with her to come. I also left her some cash so that she could catch a cab and, if need be, bring Danielle along for a few drinks. When I arrived at Nikki Beach I caught up with Mark and Jack and it gave me a real lift to see them both.

'Where's Lydia?' they asked.

Sheepishly I told them that I hoped she'd be coming along later, but, unfortunately, she didn't show up. I was gutted that Lydia wasn't there to see me perform, and, looking back, I can see that it was another signal that we were heading for the rocks. Things were now about to take a very unhappy turn.

I was due to fly back briefly to the UK to honour a long-standing commitment. Prior to going to Spain, I'd been booked to sing at the Duke of Essex Polo Trophy event (the one where Lydia and I had first met). I also had a couple of other minor singing gigs back home on the same weekend, so I'd arranged to travel back to the UK while leaving Lydia in Marbella. It was something that both Lydia and I had known about and agreed on in advance. Even though things weren't great between us in Spain at this point, we were still very much a couple and sleeping in the same bed. So, as I packed my bags and headed to the airport, I assumed everything would be fine again when my trip was over. What I didn't know was that Lydia had other plans – and they were about to hit me like a bolt from the blue.

When I arrived back in Essex, I popped around to see Debbie to say hello. Ironically, we were in the middle of talking about the minor ups and downs that Lydia and I had experienced in Spain when a text arrived on my phone. It was from Lydia and the contents stunned me. It read along the lines of,

James – I still love you and I want to be with you, but things are not working out here in Marbella. Instead of you coming back and things getting worse why don't you stay in England and visit me every few weeks.

I was shocked because I had no idea how deeply unhappy Lydia must have been in order to send me such a text. She was basically telling me that she didn't want me to go back out to Spain. I knew that things weren't right between us, but I'd assumed it was nothing serious. In truth, Lydia was probably right that we needed some personal space, but I was very hurt. I felt rejected that she didn't want me to be out there with her.

'No,' I angrily texted back. 'I don't want that, Lydia. That is so unfair.'

By now my mind was racing and I didn't know what to think. How could Lydia say such a thing? What had brought on such a change between us? It seemed like just a few short weeks ago that we'd been happily planning our future in Spain. Within a few moments of exchanging our text messages I called Lydia to demand an explanation and we got into a huge row. I pleaded with her to think again but she was adamant that she didn't want me to go back to Spain. In the end I got angry and we exchanged a few harsh words and the conversation ended on a bombshell.

'If you can't accept this then maybe we shouldn't be together at all,' Lydia yelled.

I was confused and upset after our row. I couldn't understand how Lydia could be feeling this way. I wondered whether Danielle had somehow influenced Lydia's thinking against me. I was probably being unfair to Danielle, but I got it into my head that maybe she was partly to blame because Lydia seemed to go off with her on so many occasions. One thing I was certain of was that I was still madly in love with Lydia and I hated the thought of her being in Marbella without me. Debbie did her best to console me.

'Lydia loves you,' she said. 'You'll be absolutely fine together, but she's finding it hard out in Spain, so she just needs a little time and some space.'

Much as I should have taken Debbie's advice and stayed in the UK for a while, I decided instead to take the first flight back out to Málaga after I'd performed at the Duke of Essex polo event. Mark and Jack were in agreement with Debbie that it was a bad idea to go, but I ignored them, too.

'Arg, just let's chill. Don't fly out there,' said Mark.

Mark says that I have a habit of thinking with my heart instead of my head, and this was one of those occasions. When I arrived back in Marbella I went straight to Puerto Banús, where there was a very posh Dolce & Gabbana boutique where Lydia and I would often window-shop. I knew that they stocked a bikini set that Lydia adored, because she had often commented on how much she liked it. It was very expensive and it featured a very cute Minnie Mouse design. I'd gone through most of my savings by now but I thought it would be a nice gesture to buy the bikini for Lydia to show her how much I loved her. I paid for it and decided to surprise Lydia by giving it to her at work. As I walked through the hot sun I was still convinced that everything would be all right, but when I arrived at Lydia's workplace there was no sign of her. While I was looking for Lydia, one of her workmates must have recognised me and called her, because the next thing that happened was that she rang me on my mobile.

'James, what are you doing here?' she snapped.

'I thought I would surprise you. I've bought you a nice present,' I said.

I soon discovered that Lydia was very upset and cross because I'd gone against her wishes. Despite my best efforts, things were going from bad to worse.

'Why have you gone against everything that we discussed? Why are you back out here?' she demanded.

At first I was speechless, but then I felt angry and we had yet another row. Lydia insisted that I was pushing her away by refusing to let her have her own space. I felt that I had gone out there to declare my undying love and to give her a nice present, only for it to be thrown back in my face. Wearily, I trudged round to the apartment and unpacked my things. It was very miserable there that night. I stayed in our bedroom but Lydia insisted on sleeping in Danielle's room, and that was how things carried on for the next few nights. We were living separate lives under the same roof and it was very awkward and miserable. As far as Lydia was concerned, we were no longer an item and I felt very unwelcome. Lydia and Danielle would go off and do their own thing with their workmates while I felt isolated and lonely.

The monotony was eventually broken when three of my friends arrived to stay with us. One of them was Danielle's boyfriend, Fabian. He was accompanied by two more of my mates from back in Essex, Danny and JB. I knew that I couldn't spend the rest of the summer in the apartment with Lydia and Danielle with things as they were, so I decided that I'd spend a few days with the boys. I hoped I'd patch up things with Lydia in the meantime. If not, I planned that I would fly back to the UK with Fabian, JB and Danny at the end of their holiday. I must have seemed pretty down, because the first thing the boys commented on was how low and miserable I was.

'Come on, Arg! We know you're down and depressed, but keep your chin up,' they urged me.

As far as they were concerned, they were on holiday and they wanted to have nonstop fun. I made a go of things for a few days, but my heart wasn't really in it. Then, on the last day of their holiday, the boys had arranged to attend one of the wildest parties in Marbella. It was called a 'Champagne Spray Party' at the Ocean Club in Puerto Banús. It's a fantastic all-day event, where hundreds of people descend upon the Ocean Club's luxurious pool area for a giant party with DJs and dancers and all sorts of entertainment. There are huge beds for people to relax on and everybody gets roaring drunk and sprays champagne over one another. Fabian, Danny and JB were determined to have a great time and they agreed I could come along – but on one condition: that I perk up and join in with the fun.

'We're on holiday,' they said. 'We know you and Lydia have had a tough time, but you've got to put that at the back of your mind. Just come and have some fun with us.'

'Boys, I don't want to ruin your holiday. I'm going to go for it today!' I promised.

And that was exactly what I did. When we arrived at the Ocean Club the sun was blazing and there was the usual array of beautiful women surrounding the pool. The boys had booked their own giant bed and the champagne soon started to flow. I was on good form laughing and joking with the lads and joining in with all the usual banter. I still had Lydia in the back of my mind but I was determined to finally snap out of it and give the boys a good send-off. Before I knew it, I was quite tipsy and we had a laugh slipping and sliding on our bed after it had been doused with champagne.

An attractive girl kept looking over in my direction

It was the first time I had smiled for days and I was really getting into the swing of the party. After a while I noticed that an attractive girl kept looking over in my direction. I wasn't looking out for anyone else but she caught my eye because Lydia and I had previously noticed her at a different party, and on that occasion Lydia had remarked how good looking this girl was. She had a very striking figure and brunette hair. Every time I glanced in her direction she seemed to be smiling back at me.

By now I was very drunk and, amid all the sunshine and wild chaos of the pool party, things seemed to have gone to my head. When I looked up again the girl had walked over and come up to me to say hello. We started to exchange a few words and chat about the party. What happened next wasn't planned. Events just seemed to get out of hand, and I suppose the booze was partly to blame. While I was talking to the girl my friend JB came up behind us and pushed our heads together so that our faces were very close.

'Come on, come on!' he yelled, as if to urge us to kiss.

Then it happened.

Our lips came together and snogged for a few seconds.

It was only a brief kiss and when we parted I remember thinking, What the hell was *that* all about?

I must have come to my senses a bit because the girl soon got bored and wandered off into the crowd. The whole kiss can't have lasted more than five or ten seconds and it meant nothing, although I hoped that nobody had noticed. After that we carried on partying until the evening, and my cheeky snog with the brunette was soon forgotten. Or so I hoped.

That night I went back to the apartment with the boys and slept in my bedroom, while Fabian joined Danielle, and Danny and JB slept on the sofas. I was soon fast asleep, with all thoughts of my poolside snog with the mystery girl now long forgotten. I assumed Lydia was out working and amid a boozy haze I drifted off to sleep. During the night something disturbed me and I awoke to discover somebody was opening the bedroom door. At first I thought it was one of the boys, but it turned out to be Lydia. She crept into the room and lay beside me on the bed. I could sense that she wanted to make up and she was soon cuddled up beside me.

'James, I do love you,' she whispered. 'I know things haven't really worked out for us here but I still want to be with you. I don't want us to break up. Maybe we just need to think about what we can do to sort things out.'

'Lydia, I love you so much,' I responded.

We chatted for a while and then we started kissing. Suddenly, I felt as if it was all going to be all right. It seemed as if a bad dream had ended and that finally Lydia and I might be able to get our relationship back on course. We kissed some more and then we made love. I felt that I had finally won her back.

I awoke the next morning feeling on top of the world. Lydia was mine again and I felt sure that we'd be able to put all our troubles behind us. The fact that she had said that she still loved me meant everything to me. Lydia was still asleep in the bed next to me, so I quietly left the room and went to the kitchen to get a drink and make some breakfast. I was in a good mood as I pottered around, enjoying the peacefulness of the morning while Lydia caught up on her rest. I'd been gone from the bedroom for about an hour when I heard a loud noise.

Bang!

It was the sound of the bedroom door slamming with great force. I rushed back to see what had happened and I discovered Lydia had locked the door. I could tell that something was very wrong.

'Lydia, what's up? Why have you locked the door?' I asked anxiously.

I could hear Lydia crying and screaming and it sounded as if she was throwing things around the bedroom.

'Lydia, Lydia – what are you doing? What's the matter? Open the f***ing door!' I yelled.

Lydia sounded hysterical. All I could hear was sobbing and what sounded like my clothes being ripped from their hangers in the wardrobe.

'Open the door, Lydia!' I insisted.

Suddenly, the door flew open and Lydia came rushing at me with my suitcase in her hand. She threw it at me full force and then slapped me around the face.

'Out, get out! F***ing get out!' she screamed.

I was shocked. Clearly, something had made her see red, big time. And then the penny dropped.

'I f***ing know. I know. I know,' she sobbed.

While I was in the kitchen making breakfast one of Lydia's friends had called her to explain that I had been spotted kissing the brunette girl at the Ocean Club. I was speechless and didn't know what to say. It had only been a silly mistake that had lasted a few seconds but I could see that Lydia was in bits about it. I tried to explain that it had meant nothing. I'd gone to the Ocean Club after Lydia had led me to believe that it was all over, and I had just got caught up in the moment. But the more I tried to talk my way out of it, the angrier Lydia became. I felt a complete idiot. It was obvious that I had made a big mistake, even though the kiss itself meant nothing to me and I had genuinely forgotten about it. But in Lydia's mind I had cheated on her and I could see that the thought was destroying her. She was absolutely heartbroken and she threw me out of the apartment, slamming the door behind me.

As I sat downstairs, my mind was in pieces. I'd gone from the crest of a wave to the depths of despair. Just when I thought I had managed to get back with Lydia it had all come crashing down, all because of my own stupid behaviour for a few seconds at a pool party. I felt like a prize donut. I was full of regret and remorse. I sat there wondering what to do. I couldn't envisage Lydia letting me back into the apartment, yet I had no air ticket to get home and very little spare cash on me. I was sitting in the street with a suitcase when Danielle, Fabian, Danny and JB came down to talk to me.

'It was just a stupid kiss; it meant nothing,' I explained.

I cursed JB for being the one who had pushed me towards the girl, but I knew really that the blame lay with me. I wanted to go and make my peace with Lydia but the others advised me against it. They said she was feeling destroyed. It would only make things worse if I went back up to the apartment.

'What am I going to do?' I asked. I was at my wits' end.

Amid all the fuss and confusion, Danielle had phoned her uncle, Jamie, to tell him about what had happened. I suppose she knew that he and I were friends and she hoped that he might be able to help calm me down. He was living in a huge villa with plenty of room just up the coast at Estepona, but I knew him well from back in England, where he had been part of the Essex crowd. My phone rang and it was Jamie, who said I could go and stay with him while Lydia calmed down. It was a kind gesture and I didn't have any other options open, so I decided to catch the bus to Estepona. I felt so lonely that I cried on the journey.

Jamie was a good host and I spent the next few weeks staying with him. It felt as if my heart was broken, but I did my best to try to get through it. I spent long hours working out in the gym, doing skipping and pounding on the running machine. I managed to lose a little bit of weight. Jamie was very much into self-help books that were all about the power of positive thinking. I read a few of those, which helped me a little bit; but, try as I might, I couldn't get Lydia out of my mind. The only slight bright spot was that I was contacted by a venue that invited me to sing at Buddha Beach. It was a big concert with the Drifters at the top of the bill and I supported them. It was a great gig but I was very sad that Lydia wasn't there to see me. We'd had no contact since our blazing bust-up at the apartment and I was desperate to see her again. Unfortunately, things were about to go from bad to worse.

After a few weeks, Mark and Jack came out to visit me and we arranged to go for a night out together at a club called TIBU. It was great to see the boys, and their usual banter gave me a lift, but I was about to walk into another firestorm with Lydia. When we got to TIBU I was drinking quite heavily when I saw Lydia walking

I saw Lydia walk into the club with a man

into the club with a man. He was much older than her and had a bald head, and, as they arrived, they seemed to be holding hands.

What the hell's going on here? I thought.

He looked far too old to be in a relationship with her but my head just went to pieces. I later learned that he was just a friend from work, but at the time I was fixated by the fact that they were together. I saw red and my heart started pounding. I was so angry and hurt. It felt as if there was a wild fury inside me. What I did next was stupid, horrible and immature and I will always regret it.

While I was drinking with Mark and Jack there was a girl in the bar who was all over me. She was paying me lots of attention and making it clear that she was interested in me. Cruelly, I made sure that Lydia could see everything while I flirted with her. Then, slowly and deliberately, I kissed the girl in full view of Lydia. While we snogged I could see Lydia out of the corner of my eye and her face just dropped. She was shocked and hurt and I could see her getting teary-eyed. To this day I don't know what possessed me to do it, it was as if I had a devil inside me.

As soon as the kiss was over I regretted it. It was a harsh thing to do and something that was not normally in my nature, but all the weeks of upset over Lydia had turned to anger and welled up inside me with brutal force. I felt ashamed.

F***! I've got to get out of here, I said to myself, still not quite believing what I had done.

As I went to leave, Lydia came right up in front of me.

'Oh, all right, are you, James? Having a good night, are you?' she asked sarcastically.

And with that she picked up a whole pint of water and poured it over my head. I was soaked and I left the club dripping wet, while Lydia stayed inside with a broken heart.

After that I went back to Jamie's villa for a few days. I was inconsolable because I felt that the damage I had done was irreparable, but there was one last terrible incident that seemed to put a final nail into the coffin of my relationship with Lydia. I had arranged to stay with Jamie for another week because I had one last gig to play at a private party in Puerto Banús for one of his friends. After that, I planned to go back to the UK alone.

By now everybody had warned me to give Lydia a wide berth, but I wouldn't listen. I sang at the party and had a good time, but afterwards I got paralytically drunk. In my boozed-up state I decided to go and visit Lydia at the apartment. It was another stupid thing to do but in my drunken mind I still wanted to make up with her. I was due to fly home a few days later but all that I kept thinking in my head was, Lydia, Lydia, Lydia! So I slipped away from the party determined to go and find her.

When I turned up at the apartment, Lydia was there. She was shocked to see me.

'Lydia, I'm so, so sorry,' I pleaded. 'I can't believe I kissed that girl in front of you. I was evil. I won't be surprised if you can never forgive me.'

I could tell that she was still very hurt and angry, but what she said next upset me even more.

133

'Well, don't worry about it because I've met somebody else,' she said.

My heart sank. The thought of anyone else being with Lydia made me feel sick. I used to think that when people said they had a broken heart it was just a saying, but now I knew for real what it felt like. It was as if somebody had punched me. I felt a physical ache in my body as Lydia explained that she had met a boy whom she got on with. Thankfully, she said that they hadn't slept together, but I was still devastated. The next thing that erupted within me was boiling fury. I saw red and I kicked the table and started to throw things around the apartment. Thankfully, Danielle came in at this point with a friend called Tommy, who was a nightclub promoter. Tommy and I were mates and he grabbed hold of me and calmed me down. I was still in pieces. It had been a mistake to go to the apartment.

I knew now that there was no way I'd be able to get back with Lydia while she was in Spain. A few days later I packed my bags and flew back to Essex. I was lonely and full of despair.

9

JOINING *TOWIE*: LIFE ON
THE ROLLER COASTER

Sometimes, you get your biggest breaks when you are feeling at your lowest, and that was what happened to me when I joined *The Only Way Is Essex*. When I came back from Spain after splitting up with Lydia I was distraught. I had no job, no girlfriend and no prospects. My friends could see how down I was and they tried to rally around me. Josh was now playing for Scunthorpe in the Championship and he invited me to go and stay with him at Burton Waters in Lincoln. He was living in a beautiful house on a lake with a David Lloyd gym located in the same complex. At first I couldn't even bring myself to eat properly and I spent most of the time crying about Lydia while he was out training, but Josh was a real rock and he helped me through it.

He said to me, 'Look, Arg, you have no commitments, so use this time. Get down the gym and get yourself in shape.'

I took Josh's advice and I worked out for hours on end and

lost a lot of weight. I got down to below 15 stone and I started to feel much slimmer. I had an idea that if I could shed enough bulk and look good it might help me to win back Lydia. I couldn't stay with Josh the whole time, so I would occasionally make trips back home. It was during one of these that I linked up with Mark and we discussed *TOWIE*. I'd first heard about *The Only Way Is Essex* earlier in the summer when I'd come back from Spain to sing at the Duke of Essex polo event. There was a camera crew filming everybody and Mark explained that they were interested in making a new TV show all about Essex. A production company called Lime Pictures was planning to film a pilot. The idea was that it would feature real-life characters to capture the bling of Essex, which was already famous for its spray-on tans and party lifestyle. In the States there was a show called *The Hills*, which followed the fortunes of the in-crowd in affluent areas of Los Angeles. It had already been a bit of a hit there. During the polo event, Mark introduced me to *TOWIE*'s producer, Sarah Dillistone. We had a quick chat but she didn't film me because I said I was living in Marbella. While I was in Spain, Lydia and I saw Mark appear on some early trailers for *TOWIE* on ITV2, but I never thought in a million years that I would be on the show. When I arrived back in England *TOWIE* wasn't on my radar, apart from the fact that I was happy for Mark.

I never thought in a million years that I would be on TOWIE

'This new TV series is going to be crazy, it'll be a big hit,' he said.

Then, out of the blue, I received a phone call from a woman called Liz at Lime Pictures.

'We realise that you've only just come back from Spain,' she told me. 'We haven't had the pleasure of meeting you properly but we know that you're one of Mark's best friends and it would be nice for you to come up to the office and just have a chat.'

I was flattered to receive the call, but at this stage I still didn't think much of it. I assumed that, at best, they might just want to offer me the chance to appear in the odd tiny scene. I had no idea that it would lead to a major role.

And then something crossed my mind.

Maybe if I'm on TV it'll help me to win Lydia back, I thought.

I arranged to go the offices of Lime Pictures in London and I was shown into a room with a camera.

'We'd just like to film you while we ask you a few questions,' they explained.

The producers were mainly interested in asking me about my friendship with Mark, but I spent the whole time telling them about Lydia. It seemed as if every question they asked somehow ended up with me talking about her. I think it made a bit of an impression on them, because afterwards they commented on how much I obviously still loved her.

Although I didn't know it at the time, it had been a bit of an audition and I'd obviously passed the first test. I think they were looking for somebody to be Mark's friend in the show, somebody who could be a bit of a sidekick. They wanted him to have someone he could go shopping with, talk to about his problems and have a bit of banter with. They weren't looking for a main character at all, just a bit of a lapdog for Mark to talk to. I was approached because I was Mark's best mate. They loved the fact that he and I were complete opposites. Mark was this successful ladies' man and really good-looking, whereas I was quieter and a bit chubby. But, despite our differences, we had this natural genuine friendship. They liked the fact that Mark would confide in me about his feelings. He had recently split from Lauren Goodger after dating her for nine years. In public, Mark would make out he didn't care much about the split, whereas with me he would get deep and tell me how he truly felt.

I was invited to shoot a pilot, but when it came to filming it I was completely wooden. The crew filmed me talking to Mark in his car while he drove along, but I was completely distracted by the cameras. I felt I came across very stilted and awkward. Mark was then also asked to film a set of title sequences with the other main characters, who included Kirk Norcross, Amy Childs, Mark's sister Jess, plus Sam Faiers and one or two others. I wasn't invited to take part in the titles, and neither was I asked to attend a big press launch for the show at the Embassy Club in London. I assumed that I'd been left out because I was destined to have only a tiny role, if anything at all.

It was while I was in discussions with *TOWIE* that I got a shock when I discovered Lydia was back in Essex. I'd heard rumours that she had returned and I was singing in Nu Bar one evening when she walked in with some of her friends.

My heart started banging as soon as I saw her, but my mates later told me to play it cool and not go rushing over. I felt a mixture of emotions because my first reaction was that I wanted to speak to her, but by now I had learned my lessons from Spain and I realised that going charging in head first isn't always the best thing to do. I resisted the urge to go over and say hello, but we both clocked each other. Soon afterwards I deliberately left the bar.

Later that evening I received a text from Lydia: 'Where are you, I need to speak to you.'

I didn't reply, even though it nearly broke my heart to ignore her. A while later, I bumped into a friend of Lydia's, who told me that she'd been frantically asking after me that night.

Perhaps there was hope for us yet.

I was delighted when I received a phone call from the producers to confirm that they wanted me to appear in the first ever episode of *The Only Way Is Essex*. I couldn't believe my luck – I was going to be on TV! The first thing that Mark said to me was that we needed to up our tans for the cameras.

'Arg, you're looking too pale, you've got to get under the sunbed,' he told me with his usual blunt honesty. 'This could make us rich if we get everything right.'

'Arg, you're looking too pale, you've got to get under the sunbed!'

We both spent the next few days going to tanning salons and frantically shopping for new clothes to wear on air. The money I was being offered to appear wasn't huge, but I didn't care, because I hoped it would lead to greater things. The format of the show was very interesting. The producers explained that they would speak to us about our daily lives and ask what we had coming up. They'd then ask us to be filmed in various situations discussing certain topics. The conversations are all genuine – nothing is scripted – so what the viewers see on air is what really happens.

Around this time Lauren had a birthday party coming up and all the local gossip was about whether or not Mark would go along, having just split from her. The opening scene of the first episode showed Mark and me discussing the party while we were in his car. While we were filming I was still very much a bag of nerves. I had no idea whether the show would be a hit, so I didn't tell anybody about it in advance, apart from my own family. My mum and dad were very excited but I asked them not to tell anyone. To be honest, I was worried that I would be so wooden that the whole of Essex would take the piss out of me.

In fact, the producers loved the chemistry between Mark and me from the beginning. We were like a bromance double act who were rarely seen apart. They liked the way Mark would crack jokes at my expense but I would just laugh it off. I didn't mind being the butt of his humour, because he always did it with warmth.

When it came to film Lauren's birthday party I was shocked by how explosive it turned out to be. Lauren went into a jealous fury when she spotted Mark talking to Sam.

'You bunch of *****!' Lauren screamed, using a very rude word.

I'd seen Lauren react like that in the past when she was angry, but I was still amazed at how blunt she was in front of the cameras. I thought it was quite funny and it set the tone for the future. I knew we were in for a crazy ride. It made me realise that Lauren was exactly what the producers wanted. She was fiery, opinionated and prepared to let rip after a few drinks. It was a toe-curling moment, but it was TV gold. *TOWIE* had arrived with a bang.

Watching yourself on television for the first time is a bit of a shock. I wasn't used to seeing myself on camera and I felt that I looked a bit awkward in those early scenes. The producers were keen to film Mark, Jess and me as we sat together watching the first episode, so that they could capture our first reactions to seeing ourselves on TV. We all had mixed emotions. We sat on the sofa and at times I cringed behind a pillow. It was like being on a roller-coaster. One minute we were up and I thought we looked great, the next we were blushing and wishing the ground would open up to swallow us.

Our mobile phones went into meltdown the moment the show went on air, as people we knew recognised us and began to send us texts and emails. Facebook and Twitter also went into a frenzy – but, unfortunately, for all the wrong reasons. People were going onto social media sites to slate the show. There were hundreds of tweets and posts branding *TOWIE* embarrassing rubbish.

'What is this shite?' they were asking.

People were saying that the show was awful and cringe-worthy, with some viewers claiming it was the worst thing they had ever seen on TV. Even the reaction of my friends and family was mixed to begin with. I received a text from Lydia's mum Debbie asking what the hell the show was all about and why was I on it.

I was worried that I'd never be able to show my face in public again, but thankfully it was just a storm in a teacup. The producers could see through it all and they weren't concerned, because they knew they had created something that was going to be a huge success. I think a lot of the negative criticism on Twitter came from people in the area who didn't like our group of friends, and they were probably a bit jealous of seeing us on the box. Regardless of what people said on social media, my life was about to change overnight.

I started being recognised in the street the very next day. I'd spent the night of the broadcast at Mark's flat in Abridge and I got a cab back home the next morning. After all the excitement I decided to go for a quiet walk around Woodford Green to get some peace and fresh air. As I walked along I was amazed when a couple of cars beeped at me they went by. Someone even shouted, 'All right, Arg?' through their window as they drove past.

I got to the local newsagent, where I bought a *Daily Mirror*. When I opened it there was a big article about *The Only Way Is Essex* and there was a photo of me along with some other members of the cast. I thought it was crazy. The show had been launched only the day before and already we were being built up in the media. The attention continued to grow as more episodes were shown. My Facebook account was swamped and I instantly had five thousand 'friends', the maximum you are allowed. Suddenly, everybody wanted to be my friend, and celebrities such as Alan Carr and Kylie Minogue started to tweet about *TOWIE*. Katy Perry gave us a shout-out on stage, and other famous *TOWIE* fans included Kate Middleton and Oscar-winning actress Jennifer Lawrence. People very quickly started to absolutely love the show.

Suddenly everybody started to tweet about TOWIE

Despite all the excitement of the first episode, Lydia was still very much occupying my thoughts. We'd not had any further contact since we'd spotted each other in Nu Bar, but a few days after *TOWIE* was screened she sent me a jokey text saying that she'd heard I was now a Z-list television star. We exchanged messages and Lydia told me that she was at a friend's house, so I decided to ask if I could see her.

'Why don't you let me come and pick you up in a cab and I'll take you home?' I offered.

Lydia agreed and I booked a car. I was full of apprehension on the journey to pick her up because it was the first proper meeting between us since what had happened in Spain. When she got into the minicab things were very awkward. I was sitting in the back while Lydia sat in the front next to the driver. We hardly spoke a word on the journey back to her house, apart from a polite hello. I don't think either of us knew what to say, but, as we travelled along in silence, I put my hand on her shoulder and briefly ran my fingers through her hair. It was my way of letting her know that I still loved her.

When we got to Lydia's house we went into a downstairs room. Our conversation was very subdued. I think we were both very nervous and we were just skirting around the issues, making polite conversation about nothing. Then we had a little cuddle. It felt wonderful to hold her again. And then we kissed each other briefly.

'Can I stay the night?' I asked.

'No, James,' she replied.

I left the house feeling really confused. It seemed as if there was a chance we could work things out, but nothing was resolved. I think we both probably still needed a bit more space. One thing that Lydia did confide to me was that she'd been contacted by the producers, so there was a possibility that she was also going to be invited to appear on *TOWIE*. I was pleased because I hoped it would be a chance for us to get back together.

There was a sixties party coming up in the show and I was chuffed when I was asked to sing at it. I thought it would be a fantastic way to get known as a singer. To be able to perform on national television was a golden opportunity to boost my career and I hoped I would get lots of bookings as result. I was anxious to do my best, but I must admit I was very nervous.

'I've heard that Lydia's going to be coming to the sixties party,' Mark told me on the day of the event.

It was a bit of a surprise and it ramped up the pressure. I was nervous enough about singing, but the thought of Lydia being there filled me with even more fear because I was worried about how she would react. What if things went wrong, or if she turned up at the party with somebody else? I was a complete bag of nerves. I didn't relax until I finally got on stage to sing. I performed 'Can't Take My Eyes Off You' by Andy Williams, and I got a good reaction from the audience. Amy Childs came on stage with me and did a little twirl. While we were dancing, I spotted Lydia entering the room. I was very surprised by the way she looked, because she was wearing such heavy makeup. It was caked all over her face and I'd never seen her like that before. It was so thick that she was almost dark brown. She didn't look anything like the normal Lydia. It was almost as if she were wearing a mask.

When we spoke after I came off stage I told her that she looked beautiful (I didn't mention her heavy makeup). I wanted to apologise for what I had done in Marbella and now seemed like the right moment. I didn't care that we were being filmed.

'Sorry for what happened in Spain, Lyd,' I said.

We had a brief conversation and I decided to take the plunge and ask if she would take me back.

Lydia's reply stunned me.

'I always used to see myself being with you, but at the moment I don't see anything. Sorry,' she said on camera.

And with that she kissed me on the cheek and walked off. I felt my heart sink and I struggled not to cry in front of the cameras. What I had hoped would be our big reunion had ended with my being given the brush-off. I felt a fool because I knew the whole thing would be shown on TV, which made me feel worse.

*

Facebook and Twitter went into overdrive when Lydia was shown spurning me. There were hundreds of people tweeting about what had happened between us, and Lydia came in for an enormous amount of stick. Some of it was very cruel and callous, with lots of horrible comments about the heavy makeup that she'd worn on the show. People were saying she looked like a transvestite or drag queen. The tweets were completely unacceptable. They said she was fat in the face and called her nasty names like 'pig'. It was like an avalanche of hate. People were saying that I shouldn't bother with her. It hurt me to see her being slated like that and I wanted to go and see her at home to find out how she was coping. Mark advised me against it.

'She's just said on national telly that she doesn't want to be with you! There's no going back from that, you've got to move on,' he said.

But I didn't want to move on. I knew there was still a chance we could patch things up and I was determined to go round to see her. When I got to the house, Debbie let me and I went up to Lydia's bedroom. She was terribly upset by all the abuse she'd been getting. I gave her a cuddle and things seemed to relax a little between us. I think the shock of all the nastiness she'd suffered made her let her guard down and for the first time in ages we talked in an open and honest way. Lydia said the reason she'd worn so much makeup on *TOWIE* was nerves. She'd been kept waiting to film the scene and every few

Lydia was terribly upset by all the abuse she got

minutes she'd redone her makeup because she was worried she wouldn't look her best. She just kept applying more and more without realising it.

I told her to ignore all the horrible comments.

'Lydia, you are so beautiful,' I said. 'You've got nothing to worry about. It doesn't matter what everyone says. They say one thing and then they change their minds when you're on camera again.'

I told Lydia that I was convinced that we still had a future and I could sense that she was softening towards me. We chatted for a while and then we started to kiss. Suddenly, it felt right between us again.

That night we ended up making love.

I felt so happy, although, when I asked if it meant we were back together, Lydia wouldn't give me a straight answer. I didn't see her again until we filmed a scene at a Hallowe'en party. It was at new bar called Deuces, which Mark had just opened. He'd saved hard to get the cash together for his own place, and several of the boys and I worked through the night to help him get it ready in time.

'You look gorgeous,' I told Lydia at the party. This time her makeup was perfect.

I later performed in front of Lydia during a dinner party at an Indian restaurant, where I did a rendition of 'I've Got You Under My Skin'. I told the audience that I was dedicating the song to Lydia, and while I sang I looked her straight in the eye. It had the desired effect, because afterwards when I joined Lydia at her table I could see I'd won her over. We agreed to have a fresh start.

'I love you so much, Lydia,' I told her when we were alone. 'I'm so glad we're back together again. You mean everything to me.'

Mark had experienced a terrible shock after the Hallowe'en party when somebody firebombed his bar. Thankfully it was empty at the time but it was a real blow after he had worked so hard to get it ready on time and I felt very sorry for him. To this day, we still do not know who was responsible.

I went down there the next day to offer Mark my support. He went about getting the place cleaned up and he was determined to reopen as soon as possible. It was a shame, because it took the gloss off his achievement and from that moment on we always feared it might happen again. I wondered if being on TV had made Mark a target. *TOWIE* had been on air for only a short time, but already it had become a huge phenomenon. We all went from being complete unknowns to being splashed across almost every magazine and newspaper in the country. It created lots of spin-off work as we were approached to make personal appearances and endorsements. I also experienced a big increase in the number of enquiries about booking me for singing gigs. Many of us soon started to make a very good income from all the extra work that being in the show brought us.

The big plot as the first series reached its finale revolved around the fact that Mark had challenged Kirk to a charity boxing match. It was as if the bout would settle the matter as to who would be crowned the King of *The Only Way Is Essex*. I was due to be master of ceremonies at the event, which meant that I'd have to announce the fighters from the ring.

I was nervous on the night, both for Mark and because I would be under the spotlight while doing the announcing. Unfortunately, the pressure got to me and I ended up getting drunk. What the viewers didn't see was that I brought along a large bottle of Jack Daniel's so that I could sip it with Coke to help calm my nerves. I overdid the booze and most of the fight itself was a bit of a blur to me. The producers had hoped to film a scene of me discussing the bout with some of the other cast members, but they had to scrap it because I wasn't making any sense. When Mark won the fight he became the King of *TOWIE*, but by that time I was so sloshed that I got into a muddle when I announced the result. I couldn't remember what colour corner Mark had fought in!

I wasn't too worried about my indiscretion when I awoke the next day. In the space of just a few months, my life had been completely transformed. I had come back from Spain penniless and alone. Now I had a top role in a TV show and plenty of money coming in, and I was back with Lydia.

10

FAME, FORTUNE AND A GUILTY SECRET

I fought so hard to get Lydia back – but the truth is that, just when she was ready to make a go of things, I threw it all away with my own stupid behaviour. I'm embarrassed about it now, but all the attention that *TOWIE* created went to my head. I started falling in love with myself, and my ego very quickly grew to epic pro- portions. I had gone from being Mark's sidekick to arguably the second biggest character on the show. I was fêted with adoration by fans every time I made a personal appearance and for the first time in my life I was earning decent money.

I had never experienced all this attention from girls

I received so many approaches that I found a manager, Neil Dobias, who was also looking after Mark at that time. When I first met Neil I'd tried to charge him to get into a nightclub while I was helping on the door – I didn't realise he was already working with Mark. Neil is still my manager today and we get on very well. When he left the agency that he was working for to set up on his own, I moved with him.

ITV did a huge poll asking viewers what they thought of the cast and I was voted the second most popular character behind Amy Childs. One thing that I had never experienced before was all the attention from girls that it created. After I appeared in the first series, they started to throw themselves at me. I couldn't believe how blatant they would be. I would be standing at a bar while making a personal appearance and they would come right up and offer to sleep with me out of the blue. At first I wasn't interested, but as time went on there were occasions when I succumbed to temptation. During the second series of *TOWIE* there were lots of rumours going around that I had been unfaithful to Lydia, which I denied at the time. I am ashamed to admit it now but I did cheat on Lydia, which is something that I will always regret. All I can say is that I was young and foolish and, if I could turn back time, I would.

For a very brief period after we got back together, it seemed as if Lydia and I would be happy. As Christmas 2010 approached, I was determined to buy her a special present to show how much I loved her, so I decided to get her a micropig. It was a cute little animal we called Mr Darcy. When I gave him to her at Christmas our relationship was already under strain. Things had started to change between us after I had become a hit in *TOWIE*. In the past Lydia had been the one who wore the trousers, but as my confidence grew my ego started to take over. I was spending more and more time with Mark out partying, which had started to cause friction between Lydia and me.

'It's feels like you're two-timing me with Mark,' she told me. 'You're always out with him instead of me. It's embarrassing that you're so far up his backside.'

'What do you mean?' I protested.

'You'd jump off a cliff if Mark told you to. If you keep listening to him you'll lose me.'

'Oh, leave it out, Lydia,' I replied.

'No, I won't leave it, James. He's coming between us because you spend so much time with him. I've hardly seen you recently.'

Aside from our arguments over Mark, I also had one very guilty secret that I kept from Lydia, and it concerned Amy Childs. I had known Amy as part of the Essex crowd since pre-*TOWIE* days and we'd always got on very well. She's a lovely, bubbly, pleasant girl and I always found her easygoing company. During the *TOWIE* Christmas Special, on which I'd presented Mr Darcy to Lydia, I'd also been filmed chatting alone to Amy in the kitchen. It was quite a flirty scene in which Amy suggestively held up a couple of Christmas puddings in front of her boobs and asked me if I wanted to sample them. Amy asked me on air what Lydia would do if she caught us chatting. I replied that Lydia wouldn't mind because we were just talking as friends.

'Even though you fancy me a little bit, isn't it true?' said Amy.

It was an awkward moment because the cameras were rolling, so I denied that I was attracted to Amy. I think the viewers just assumed it was a bit of harmless flirting, but the truth was that, away from the public eye, Amy and I were already starting to grow quite friendly. We'd secretly been involved in a very embarrassing moment at an ITV dinner, when Sam Faiers caught us snogging passionately in a loo. It was at a hotel in Mayfair at a Christmas function that was arranged by the boss of ITV, Peter Fincham. He said his two biggest successes of the year were *Downton Abbey* and *The Only Way Is Essex*. In the case of *TOWIE* it had gone from being a bit of an experiment to an overnight phenomenon, so a small group of cast members were invited along to the dinner to celebrate. Only about six of us went, including Amy, Sam and me. The producers were very excited and they told us all to be on our best behaviour because it was a real honour to be invited to such an important event.

Amy arrived in a dress that was typically stunning and showed off her boobs. Despite being told to watch ourselves, we were all soon getting up to mischief as the drink flowed. We were being very loud and we started to sing songs as we got into the party spirit. Peter didn't seem to mind that we were being ourselves and we all got very merry. When I chatted with Amy our conversation was quite flirty and I could feel a spark of attraction. At first I didn't think too much of it, because Amy loves getting attention from boys and I assumed she was just being a bit of a tease. But as the evening wore on, I got pretty drunk and I found myself getting caught up in the moment. Here was the sexiest and most famous star of the show and she was lavishing her affections on me. None of the other guests were aware of what was going on and it felt exciting and sexy.

It was clear that she was giving me the come-on and my ego loved it. But at the same time I still wondered if she was just winding me up by having a little bit of banter. For the time being my attention returned to the party and I entertained everyone by singing 'Let It Snow'. Afterwards, I walked away from the dinner table towards the toilets, which were unisex. Amy was standing outside on her own and her face lit up when she saw me. It felt unreal as we pulled each other inside the loo. There was a big wash area with mirrors above the sinks where we embraced and began to kiss. It felt incredibly sexy to be alone with Amy, but after a few seconds I pulled away out of guilt.

What about Lydia? I thought.

But Amy looked so attractive and the truth was I did fancy her. The drink had got the better of my judgement, so I carried on kissing and cuddling her. Things had just started to get pretty steamy between us when suddenly we both got a huge shock. The door flew open and in walked Sam, catching us together in each other's arms. We didn't see her until she was standing there right beside us. I was so embarrassed that I didn't know where to look! Sam's first reaction was to burst out laughing, but then her attitude hardened. I can remember her saying something along the lines of, 'This is out of order! Arg. You're with Lydia and you'll f***ing regret it if she finds out.'

Thankfully, Amy and I came to our senses and the spell was broken. We went back into the party. The other guests seemed unaware of what had happened, but I wondered if any of them had secretly worked it out. It must have looked odd, the pair of us disappearing together like that. I didn't blame Amy – she was single at the time, so she hadn't done anything wrong. But I was mortified that Lydia would find out. I hoped that I could trust Sam, as she was one of my oldest and best friends from back in Essex.

The next time I saw Amy was when we were back on set. When we got a private moment alone I asked her how she was feeling.

'I'm fine, Arg,' she said, and she winked. 'How are you?'

'I'm good, Amy. You're looking well.'

Neither of us said anything about our secret kiss and cuddle. It was one of those things that are easier to leave unspoken. Rumours about Amy and me later started to circulate around the set. I guess there was just a chemistry between us that we found hard to hide, although at this stage Lydia didn't suspect anything. As far as I know she never got to hear about the incident in the loo. I felt stupid because I loved Lydia dearly and I didn't want to be with anyone else, but at the same time I was young and all the attention I was getting was too much to handle. I felt a fool because I'd worked so hard to get Lydia to forgive me for the stolen kiss I had with a girl at the Ocean Club – and then I'd gone and done the same thing again with Amy Childs. I knew I was being selfish but

I knew I was being selfish

it never crossed my mind to let Lydia go. I was naïve and thought I could have the best of both worlds.

I piled on a lot of weight over Christmas and in the months that followed. By the time the new series of *TOWIE* started in March I had ballooned to 17½ stone. Just a few months earlier I had tipped the scales at around 14½, so I had gained 3 stone in a few short months. When I saw myself on screen I was shocked by how big I looked and it became a bit of a talking point in the show. Mark made a joke about how he wanted to organise some pool parties, but he was worried about my size.

'You'll be jumping in the water and all the water'll be jumping out,' he quipped on air.

Meanwhile, Lydia and Debbie (who, despite her initial reservations about the show, had joined the cast by now) persuaded me to join a diet class. My weight is a big factor in my life, so naturally it became part of the show. The reason I'd gained so much was partly the lifestyle I was leading away from cameras. Before the start of the new series I'd been making four or five personal appearances a week at nightclubs up and down the country. The clubs would obviously encourage you to have a good time, so I was drinking quite a lot and then following it up with a kebab or a visit to a twenty-four-hour McDonald's every night. It was a vicious circle of booze and junk food. There would be crowds of girls queuing to speak to me at every club and my personality began to change. I think Lydia could sense that I was becoming more independent, and she hated my going off partying all the time. Although she enrolled me in a diet class, Lydia didn't seem overtly worried about my weight gain, and I wondered if secretly she felt a bit more secure about me because it made me less attractive to other girls. In fact, Lydia used to like cuddling up to me because she could lie on top of me, and she said I was like a big comfy waterbed. What did concern her, however, was the amount of time I was continuing to spend with Mark or away making personal appearances, which we always referred to as PAs. I'd receive requests from all over the country to attend nightclubs, and when I arrived the place would be packed out. It sounds silly but it felt like pop stardom because there was so much interest. Jack Tweed's brother Lewis drove me to the events. He had a little Smart car and we would sometimes travel up the motorway in it for hours on end. It was cramped inside but it did the trick just fine. If the venue we were visiting was more than two or three hours away we would usually be put up in a hotel, which meant I was away overnight. I earned good money from all the PAs, but for long periods of time I was away from Lydia and it's hard to keep in contact by phone when you are in the middle of a nightclub. I think the stress of wondering what I was getting up to started to take its toll on her and she became very insecure about our relationship. The balance seemed to have tipped away from her slightly and, even though I still wanted be with her, my head had been turned by the showbiz lifestyle. Of course, she was on *TOWIE* herself, but I seemed to be the character who was getting all the interest from the public. I think Lydia was affected by the fact that I'd changed a little, and I think it knocked her confidence.

At first, Lydia put on a brave face and suggested the time was right for us to show a bit more commitment by moving in with each other. She said we could find a flat, or, better still, a cottage where we could bring along Mr Darcy and make a happy home for the three of us. I agreed and we started to look around. When an apartment became available in Abridge it seemed like the perfect solution. There was only one potential drawback: it was directly below Mark's flat and I knew Lydia wouldn't want to be so close to him.

'How can you have a serious relationship and then have your best mate living upstairs?' she complained.

We later dropped the idea.

It was while I was making a personal appearance in the West Country that I cheated on Lydia by sleeping with somebody else for the first time. I am not proud of it. Mark and I were appearing at a nightclub in Bristol for a couple of nights in a row when it happened. The club was packed to the rafters and there were a group of girls who looked like glamour models who came back to our hotel afterwards for a drink. Up until now I'd resisted the temptation to stray from Lydia, but a definite change was starting to come over me. I'd never known women to throw themselves at me like this before, and I found the heady mix of adulation and fame too much to handle. I was also drinking a lot and on this occasion I was very drunk. One of the girls followed me to my room and we

A definite change was starting to come over me

had sex. It didn't last long and she went home straight afterwards. I hated myself for it – I felt terrible. The next morning I was very homesick and I felt guilty about Lydia.

I don't know why I did it, other than to say that I was young and foolish. I guess boys will be boys, although that's no excuse: Lydia deserved far better from me. The horrible thing was that, after it had happened the first time, it got easier to slip again in future. I cheated on Lydia several times with girls who threw themselves at me while I was making nightclub PAs. The strange thing was that I never once enjoyed it. I think it was just a power thing: a part of me wanted to be a bit of a geezer to impress my mates. But feelings of guilt and remorse soon followed. It was driven by my ego. The only time I enjoyed sleeping with someone was when I was with Lydia, so it wasn't as if any of these girls were satisfying me in that respect. I just did it because I could. I suppose there was a side of me that wanted to sample a single lifestyle. I was twenty-two and the only girl I had even been with up until now was Lydia. I wanted to have my cake and eat it. It didn't happen every week, but I continued to be a naughty boy over a long period. It was never a case of having to work for it: the crazy thing was that, because I was on the telly, girls would just come up and blatantly offer it to me on a plate. On one occasion I came very close to being caught by the press. It was about a year after I'd first cheated and it again occurred in the West Country. I was drunk and I was flirting outrageously with some girls during one of my nightclub appearances. One of them whispered in my ear, 'Arg, let's have sex.'

It was the sort of offer that most young blokes in their early twenties can only fantasise about, and I admit I was openly tempted. My head was spinning from the booze and in truth I didn't have a clue what was going on, but I agreed to leave the club and I ended up cheating again.

I got a terrible scare a few days later when somebody started posting comments about me on Twitter, saying words to the effect, 'I know what you did after the nightclub.'

A few days later the media got to hear about it and the *TOWIE* press office received a call from a national newspaper. I was in a terrible state over it because the call came in on the day that I was with Lydia's dad, Dave, who was accompanying me to a show that I was performing at in Birmingham. The story was due to be published on my birthday, but I denied it and thankfully it never appeared. It had been a close shave and it shocked me into behaving myself.

Rumours of my infidelity started to circulate on the *TOWIE* set, and it wasn't long before they started to be alluded to on air. Of course, I denied them, but it was a case of no smoke without fire. Ironically, at the time that I was playing the field, Mark took the plunge and vowed to settle down with Lauren. He proposed to her on the show and they went about organising a huge engagement party. I couldn't believe it when he popped the question, but it was typical Mark – always causing a stir. Lauren was like the cat who'd got the cream and she immediately began to move all her things into his apartment. For a while it really did look as if Mark was loved up and finally ready to settle down. There was a funny scene in *TOWIE* in which his grandmother, Nanny Pat, told him it was finally time to throw out his lucky pants, which he wore when he was on the pull. When the engagement party came along it was suitably grand. Mark and I arrived on a pair of white horses to be greeted by all the other guests, while Lauren followed us in a white Rolls-Royce. There was a funny moment with the horses because I weighed so much. I had trouble getting mounted and I had to be helped on and off.

At the very moment that Mark and Lauren were loved up, the friction between Lydia and me started to surface. We were still hunting for somewhere to live together and I found what I thought was a great option. I'd been earning good money and my dad and I decided to invest jointly in a town house in Woodford Green. It was derelict and needed renovation but I thought it would make an ideal home. I bounded round to Lydia to tell her the news, but, instead of her being delighted, we had a huge row.

'You've hardly spent any time with me recently, so how can you be ready to move in with me?' she complained.

I was defensive, but Lydia gave me a whole list of reasons why she was unhappy with me. She said that I never answered her phone calls, that I was always with Mark and that I never took her out. Lydia was also upset about a conversation that she'd had with Mark a few days earlier. He'd told her that, even though everybody thought I was a good boy, I was actually worse than he was when I was out. It was a throwaway comment that Mark made because he was fed up with always getting the blame for leading me astray. To

Lydia it was like a red rag to a bull and things came to a head during a scene on *TOWIE*.

'He turned round to me and said that you basically cheated on me,' she told me in front of the cameras.

I tried to reassure her that Mark had meant it as a wind-up, but Lydia started crying. At times like this we'd get swept up in the emotions of the moment, regardless of the fact we were being filmed. I felt awful standing there listening to her while she was so upset.

'I just have got no trust in you whatsoever. You lie all the time about where you're going; you have girls; you're disrespectful,' Lydia told me in front of the cameras.

Our row ended with Lydia getting hysterical and afterwards she refused to see me for a while. I tried going round with flowers but Debbie refused to let me in.

Debbie was so angry over the rumours that I had cheated that she later confronted me in the street about it, but I denied everything. I was worried that, if I admitted it, Lydia and I would never get back together. I was just too much of a chicken to come clean. I was scared of what the consequences would be and I was too cowardly to admit it.

When Lydia quizzed me about it I became extremely defensive.

'I didn't cheat on you, so don't start accusing me of things,' I would say.

We had another blazing row in front of the cameras, which ended with Lydia telling me, 'I just hate you so much, James.'

By now Lydia was sick of me. She'd made it clear to me that she regarded herself as single and we split up for a while.

I was unhappy about it, but I still hoped there was a chance we could turn things around in the future.

At the time that Lydia was hearing rumours about my cheating with girls in nightclubs, she was also becoming suspicious of my friendship with Amy Childs. Amy and I had continued to flirt occasionally since our secret Christmas kiss, and we appeared together in a number of scenes on *TOWIE*, including when I asked her to be my tennis partner in a sexy tennis outfit. Eventually, Lydia became so upset with it all that she confronted Amy, who told her nothing was happening between us.

Looking back, I am not proud of the way I treated Lydia, and I would like to apologise to her for the way I behaved. The crazy thing was that, even though I cheated on her, if Lydia were to go near anybody else it would still make me insanely jealous – as I was about to find out.

11

A Boy Called Joey and a Fracas at a Pool Party

I didn't know it at the time, but Lydia was about to give me a dose of my own medicine. It happened at a pool party that Mark organised in the Essex countryside, and it shocked me into mending my ways. Lydia and I had remained apart after our recent string of rows, which meant that in theory we were both single and therefore free to date other people. In reality, the thought of Lydia being on the arm of anybody else still made me feel physically sick. I admit I was being hypocritical, since I'd done my fair share of cheating, but my own behaviour was still a secret that I was trying to deny. Call me old fashioned, but I wanted Lydia to stay well away from other boys while the feelings between us were still so raw. There had been a brief scene on *TOWIE* where she had bumped into a boy called Rob in the street, and later it emerged that they had exchanged telephone numbers. At first I didn't think too much of it, because I was convinced nothing would come of her and

165

Rob. He was a good-looking boy, but he just didn't seem her type and there wasn't any chemistry between them. It never occurred to me that Lydia would invite him to an event at which I was present.

When Mark announced that he was planning to hold a pool party I knew that he'd want to do it in style.

'What do you mean, a pool party?' I asked.

'We're talking champagne sprays and Playboy girls,' he told me with his usual swagger.

Mark's idea was to recreate the glamour of Marbella in the Essex countryside and he arranged to borrow a luxurious mansion, which was out in the sticks near a village called Theydon Bois. It was a fantastic property that had a large terrace and garden, plus, of course, an all-important outdoor swimming pool. It was the ideal spot to host a fantastic champagne bash. I agreed that was a great way of getting loads of gorgeous women to show off their bodies in bikinis while all the boys relaxed in their swimming shorts. The producers of *TOWIE* loved the idea and all the cast were invited to attend. For Mark it was also a way of sending out a message that he was still the No. 1 man in the show.

There was a new kid on the block by this stage in the shape of Joey Essex, who'd joined *TOWIE* in Series 2. Joey had caused quite a stir by organising a series of 'reem parties', which were a huge success (reem is Joey's favourite term for something that is fantastic). All of a sudden, it was as if he was the new up-and-coming Essex

There was a new kid on the block in the shape of Joey Essex

boy. Joey is a wonderful character. I knew him before he joined the cast and we were good friends, and we still are. The first time I'd spoken to him was while I was on a holiday in Marbella. Lydia and I were at a club called News Café and I went out onto the balcony to get some fresh air. Joey was there with a phone clamped to his ear while having a furious argument with the girl he was dating at the time. They had been childhood sweethearts.

'I'm not outdoors. I'm being good. Leave me alone!' he shouted into the phone.

I'd seen Joey's face around Essex a few times in the past, but we didn't really know each other. After he finished the call I asked him if he was all right.

'Yeah, I'm just rowing with my bird. It's a nightmare. How are you, mate?' he asked.

We introduced ourselves and I offered to take him inside and buy him a drink. Joey is a very kind-hearted, nice boy. You could tell straightaway that he loved getting up to mischief and in many ways he is like a big friendly kid. Back then he was obsessed with sunbeds and he looked so brown that I imagined he must have spent a lot of time on them. He was almost orange and I thought he looked a bit like a Ken doll. I talked to him a little bit about his girlfriend, whom he later split from before he joined *TOWIE*.

After our conversation in Spain, Joey and I would shake hands if ever we bumped into each other around Essex and we later arranged to go on a night out together to a club called Funkymojoe in South Woodford. Joey had only just broken from his girlfriend at this stage but he didn't let it get him down. He was this cheeky chappy who went around the club snogging girls. He wasn't on the TV at the time but he still seemed to have girls queuing up to kiss him. We bumped into Sam Faiers and Jess Wright in the club and the four of us posed for some photos together. Joey was in a great mood and I suspected that he secretly knew that he was about to join the cast, although nothing had been announced. After we left Funkymojoe we went off for a kebab together and he ended up coming back to my house in a cab. We crashed out together on the same bed, snoring our heads off. When we woke up the next morning we had terrible hangovers, and our friendship grew from then on.

Mark and Joey are very different characters. They are both successful Essex boys who are great at nightclub promoting, but that's where the similarity ends. Joey is like the class clown, whereas Mark is older and more business-minded. Nonetheless, even though they got on very well, Mark was keen to keep his crown as the top man in *TOWIE*.

'No one's taking that role from me,' Mark told me. 'I'm the man here and I'm coming back, Arg. I've been gone but the show needs me back, you need me back and *I* need me to be back!'

'You're right, Mark. The show just isn't the same without you getting up to mischief,' I agreed.

It was no surprise to me that cracks soon began to show between Mark and Lauren. He just missed his old lifestyle too much. Towards the end of the second series of *TOWIE* they were constantly arguing and just didn't seem to be enjoying each other's company. Mark and I were still spending a lot of time together and it sometimes felt as if I were a third person in their relationship. I would often stay in their spare room. We all got along well together, but I began to get the feeling that the engagement wouldn't last for very long.

Meanwhile, I was technically single. I went on a date with a girl whom I got talking to during a personal appearance in Romford. Her name was Ebru and she looked the spitting image of the actor and model Megan Fox. I invited her to come and watch me sing at one of my gigs, and she agreed. We shared a little kiss after I performed on stage, but that was all. I didn't sleep with her.

When it came to the day of the pool party everything started out well. We were terrified that the weather was going to ruin it because it had rained the day before, but we were blessed with sunshine. The idea was that anyone who was anyone in Essex would be present. Guests were wandering around in swimwear, sipping cocktails and generally just having a great time in the spring sunshine.

Amy Childs was looking stunning in a fuchsia-pink bikini. I had been in several scenes opposite her by now and we were quite flirty. Away from the cameras, we had recently been on a shopping trip together and I felt there was a bit of a spark between us. But, when I went over to say hello at the party, Amy was fuming with me because Lydia had asked her if we were sleeping together. For the record, Amy and I have never slept together, but our secret kiss at Christmas had stayed at the back of my mind. Foolishly, during an argument with Lydia, I'd made the mistake of alluding to my friendship with Amy. I can't remember exactly what I said, but it was along the lines of claiming that, if Lydia didn't want me, then maybe Amy would. I don't know why I said it – perhaps deep down I thought it was a way of making Lydia jealous and shocking her into taking me back. It was a daft thing to do – and it backfired, because Amy was angry and she gave me a right mouthful.

I felt a right fool, but there was worse to come when Lydia made a grand entrance to the party with the boy she'd met in the street, Rob. I felt as if I had just been hit by a very heavy weight. My pulse raced and I felt sick inside. Even though Lydia and I were officially apart, I still regarded her as my one true love and the thought of her with another boy was just too much to handle. I also felt humiliated. Here I was at my best mate's party and the girl I loved was rubbing my nose in it by parading around with another bloke. Seeing this shocked me into realising just how deep my feelings for her were. If I am honest, I had not shown Lydia much respect, either, in recent months. After all, I'd secretly been on a date with the girl I met in Romford, but I hated it now that the tables were turned.

Seeing Lydia with another boy shocked me

But, if the fireworks that were caught on camera were dramatic, they were nothing compared with what happened after we stopped filming. I'd been getting more and more wound up as the afternoon went on, and by the evening I was ready to snap. What the viewers didn't know was that, when it was time for everybody to go home, I was involved in a fracas. I frantically looked around for Lydia and I spotted her with Rob, gathering their stuff together and walking towards the front of the house, as if they were about to leave together.

There's *no way* I am going to let her go home with him, I vowed to myself.

I followed the pair of them outside and it was obvious that Lydia was about to get into Rob's car. I saw red. I went running over and caused a huge scene.

'You are *not* getting in a car with that boy! You are taking the piss, Lydia!' I yelled. 'You've only just broken up with me. Don't do that in front of my eyes.'

Lydia stared back at me. She looked shocked, but I also got the impression that part of her was enjoying the fact that she was making me squirm.

'It's none of your business. He's just going to drop me home,' she replied.

'You're not getting in! You are *not* getting in!' I screamed.

A bit of a commotion followed, during which I somehow managed to grab hold of a pair of Lydia's shoes, which I think were on the floor. I assume that she must have still been wearing flip-flops from being at the pool, hence she wasn't wearing the shoes. I was determined to hang onto them: there was no way I wanted her to leave with Rob. It sounds daft that I tried to hold a pair of shoes hostage, but that's exactly what I did.

'Mind your own business,' repeated Lydia.

Meanwhile, Rob didn't seem to know where to look. I could see that it wasn't his fault. He'd just blundered into a situation while doing a bit of filming for *TOWIE*. I didn't bear him any personal malice, apart from the fact that there was no way I was going to let him drive off with Lydia! Mark was by my side and he offered to have a quiet word with him.

'Look, Rob,' Mark said. 'Lydia's single or whatever, but you know Arg's just broken up with her, so this is not nice.'

'Honestly, Mark,' Rob replied, 'I've come here with Lydia but we're not dating. Arg's got nothing to worry about.'

I was still extremely upset with Lydia and I must have looked like a bit of a mad man standing there. Several of the crew had come over by now to see what all the fuss was about and I spotted a girl who I knew was one of the producers.

'Can you drive her home instead of him?' I suggested to the girl.

A bit of a standoff followed, but in the end Lydia relented.

'Fine, I'll get in this car, then,' she said, and she got into the producer's vehicle.

I had been driven mad and I had finally cracked for the first time since Lydia and I had been in Spain. Lydia had the power back and had proved she was wearing the trousers. I was in bits. As the producer and Lydia drove off I was still in a jealous craze and I was convinced that Lydia and Rob would either get back together as soon as they were round the corner or arrange to meet up somewhere else.

'Mark! Mark!' I yelled. 'Get your car and please come quickly. I need to follow her to know where she's going.'

By this point, even Mark thought I had lost it.

'Shut up,' he said. 'She isn't going to be with that boy.'

'No, Mark. I've got to go to her house.'

'You're mug,' he said. 'You do it all the time. You always make the wrong decisions.'

'No, Mark. Just drive me to her house. I just need to know if she's in,' I persisted.

'Arg, you're such a donut,' he told me. 'I've never seen a boy act like this over a girl. It's pathetic – you're an embarrassment.'

Despite his reservations, out of loyalty Mark eventually agreed to drive me to Lydia's house. He was a true mate, even though what I was asking him to do was slightly mad, and I was very grateful. When we arrived at Lydia's home, Mark parked up a few metres away and waited in the car while I crept up to the front door on my own, trying to be as quiet as I could. All the lights were on and I sensed that all Lydia's family were at home. Moving as quietly as a mouse, I opened up the letterbox and peeped through. It was a crazy situation: here I was bent double and holding my breath, while I spied on the love of my life. I listened carefully and I was relieved when I heard Lydia and Debbie talking together in the kitchen. I was glad she had made it home and that there seemed to be no sign of Rob. I could barely make out what they were talking about but I heard Lydia say, 'I'm going to bed. Goodnight, Mum.'

Yes, thank God! I thought.

I ducked down out of sight while I heard Lydia walk up the stairs, after which Debbie came out and bolted the front door. I crept back to Mark's car. Lydia and Debbie never knew I was there.

The following morning I woke up at seven, having spent

the night at Mark's flat. I was no longer angry with Lydia, but I groaned as I thought about the events of the day before. For the first time, it fully hit me how upset she must have been to parade Rob in front of me like that at the party. Up until now, whenever she had told me it was over between us, I'd taken it with a pinch of salt because something had always told me that we would get back together. But this was different. It had shocked me and it made me realise how much I'd been risking with my appalling behaviour towards her.

That's it, I thought. I'm changing my ways now, and I'm going to treat her better.

Lydia had just proved to me in my mind that sometimes you don't realise what you have got until you've lost it. Seeing her with Rob had made me feel as if I'd lost her for the first time. I vowed to myself that I would not cheat on her any more and that I'd make proper time to be with her, rather than spend most of my time out clubbing.

I knew I wanted to see Lydia as soon as possible, so I went straight round to her house that very morning after the pool party. Debbie reluctantly let me in and I went upstairs to see Lydia in her room. At first she told me to get out, but I think part of her was expecting to see me, and after a while she agreed to listen to me. I think that after all the fireworks from the night before we were both feeling emotionally drained. I told Lydia how I felt about her and after a while we cuddled. I suspect that Lydia knew that she'd successfully made her point and she'd got me right back where she wanted me.

It might sound crazy, but we began to make it up there and then. Less than twenty-four hours previously, Lydia had told me that she couldn't think of anything worse than being with me, yet here we were talking and cuddling again. Unfortunately, that was how our relationship continued for some time. One minute it was on; the next it was off. Slowly, we talked things through and eventually we decided to make another go of things. By now Lydia was obviously well aware of the rumours that I had cheated on her, but I continued to deny them. Looking back, I realise she didn't question me about it as closely as you might have expected. I don't think she wanted to find out the truth, because she knew it would be too painful. One thing I was sure of was that I wouldn't get away with treating her like that any more. I had a choice: either break up and have my fun or stay with her and sort out my life. I chose to make a go of things with Lydia. We stayed together for another nine months after our pool-party bust-up, but there were plenty more ups and downs to come.

12

A BAFTA FOR *TOWIE* AND A FAMILY SHOCK

If you work in television, winning a BAFTA award is like winning the World Cup: nobody can argue with you once you've achieved it, and you're officially recognised as the best in the business. On *TOWIE*, we were just a bunch of kids who grew up together in Essex, and most of us never would have dreamed that one day we'd be honoured by the British Academy of Film and Television Arts. Yet in May 2011 that was exactly what happened. *TOWIE* was nominated for the BAFTA YouTube Audience Award alongside the very best of British television. We were up against two of the most critically acclaimed TV dramas of recent times: ITV's mighty *Downton Abbey* and the BBC blockbuster *Sherlock*. Also on the list were *Big Fat Gypsy Weddings*, *Miranda* and *The Killing*. It meant that the likes of Mark Wright and Sam Faiers were up against great theatrical actors such as Hugh Bonneville and Benedict Cumberbatch for telly's top gong.

Few people fancied our chances and, to be honest, I didn't think we would win either – not that I didn't believe we deserved to. In the space of less than a year, *TOWIE* had become one of the nation's most talked-about TV series of all time – and I loved every minute of it. But, despite its huge popularity with the public, in some circles people continued to look down on the show for whatever reason. I think there can sometimes be a bit of prejudice against reality television in general, due to the idea that it somehow isn't in the same class as heavyweight dramas featuring classically trained actors. People are entitled to their views, but I think it's unfair because the truth is we make a great television show and the viewers love watching us. That said, we continued to get a bit of stick on Twitter from time to time from people who would brand us as thick or take the piss out of the show for being cringeworthy. Some of the criticism continued to be led by local people in Essex who I suspect were still envious that they weren't on the show themselves. I'm sure there were also a few people in the business who were a little jealous of us because we'd achieved all this fame but we weren't actors.

The first I knew about being nominated was when Rachel Hardy at the *TOWIE* press office sent us all an email to tell us the good news. I was so excited that I couldn't wait to tell my mum and dad.

'We've been shortlisted for a BAFTA!' I told them.

It was the television equivalent of being nominated for an Oscar and I was full of excitement. It reminded me of winning my Kenny all those years ago at the Kenneth More Theatre!

Lydia and I had had recently got back together after our fracas at the pool party, but we had decided to keep our relationship low key. We didn't want to make a big deal about the fact that we were an item again because we knew it would only create more fuss, and we'd just been through all the pain of breaking up in front of the cameras. But the BAFTAs represented the ideal occasion for us to show the world we were back in love. I was delighted when the *TOWIE* press office confirmed that I was one of the cast members who were selected to attend the event, which was being held at the Grosvenor House Hotel in London. Unfortunately, there were initially one or two big-name cast members who were left off the invitation list. A flurry of emails was exchanged as various people argued their case for who should go to the awards ceremony. In the end, nine of us were selected. They were Lydia and me, Joey Essex and Sam Faiers, Kirk Norcross and Amy Childs, Nanny Pat and, of course, Mark and Lauren. In addition, lots of producers and crew were deservedly going, too, including Sarah Dillistone (series producer on Series 1), Claire Faragher (series producer on Series 1 and executive producer on Series 2), Nicky Hegarty (executive producer on Series 1) and the co-creators of the show, Ruth Wrigley and Tony Wood.

Meanwhile, the *TOWIE* press office told the cast members that we would be arriving at the event in style. The idea was that each of us would travel in a car with a theme that captured the fun and bling of *The Only Way Is Essex*. After all, this was our big moment and we were out to have maximum fun. Mark and Lauren were to be in a brand new, white Rolls-Royce Phantom, which summed up the fact that they were engaged to be married. Amy and Kirk were given a pink Hummer limo (you can't get more bling than that). Joey and Sam were given a white, soft-top Mini (so they looked just like Barbie and Ken). Meanwhile, Nanny Pat was to have her own horse-drawn carriage. Lydia and I chose a vintage, cream Rolls-Royce, which we knew would look stylish and swish.

Lydia was terribly excited.

'I can't wait to choose a nice dress,' she told me.

She opted for a grey and silver, flowered Dynasty gown that was off the shoulder and billowed out at the bottom. She looked absolutely stunning on the night.

'Lydia, you look so beautiful,' I told her, and we posed for pictures together before we left for the event.

I bought a new black suit and I wanted to wear a long black tie with Swarovski crystals embedded in it. My friend Adam, who owns Nu Bar in Loughton, had a tie just like it and he agreed to lend it to me (although I don't think I ever got around to giving it back).

Our cream Rolls-Royce was the perfect vehicle for us and as we approached the Grosvenor I felt like royalty. We could hear the crowds screaming and cheering and, as we neared the red carpet, all I could see were hundreds of camera flashguns going off. There were photographers and journalists everywhere. I first I assumed the cameras were flashing for somebody else but it was Lydia and me whom they were excited about. What amazed me was that all the

We could hear the crowds cheering as we neared the red carpet

reporters were fighting to talk to anyone from *TOWIE*, while ignoring a lot of the more established names who were there. It was a good omen and a bit of me began to wonder if it was going to be our night. It felt amazing as Lydia and I walked up the red carpet and went into the hotel. When we got inside, I admit that at first I was a little bit starstruck, because there were so many great celebrities whom I'd grown up watching on TV or in films. I was thrilled to see Martin Freeman in the flesh and I remembered how my dad and I used to laugh our heads off at him when we watched *The Office* together. Martin won the award for Best Supporting Actor later that night for playing Dr Watson in *Sherlock*. Then I spotted another personal favourite of mine.

'Look, there's Steve Coogan!' I said to Lydia.

Steve had starred in *Tropic Thunder*, the movie that Lydia and I had watched over and over again during our holiday in Gran Canaria. I went over to Steve and we said hello and he agreed to pose for a photo with me. I also had my picture taken with Graham Norton, who later won a BAFTA for Best Entertainment Performance. Graham was charming and fun, just as he is on the telly. We pestered lots of people for photos over the course of the evening. The funny thing was that all the other celebrities were used to rubbing shoulders, so they weren't bothered about having their picture taken with each other, but for us it was a big deal. Lots of *TOWIE* cast members seemed to be running around with their phone cameras asking people to pose with them. We were still relative newcomers to the scene, and the BAFTAs was the first time I'd experienced a showbiz event on this scale.

When the awards ceremony started we settled down at our tables and crossed our fingers. The category in which we were nominated was due to be presented by Simon Bird, Joe Thomas and Blake Harrison of *The Inbetweeners*, who had won the same award the previous year. As the lads made their way on stage I held my breath. As I said, we didn't really expect to win, but maybe . . . just maybe . . .

'And the winner of the YouTube Audience Award is . . . *The Only Way Is Essex*!'

Yes!

We were ecstatic. A giant roar that sounded a bit like a football crowd erupted from the tables where the *TOWIE* crowd were all sitting together. It was a huge upset when the award was announced and I got the impression that nobody else in the banquet hall had wanted us to win. I jumped to my feet and hugged several of the producers. We were beside ourselves with joy and we could hardly believe it. Unlike the other BAFTA categories, the YouTube Award is decided via a public vote, so we knew that we owed our success to our fans. If it had been left to a stuffy committee to decide, then I doubt we'd have won against the likes of *Downton Abbey*. The fact that the public had chosen us made the feeling of victory all the more sweet. This was our moment and we wanted to savour it to the full. Together we all made our way up onto the stage to accept our BAFTA in front of the cream of British showbiz. The producers said their thanks on stage and Mark also made a short speech.

'What does that say?' he said, grabbing the trophy and pushing it towards Joey Essex. 'A BAFTA!'

Proud parents: Mum and Dad with their little bundle of fun – yes, that's me as a baby in my dad's arms!

Baby smile: As you can see, I was a happy toddler. I'm aged just twenty-one months here!

Festive fun: Me and my little sister Tash pose together in front of the Christmas tree. That's a great waistcoat!

Happy family: Mum, Dad, Tash and I pose for a family photo. Mum keeps a framed print of this picture at home.

Making a splash: Look at that six pack! I'm about six here, on a trip to Brighton.

Footie fans: That's me in my Spurs shirt with Granddad Seamus, when I was aged about seven.

Trinity boy: In my uniform for Trinity Catholic High School.

© Vincent Banks/Cox photography

Cheeky chappie: This is me as the Artful Dodger in *Oliver!* It's one of my favourite photos from my amateur dramatics days.

Toys are us: Tash and I proudly show off some of our Christmas prezzies in 1995. That's Nanny Colette and Uncle Gerry behind us.

Celebration time: Here I am on my twenty-first birthday with Lydia and Tash.

Lydia's mum Debbie and I share a drink together.

Big grins: Mum with a glass of bubbly at a family party with Lydia and me.

Squeeze: Here's me giving Nanny Brighton a cuddle.

Magic Granddad Tom, who would entertain us with his conjuring tricks.

Dressed to the nines: Lydia and me, about to go to the wedding of Jack Tweed and Jade Goody.

In love: Lydia and me, all glammed up together during a night out. Lydia looks great in those leather trousers.

Happy couple: Me giving Lydia a hug from behind, on a night out in Sugar Hut.

Bikini babe: Lydia and me, enjoying a bit of sunshine in Marbella.

Party fun: Lydia motorboats my moobs while Jack Tweed looks on during some fun in Marbella.

Bath time: I raise a toast while relaxing in the tub, while Mark points the way ahead in his yellow pants!

Hot shop: Mark, Lydia and I pose together proudly at the opening of Lydia's shop in Loughton.

Dig the jumpers: Mark and me, in our best festive pullovers.

In Marbs: Joey, Sam and me, having fun over dinner in Marbella.

Holiday romance: Gemma and me, enjoying a fantastic time in Turkey. I love the way the rose matches her dress!

Men about tan: Joey Essex and I soak up some sunshine together on our last day during a recent trip to Las Vegas.

Party pals: Me out on the town with my *TOWIE* mates Diags and Tom.

Spa very much: Helen Flanagan and I had a great time on the set of *Celebrity Super Spa*.

It's Will: It was a real honour when I finally got to meet my childhood idol Will Young (after missing out when I was in my teens).

Kelly nice: I got a special treat when Kelly Brook fed me carrot cake after we met at a Rihanna concert at the O_2 arena.

Top band: The lads from One Direction gave me a warm welcome when I met them at the ITV studios.

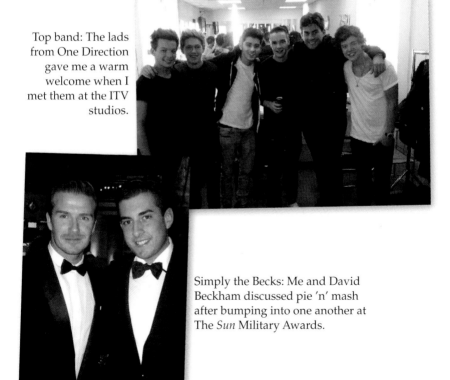

Simply the Becks: Me and David Beckham discussed pie 'n' mash after bumping into one another at The *Sun* Military Awards.

Crooners: Debbie looks on while Tony Roberts and I sing our hearts out.

We did it! From Kenny Award to Bafta. Here's me holding the award on the big night at the Grosvenor House Hotel.

Marathon man: Me with my finisher's medal after completing the London Marathon. No one believed I could do it.

TOWIE family: The cast and crew pose with our BAFTA.

Mark then proceeded to tell the world just how much the award meant to us.

'We are absolutely overwhelmed to even be invited tonight, even nominated, but to win it is ... you know ... incredible!' he said.

We were all on cloud nine for the rest of the night and we celebrated the way we know best in Essex: with plenty of champagne. It was a huge achievement. Winning the BAFTA was good for all of us because from that moment onwards people in the media seemed to give the show a lot more respect. Until now, the public had loved us, but we'd not been embraced with quite the same warmth by the rest of the TV industry. I suspect that we'd been regarded in some quarters as upstarts, but that perception changed and people now acknowledged *TOWIE* for what it is: a great TV show. You can't argue with a BAFTA! It raised the profile of *TOWIE* a great deal and the number of invitations we started to receive to appear on other shows rocketed. In the weeks and months that followed I was asked to make guest appearances on lots of top TV programmes such as *Loose Women*, *This Morning* and *Daybreak*. It was if we were welcomed into the heart of the TV establishment.

Lydia and I were slowly rebuilding our relationship as the summer of 2011 approached, but there was still one nasty shockwave in store. Prior to our getting back together, I'd been on my brief date with Ebru, the girl I had met in a nightclub in Romford. I saw her only briefly while I'd been split from Lydia and we'd done nothing more than share a kiss. The problem was that we'd been photographed backstage together at my singing gig – and a picture of us kissing was about to surface in the media. The trouble flared when I received a phone call from *Now* magazine.

'Hello, Arg. We've got some photos of you kissing a girl and we want to know if you wish to make a comment,' they told me.

'What? Why the f*** are you printing this story? That was nearly two months ago,' I protested.

'We have to print it. It's still relevant,' they insisted.

I was furious, because the picture had been taken before Lydia and I had got back together, so I couldn't see the point of dragging it up. The photographer was somebody I knew and I'd asked him not to publish it at the time, but now it was about to be made public several weeks later. After everything I'd been through with Lydia, I knew this would create yet another storm. Ironically, on this occasion I hadn't actually cheated on Lydia – it had just been an innocent date at a time when we were single. I was terrified of what was going to happen next, so I thought it would be better if I were to warn Lydia, rather than have her just open up the magazine and get a nasty shock. At least that way I could explain the circumstances in advance before she saw the photo for herself.

The question was, how to tell her?

I decided to pick my moment by taking her for a nice meal and then on to the cinema. I planned to confess at the end of the evening while she was hopefully in a good mood. Call it a mad idea if you like, but it seemed to make sense at the time. To begin with it worked like a dream and we had a great time.

'It's been a wonderful night. I can't believe how nice you've been,' Lydia said to me as she drove me home at the end of the evening. I decided the time was right to own up just as her car was approaching my house.

'Er . . . well. I have something to tell you, Lydia,' I replied. 'There's going to be an article in *Now* magazine tomorrow. I kissed a girl a while ago when we weren't together and they're going to print a photo. I'm being completely honest with you when I say it was just a brief date, nothing more happened.'

Lydia erupted.

'Get out!' she screeched. 'Get out of the f***ing car!'

'Lydia! Lydia! I'm sorry, but there was nothing to it.'

'Get out! Get out!'

And with that she went into a blind fury. I could see she was in no mood to be reasoned with, so I made a hasty retreat indoors. Later that night I texted her to try to explain things, but it made no difference. I was back in the doghouse. The next morning was extremely awkward because Lime Pictures had arranged for some of the cast of *TOWIE* to go up to Liverpool to visit the set of *Hollyoaks*. It meant that Lydia and I would have to be on the same coach together with the rest of the cast. She would have no time to cool off and I didn't relish the thought of coming face to face with her in front of everybody else on the coach, but I had no choice. Feeling sick and sheepish, I crept onto the bus and took a seat near the front. Lydia was sitting towards the back. My heart sank when I saw that somebody had arranged for copies of all the magazines to be passed around the coach, including *Now*. I sat there scared and trembling while I wondered what Lydia's reaction would be when she saw the photo. I felt like a fool because I'd only just won her back, and here we were in the middle of another crisis. I glanced over at Lydia, but she wouldn't even look at me, let alone talk to me.

This is the last place on Earth I want to be at this point in time, I thought.

Our journey began and I tried to keep my head down. Then, all of a sudden, Lydia stood up at the back of the coach and started to scream. She was waving a copy of the magazine and shouting at the top of her voice, while the rest of the cast looked on in stunned silence.

'You idiot!' she screamed. 'You fat prick. Look what you've done.'

She then started to rip the magazine to shreds. I had never seen her so angry – but the firestorm was only just beginning. Even though the coach was moving by now, Lydia sprinted down the aisle to where I was sitting at the front, and she proceeded to slap me around the head with the remaining bits of the magazine. I curled up in a ball to try to protect myself from the onslaught. There were bits of paper and torn pages everywhere. It was a total shambles, but I couldn't really blame her. I'd been just as jealous at the pool party when I'd nicked her shoes; now it was her turn. That was the

Lydia sprinted to where I sat and slapped me around the head

thing with Lydia and me: despite our troubles we felt we that owned each other, so nobody else could go near either of us without there being fireworks. I was still cowering beneath a flurry of blows from the shredded magazine when Jessica Wright and a couple of the producers came over to try to break it up. Eventually, Lydia went back to her seat and I spent the rest of journey up to Liverpool in stony silence.

When we arrived at the *Hollyoaks* set I felt as if I was in the middle of the worst day ever; the tension within our group was terrible. I spent most of the time in a bit of a daze while we were given a tour of the studios. Mark had arranged to meet us up there and it was good to see him, but nothing could lift my spirits. We were introduced to Jorgie Porter and Jennifer Metcalfe from *Hollyoaks*, who both looked very beautiful and were very charming.

I tried to break the ice with Lydia on a couple of occasions but she ignored me. That night, we all went to dinner together in Liverpool, after which Mark and a few of the other boys decided to stay on and have a party. I wasn't in the mood, so I trudged back to the coach on my own. I curled up in a ball behind a seat and went to sleep, feeling miserable. While we were on the way home I awoke to hear Lydia talking. She must have failed to spot me when she got onto the coach, because she was talking about me as if I weren't there.

'Where's Arg?' I heard her ask. 'Has he stayed behind with Mark?'

'Yes, I think so,' somebody replied.

'The idiot!' rasped Lydia.

Hearing that, I sat up in my seat to protest.

187

'No, Lydia, I didn't stay. I'm here,' I said.

Lydia glared at me and didn't say a word, so I curled up and went back to sleep. After we got back to Essex it took a bit of time for Lydia to get over the shock of the magazine article, but after a few days she began to cool down. It was just another example of one of our huge bust-ups, from which we quickly made up.

My family and I were about to receive a nasty shock that came in the middle of the summer. My sister Natasha suffered a terrifying problem with her health that took us all by surprise and could so easily have killed her.

It happened just at the time when interest in *TOWIE* was going through the roof. We were riding high after the BAFTAs and I was swamped with requests to appear on TV chat shows or to make personal appearances. What happened to my sister put everything into perspective. It made me realise that, no matter how successful you are, life can still throw you a curveball at any time.

Natasha and I (or Tash, as I call her) are very close siblings. We were born less than two years apart and, as I've said before, we were very happy playmates as kids. I have fond memories of going roller-skating with her close to where my Nanny Brighton lives on the south coast. As we grew up, our shared passion for tennis stayed with us and we still enjoy a good game today. Natasha is always so healthy and full of beans. She's a positive person who never lets anything get in the way of what she wants to achieve in life. She had to work very hard to gain her credentials as a professional tennis coach and she has a heart of gold. In fact, Natasha is everything you could hope for in a little sister and she will do anything for me.

Natasha was the last person we expected to become seriously ill. It all began with a bowl of blackberries. We have a big garden at our home in South Woodford and on warm days my family would pick the juicy blackberries that grow there, and we'd eat them for our tea. One particular afternoon, Natasha had eaten her fair share and had gone to bed that evening as normal. I was due to fly to Marbella the next day with Lydia for a short break so I decided to get a good night's sleep, too. During the night I was in my room when the noise of somebody crying awoke me. At first I thought maybe I was dreaming but, as I aroused from my deep sleep, I realised that someone was in our bathroom. It was Natasha and I could hear that she was in a lot of distress, so I went to investigate.

The sight that greeted me was very unpleasant. Poor Natasha was hunched over the toilet bowl in her nightdress and she was clearly feeling very sick.

'Tash, are you OK?' I asked.

'Oh, James. I feel really ill,' she gasped. 'I can't stop being sick and I'm in terrible pain. It hurts so much.'

Natasha looked deathly pale and was drenched in sweat. She told me she had been projectile-vomiting and that the whole of her abdomen was in agony. I stayed with her, gently rubbing her back to try to comfort her while she fought her way through waves of nausea. My mind wandered back to the blackberries that she'd eaten earlier in the day. I hadn't liked the look of them very much, because they were the last of the crop and they didn't seem very appealing.

'You've probably picked up a stomach bug from the black-berries. You'll be all right when it passes,' I told Natasha.

'No, you don't understand,' she replied. 'This feels different to an upset stomach. I've never felt pain like it.'

I didn't know what else to do so I went to wake up my parents and my mum took over looking after Natasha. At this point, I still assumed that it was nothing more than a stomach bug and after a while I went back to sleep. We all hoped she would be fine and the next day Lydia and I went ahead with our plans to fly to Marbella. My mum and dad reassured us that it was probably nothing to worry about, but as a precaution they decided to take Natasha to hospital. I was naturally worried, but at this stage, despite Natasha's obvious discomfort, I had no reason to suspect that it was anything serious.

My theory about her having a tummy bug proved to be very wrong.

After Lydia and I arrived in Spain, we learned that my mum and dad had been frantically trying to reach us by telephone. My mobile was playing up and they hadn't been able to connect with me, so it was Lydia who eventually took their call. My mum explained that the doctors had discovered serious internal complications in her bowel and that Natasha would need major surgery.

'I don't think you realised how ill your sister is, James,' Lydia told me. 'She needs a major operation and the doctors are very worried.'

Our first thought was to fly back to the UK immediately, but my mum and dad said everything possible was being done to help Natasha and that there was nothing else that we could do. Lydia and I were due to stay in Marbella for only a couple more nights, so we decided to keep in touch by phone and catch our original flight back. I was worried about Natasha, but part of me was still convinced that she would be fine. I think that when I receive bad news about a loved one it doesn't always sink in. I'd refused to believe how ill Granddad Seamus was until the cancer finally beat him. It was the same with Tash. Even though I was worried I didn't take in the full gravity of the situation until I saw her again for myself.

After Lydia and I returned to the UK we went straight to Whipps Cross Hospital, where Natasha was being cared for. The sight of her in her hospital bed was a complete shock. She had bloated up to enormous proportions and had tubes running in and out all over her body. She was very weak and looked spaced out from all the drugs that the doctors had given her. She was so groggy that it seemed as if the old Natasha wasn't really there. It made me feel sick inside to see somebody I love in such a state. My parents said Natasha's illness had nothing to do with the blackberries. She had suffered a twisted bowel that had become gangrenous inside her body. It had been a massive shock to her system and she needed six hours of surgery to correct it. It was extremely serious and the doctors had warned that, in the worst-case scenario, the condition could be fatal.

The doctors warned that the condition could be fatal

'But surely Natasha isn't going to die?' I asked my mum when we were alone together.

'She's very ill, James. All we can do is pray for her.'

I took my mum's advice and prayed for my sister. I was obviously desperately worried about her, but despite everybody's fears I knew deep down in my heart that she would pull through. Natasha is too much of a battler to let an illness ruin her life, so I never stopped believing in her for one moment. It's at times like this when religion is a great comfort to my family. As a child I regularly went to six o'clock Mass on a Saturday evening with Granddad Seamus and Nanny Colette. I also attended church on a Sunday morning quite often throughout my early teens. Nanny Colette is a Eucharistic minister, who gives out the bread and wine during Mass. As I've grown older I have never stopped believing, but as you get busier in life you tend to go to church less often, and nowadays it is mainly just Christmas and Easter that I attend.

During Natasha's illness we all did a lot of praying for her. Her operation was just the start of a long and gruelling road back to recovery, and there were several nasty complications along the way. Natasha needed a second major operation and she also contracted the hospital bug MRSA, which in itself can be fatal. The doctors ended up cutting her stomach in half and removing a large section of her bowel, which had become infected. It was a huge trauma for her body to go through.

The whole situation was very disheartening. I was used to Natasha being the sporty athletic one who was always up in the morning, playing tennis all day and driving here, there and everywhere. She was always busy, so it was so sad seeing her there in the hospital bed like that. She was in and out of hospital for about four and a half months, during which time I visited her whenever I could.

While Natasha was recovering I was invited to sing on *Loose Women* on ITV. It was the first time I had performed live on TV and I thought it would give me the perfect opportunity to wish Tash well.

'I'd like to dedicate this song to my sister, Natasha, who's currently in hospital,' I announced on air.

I then sang a rendition of 'Can't Take My Eyes Off You' by Andy Williams. Natasha later told me that she'd been watching from her hospital bed. She'd been so weak that she could hardly open her eyes, but she told me it meant a lot to her.

Natasha dealt with her predicament with amazing bravery. Whenever I went to see her I tried to be as upbeat as possible and I'd cheer her up with all the latest gossip from the *TOWIE* set. I would cycle to the hospital and sometimes stop off at Lydia's house on the way to collect her little brother, Freddie, sister, Roma, and some of her foster siblings, and they'd join me on their bikes.

Lydia, meanwhile, was fantastic. She went to visit Natasha loads of times on her own while I was out working, and she even took her beloved *Sex in the City* DVD collection into the hospital. Natasha watched them all on her bedside TV and she said it gave her a real lift.

As Natasha slowly got better she became strong enough to come downstairs to meet me at the W. H. Smith store within the hospital. We'd stock up on sweets and magazines while I made sure she had everything she needed. When the hospital served up her food I'd occasionally finish off her dessert when she couldn't manage it – and I could tell from the big smile on her face that the old Tash was coming back!

Slowly but surely she began to get stronger every day.

Although, as I learned, those blackberries had nothing to do with her illness, I must say that it has still put me off them. It was a long, hard struggle for Natasha but she has now made a full recovery and she is working again as a tennis coach. Her job takes her all over the world, and I'm very proud of her. She fought off the MRSA and all the other complications she suffered.

I'd just like to say here: Tash, it's great to have you back! I'm so glad you'll always be my little sister.

13

FAREWELL TO
THE KING OF *TOWIE*

My friendship with Mark Wright had become a national institution on *TOWIE* – so it came as a real shock to me when he decided to quit the show. In fact, the thought of his not being there made me quake with fear because, until now, we'd done everything together. Mark was the one person guaranteed to get viewers hot under the collar. People seemed to love and loathe him in equal measure and he was always in the headlines, usually for breaking somebody's heart. If there was an argument, a break-up, a bust-up or a row, Mark was at the centre of it and I was always by his side. The first two series of *The Only Way Is Essex* were dominated by his antics and I was proud to be in lots of great scenes with him. So I was gutted when Mark told me that he was thinking of leaving

> *I was gutted when Mark told me he was thinking of leaving*

at the end of Series 3 in autumn of 2011. I just couldn't imagine life in the show without him. Officially, Mark left to take up an opportunity to appear in the jungle on *I'm a Celebrity . . . Get Me Out of Here!* but it was also due to the fact that he'd gone as far as he could in *TOWIE*. He'd been there, done it and had the T-shirt.

Mark's decision to leave had a huge impact on me, because the majority of my scenes had been filmed with him. We were inseparable and I just didn't know if I would be the same person on screen without him. I looked up to Mark because he exuded a confidence on camera that rubbed off on me. When we were together it felt so natural and our scenes would flow of their own accord. I couldn't envisage having the same rapport with anybody else on the show. It never crossed my own mind to quit at the same time, but I was genuinely worried that it might badly affect my future. Aside from my scenes with Lydia, virtually everything I did on the show revolved around my relationship with Mark.

I was happy with the way things were going in the show, so, when Mark confided to me about his plans, it came as a bolt from the blue.

'Arg, there's something I need to tell you,' he said to me while we were alone in his flat. 'I don't know how much longer I'm going to be in *TOWIE*.'

'What do you mean, Mark? Everything's going so well. You're the top boy and everybody loves us when we're together in the show.'

'I know, but I don't want to be known as the guy who

breaks hearts in *TOWIE* for the rest of my life. I've been there and done that. I want to do other things with my career.'

'But where does that leave me?' I asked. 'I only got onto the show in the first place because of you. Are you sure you've thought about this properly?'

'I've thought about it a lot, Arg. I've got a new management company in place and they're putting together a plan for me to do other stuff. I feel bad for you but I know you'll be all right – the fans love you.'

I understood his reasons for leaving and I didn't want to stand in the way of his plans, but at the same time part of me prayed that he would change his mind. There were a million thoughts running around inside my head because I had so many unanswered questions. Would the viewers still be interested in me? How would my career develop without him at my side? Who would I film my scenes with? Worst of all, it felt as if I were losing my best friend.

One of the reasons Mark and I worked so well on screen together was that we shared a genuine friendship. It wasn't something that was created just for the cameras. ITV ran surveys that revealed that viewers loved the chemistry between us. Our so-called 'bromance' blossomed on screen and people even began to refer to us by the joint nickname of 'Marg' (short for Mark and Arg!). I love Mark to bits, he's always pulling pranks, and whenever I would stay at his flat, he often woke me up by splashing a cup of water on my face – while he filmed it on his phone! Whenever I felt down, Mark would always be there to cheer me up. If I was feeling sorry for myself over a problem with Lydia, he'd put his arm around me and tell me to stop being such a donut. Mark had a knack of knowing what to say to me and his advice normally worked. I felt that he was my shoulder to cry on throughout my constant ups and downs with Lydia and he was a pillar that I often turned to for support. He was my rock, both professionally and privately.

Mark's decision to leave *TOWIE* came at the end of a difficult period for him. His engagement to Lauren had been bumpy for some time, so I wasn't surprised when they announced at the end of summer 2011 that they were splitting up. My view was that they'd done the right thing by calling a halt to things, because the relationship was causing them both too much pain. Mark's only comment in public at the time was a brief line on Twitter in which he confirmed they had separated and he said that Lauren would always have a place in his heart.

Behind the scenes, Mark was in a lot of distress. The writing had been on the wall earlier in the summer when Lydia and I had joined Mark and Lauren on a holiday to Portugal. We had travelled there as a foursome to attend the wedding of a friend of ours. His name was Timothy Langer and he was marrying his fiancée Kathryn at the luxury resort of Vilamoura. Lydia and I were getting along OK at this point, having temporarily put our own problems behind us while I concentrated on trying to rebuild things between us. It was a hard struggle, because a lot of the trust had gone out of our relationship. Lydia had taken to checking my phone for messages and, while we were in Portugal, she found one from a woman that made her suspicious. It was actually an innocent enquiry about a booking I'd done in Malia from somebody I didn't know, but it caused a bit of friction.

Meanwhile, Mark and Lauren seemed to be constantly at war. They grated on each other's nerves throughout the Portugal trip and they both knew exactly what buttons to press in order to annoy each other. Their rows sometimes put me in a difficult position, because I got on well with both of them, but when the chips were down Mark was my best mate and he was the one I sided with. One source of friction between them seemed to be that Lauren hated it whenever Mark would show off his body by taking off his shirt. I think she was a bit conscious of the fact that Mark had a chiselled six pack, whereas she was slightly curvier and therefore not quite so proud of her own figure. I felt that Lauren could be a diva when she wanted to and she gave Mark a lot of stick that other people didn't know about.

The wedding ceremony in Portugal went very well and afterwards Mark made a short speech, which he ended by making a joke about *TOWIE*.

'I better stop speaking now before you all tell me to "shhhut up!"' he quipped, using Amy Childs's famous catch-phrase from the show.

Unfortunately for Mark, nobody found the phrase 'shhhut up' very funny and his joke went down like a lead balloon! I later sang a few songs at the reception, which were well received. As part of the celebrations, Timothy and his best man were filming a video montage of the day and they wanted to shoot a sequence in which a group of the boys all stripped off to their boxer shorts and jumped into the pool.

Mark naturally peeled off and joined in with the fun – but it seemed to send Lauren into a fury.

'Why the f*** did you do that, Mark?' she demanded.

Lauren and Lydia had spent most of the afternoon drinking together and the sight of Mark undressed seemed to make Lauren weirdly jealous, so much so that she caused a scene by threatening to strip off herself in retaliation.

'You're just showing off by getting your body out,' she screamed. 'If you're going to do it, I'm doing the same!'

'Don't be so stupid. You're out of order,' Mark replied.

Mark was horrified and he had to persuade Lauren not to take her dress off right there at the reception. I suspected that Lauren was drunk and I got the impression she really would have jumped into the pool if Mark had not stopped her. When Lauren and Lydia got together they could drink like there was no tomorrow.

When Lauren and Lydia got together, they could drink like there was no tomorrow

Mark and I were soon pleading with them to take it easy.

'We're at a wedding and there are friends and family here,' Mark told them. 'You two are causing a scene by getting paralytic. You need to pace yourselves and calm down.'

I offered to get the girls some water and they agreed to curb their drinking, but, as soon as Mark and I went off to chat with some other guests, the girls were at it again. As I looked over my shoulder I saw them swigging from a bottle of champagne that they were passing back and forth to each other. Part of me found it amusing, but it was infuriating at the same time.

Mark and Lauren seemed to spend the rest of the time in Portugal arguing, and after we got back to the UK it seemed as if he had been pushed to the limit.

'Look, Arg, part of me loves her but I just know this isn't right,' he told me. 'I can't see us lasting. It's just not working. We make each other miserable.'

In the end they had a heart-to-heart and agreed to go their separate ways. I was sad because I could sense they were both hurting, but I'd seen their constant fighting and I knew it was better for both of them to be apart. Meanwhile, I suspected that Mark's family were secretly quite relieved. Even though they had welcomed Lauren for the sake of Mark, I got the impression that they never really felt she was the one for him. They'd gone along with the relationship because Mark had been with her from a young age and they wanted him to be happy, but I suspected that deep down they didn't think that she was good enough for him. I got the impression that they greeted the engagement with surprise rather than delight, and they saw it as a passing phase.

Even though Mark knew he had to end things with Lauren, it didn't stop him from hurting a great deal. They had gone through secondary school and spent their late teens together and, despite their many break-ups, it was obvious that this time their split was for real. They'd made a big show of getting engaged on TV, which made things all the more painful.

Mark needed me as a mate more than ever, but it came at just the same time as I started to spend a bit more time with Lydia. My relationship with her was still troubled but for a while we seemed to be getting back on track. Lydia had thrown herself into her lifelong ambition of opening a fashion boutique, which I was happy to help her with. We had often spoken about opening a shop in the past, and, now that Lydia was beginning to earn well from doing the odd endorsement off the back of *TOWIE*, she decided to give it a go.

'I'm so excited, James. I've always wanted to do this,' Lydia told me. 'I want the shop to be a big success. I've got so many ideas. I don't just want to sell clothing: I want the shop to stock delicious things to eat as well.'

'That's brilliant, Lydia. I'm proud of you,' I told her.

Lydia and I had previously enjoyed watching a romantic comedy called *It's Complicated*, in which Jane, a character played by Meryl Streep, ran a bakery. Lydia wanted her shop to sell cupcakes and candles, just like in the movie. I thought it was a great idea.

Lydia found a vacant shop in Loughton and put together a business plan. She put up all the money and gave her sister Georgia a half-share in the venture. I was surprised that she chose to cut in her sister in like that, but it was Lydia's money and it was a nice gesture.

Meanwhile, I did my best to help to promote the opening by persuading everybody I knew to come along. It was an exciting venture and it felt as if Lydia and I were enjoying being in love again. Things seemed to be picking up for me: I was still glowing after our success at the BAFTAs and I had my girlfriend back.

I was so tied up in my own world, that I failed to see how

desperately low Mark was after breaking up with Lauren, and for a while I neglected to see him because I was with Lydia all the time. When Series 3 of *TOWIE* started to film Mark let rip at me over it during a scene in his flat. I arrived expecting to film a sequence consisting of our normal banter, but I could see straight away that Mark had the hump.

'What's the matter?' I asked him while we were being filmed.

At first Mark avoided giving me a straight answer and claimed there was nothing wrong, but when I persisted his frustrations with me came tumbling out.

'Can you sit there and tell me that you've been there for me?' he said.

I knew he had a point and I said sorry on air.

Later on, when we discussed things in private, I apologised again.

'I'm sorry, Mark. I've been trying to make things work with Lydia and I know I've neglected you,' I told him.

'You're going to smother the girl,' he warned. 'One minute you're out with the boys and then suddenly you're spending every waking moment with her and you don't want to be with anyone else. You've got to grow some balls and learn to divide up your time.'

'I know. I never get the balance right,' I said. 'It just seems that I'm either always with you and she's got the hump, or it's the other way round and I'm blanking all my mates.'

I felt awful when Mark reminded me of all the times he had been there for me in the past. When I had come back from Spain in pieces he'd been the first to console me. Mark explained that the reason he was in so much pain was that he knew that this time his split from Lauren was for real, unlike all their previous break-ups. I was so carried away with being around Lydia that I had completely forgotten about Mark and I had just presumed he would be OK.

Although Mark had the ability to wrap most women around his little finger, Lydia could see through his bluster and she blamed him for leading me astray.

'I'm fed up with always being made out to be the bad guy,' Mark told me. 'I've worked really hard to get on with Lydia, but how do you expect the girl to respect me when you're the one who's telling her that your behaviour is my fault?'

'I know, Mark, but it's only banter,' I replied.

'Yeah, but the truth is you're worse than me for looking at other girls when we're out together. You need to either man up and put Lydia in her place or stop giving her excuses to be on your case.'

'But it's hard, Mark. I love her and I don't want to lose her again,' I said.

'I know that, Arg, but you've got to be firm. You gotta make it clear that there's going to be times when you're out with the boys and she has to accept that. Everyone thinks I'm to blame and, to be honest, I'm sick of it. I'm fed up of hearing that I'm in the wrong.'

There were times when I felt terribly sorry for Mark

There were times when I felt terribly sorry for Mark. He loved being the star of the show, but it came at a heavy price. A lot of people disliked him for the way he treated girls, and it resulted in his suffering a lot of abuse when he was in public. It was true that he messed with people's emotions, but my own view was that Lauren, Sam and Lucy always chose to come running back for more. The negative fallout it created caused people to give Mark a lot of stick in nightclubs because they didn't like what they'd seen him do on screen.

I know it happened a lot because I witnessed it at first hand. He'd often receive threats and people would try to pick fights with him. On other occasions, he would have abuse shouted at him in the street and he was constantly being caned on Twitter.

'It's all getting a bit much, Arg,' he told me. 'I want people to see a different side to me. It's not my fault if birds kick up a fuss when they don't get it all their own way.'

The criticism that Mark received was something that had been happening ever since *TOWIE* first hit the screens. The situation had become so inflamed during the first series that for a while the producers hired special protection for Mark. He was assigned a bodyguard, who stayed in his apartment and shadowed him during the day. It was around the time that Mark's bar had been firebombed and for a while it seemed as if he was in real danger. It went on for several weeks, but in the end Mark decided that he didn't need the bodyguard any more and his security was scaled down.

I don't seem to generate the same reaction from people because I'm perceived as a very different character. People think of me as being much calmer, so they tend to be friendly towards me when I go out in nightclubs. Mark and I were like chalk and cheese in that respect. I think part of the reason we worked so well together is because we are different personalities, but still we get on. I thought that a lot of the flak that he received was very unfair, especially as the women around him knew the score and should have realised that they were in for a bumpy ride.

When a possibility arose of his appearing on *I'm a Celebrity ... Get Me Out of Here!* it was an opportunity for Mark to show the public the warmer side of his character. Mark started dropping hints to me in private that his management team were in talks about his going to the jungle. We had been through thick and thin together on *TOWIE* and my first thought was, How the hell will I cope without him?

We were out in Mark's car driving through Essex when he told me he had now gone ahead and set a date to leave.

'Arg, I just need to let you know that I've been confirmed for the jungle. I've been signed up,' he told me. 'I feel bad about it, though, Arg. I feel guilty about leaving you. At the end of Series 3 I'll be leaving *TOWIE* for good. My management want me to start doing presenting and maybe acting and I think it's the right time for me to move forward.'

At first I tried not to show my feelings because I didn't want to look selfish. I knew that it was a big break for him.

'Oh, mate,' I replied. 'Obviously I'm proud of you and whatever, but I'm gutted – and I don't want you to leave. I still can't imagine the show without you.'

'I don't think I can do any more in *TOWIE*,' Mark said. 'I don't think I can get any bigger, and now's the right time to think of my future. I need to go down a different path for the good of my career.'

I was quiet for a moment while I let the news sink in. I was emotional because it felt as if I was about to lose my best friend in the whole wide world. I thought back to when we had first started the show together, when we had no idea in the early days whether it would be a success or a failure. All my best memories were of those scenes that we had filmed together. The thought of doing it all alone without him seemed inconceivable. When Mark was alongside me on screen I felt secure and confident, but without him I just didn't know if things would be the same.

'Don't worry, we'll always be best mates,' Mark reassured me. 'I feel guilty about leaving you, but you'll still do well by yourself.'

Even though I knew he'd made up his mind, it didn't fully sink in for me until it came to filming our final joint scene together for his last episode. Up until that point I think I'd still secretly been hoping that Mark would do the jungle and then agree to return to *TOWIE* afterwards, but it was not to be.

When the producers learned the news they filmed Mark and me in his flat while we discussed his plans. Until now I had been putting a brave face on things and it wasn't until he picked me up in his car to go and do the scene that my heart began to beat quickly.

'Arg, you do realise this is the last scene that you and I will probably ever do alone together,' Mark said.

I started to reply but I found it hard to speak. I was beside myself with emotion and I felt embarrassed.

'Mark, I don't want this to be our last scene. I don't want you to leave,' I said.

'I know, Arg, but I have to. I feel so bad.'

It kept going through my mind that I was losing my best friend. We'd formed a special relationship, and I was afraid of losing that.

What am I going to do? I kept thinking.

When I look back at things now it makes me laugh because I was being such a big baby, but the emotions that I was feeling at the time were very real.

'Arg, you'll be absolutely all right,' Mark tried to reassure me. 'After me, you're probably the next biggest star of the show. You're not just my sidekick any more: you're a character in your own right. You're going to be fine. This is going to be good for you.'

When we arrived at his building I tried to keep my emotions in check as we walked upstairs to his apartment. The producers and the crew were already there setting up their lights. Everyone could tell I was upset but I didn't want them to see me like that, so I walked into Mark's bedroom and closed the door behind me. Within seconds I was in floods of tears. Some blokes have problems letting their emotions out, but on occasions like this I am not one of them. Nanny Pat came into the bedroom while I was in a bad way and sat next to me.

'Come on, it'll be all right, it'll be all right,' she said.

Then Mark came in and gave me a cuddle.

'I don't want to do this scene. Please, Mark, I can't do it,' I protested.

A couple of the producers came in to talk to us and I calmed down a little bit. The crew had already set the cameras up and they were keen to capture all the emotion while it was still raw, without missing anything. We went into the living room and began to film. Mark began by explaining his reasons for leaving, although he made no mention of going up the jungle. By the end of the scene we were both in tears.

'You're my bestest friend in the whole world and you're going to be in my heart for ever,' he told me in front of the cameras. 'I know I've got to go and it's time for me to just walk away from everything, Arg. I've got to move on and grow up.'

Everything the viewers saw on screen was completely real: we really were both hurting like hell. After we finished filming the producers hugged us and told us it had been an amazing scene.

It felt a bit like a marriage break-up, and in a way I suppose it was. We had been soulmates throughout *TOWIE* and to me it felt like the end of an era. There was a huge party planned for that evening, where the crew had arranged to film the grand finale of the series. Mark and I dried our eyes and began to sort ourselves out.

'We're not going to cry any more, Arg,' said Mark. 'You've let it all out now and we're gonna go to the party and have a great time.'

I still miss Mark on *TOWIE* to this day. But he was correct to say that things would work out all right for both of us, and

I still miss Mark on TOWIE to this day

we have maintained our friendship. Mark's career went from strength to strength and he eventually landed a number of different roles presenting on TV. He was also a huge success in the jungle. I watched him from back home and I was very proud of everything he achieved. *I'm a Celebrity ... Get Me Out of Here!* proved to be the perfect vehicle for Mark to show the kinder side of his personality. That's the thing with Mark: he may have had an abrasive edge in the way that he used to treat women, but he also has a very warm and generous side. Viewers saw that in the jungle, and Mark became the bookies' favourite to win, although he was eventually pipped into second place behind Dougie Poynter of McFly. I was the first person to speak to Mark on the phone when he came out of the jungle. His parents, big Mark and Carol, had travelled to Australia to be with him and they passed the phone to Mark when I called. I told him how proud I was of him and how well he had come across on screen. Everybody had loved him and I genuinely believe that going into the jungle helped change people's perceptions of him.

'I can't wait for you to get home,' I told him.

When Mark arrived back in the UK, we all threw a coming-home party for him at Nu Bar, where I did a big speech and then got wildly drunk. It was just like old times.

If I can fast-forward to today, I can say that Mark has now matured a lot since his days on *TOWIE*. He takes his career and his image very seriously and he works very hard. His days of being a lady killer are well and truly behind him.

When he left *The Only Way Is Essex* he opened up a new chapter in his life. At the end of summer 2013 he got engaged to Michelle Keegan, who is adored by fans for her role as Tina in *Coronation Street*. Michelle is a really beautiful and lovely girl and I am so happy for Mark that he has now found the one. I have been fortunate enough to meet Michelle on many occasions and she has been round to my house to meet my family. I am glad that Mark finally found true love. I hope that one day I can settle down in the same way.

It was very strange going back to *TOWIE* without him, but I was lucky that I began to form new friendships. In particular, Joey Essex and I began to film a lot of fun scenes together and we were often joined by Diags (James Bennewith) and then, further on, also by Tom Pearce. But I'll tell you all about that later.

As for Mark and me, we are still best mates. Our respective schedules obviously mean we don't see each other as much as we used to, but we are always just one phone call away.

14

A CHRISTMAS COOKALONG AND A BROKEN HEART

Christmas was traditionally a very special time that Lydia and I enjoyed together, and, as the festive season approached at the end of 2011, I was looking forward to the celebrations. In the weeks leading up to the holiday period my manager Neil received a phone call from Channel 4, who had a very interesting proposition.

'Gordon Ramsay's going to be cooking Christmas lunch on air and he'd like Arg to join him,' the broadcaster said.

It sounded like a fun show and it was to be broadcast live on national television on Christmas Day itself, so it would be great exposure for me. Various people would be joining in from around the country, and Channel 4 planned to turn it into a huge event. I was very honoured. After all, it's not

It's not every day you get invited to lunch by Gordon Ramsay every day that you get invited to lunch by the most famous chef in the country. But I assumed that the drawback would be that I would have to be away from home – and it would mean that I'd miss Christmas lunch with Lydia's family. Every year we'd always have a great time opening presents together with the children at Debbie's house, after which we'd sing songs and play games. It was always a wonderful time and I didn't want to miss out by having to film all day.

'I'm very flattered but I just don't want to give up my Christmas,' I said.

Channel 4 then came back to clarify things and they explained that Lydia, Debbie and I could film the show from home, which meant we wouldn't have to sacrifice the whole of Christmas Day.

'You'll be joining Gordon via a live TV link,' they said.

The idea was that we would follow Gordon's lead stage by stage while he prepared a sumptuous seasonal lunch with all the trimmings. We'd use his advice in order to cook up our own banquet at home. The show was called *Gordon's Christmas Cookalong Live*, and it sounded as if it would be a good laugh. Lydia and Debbie loved the proposal, so we all agreed to take part. It was a mad, crazy idea – but it was too good to turn down.

'It's a deal,' I said.

With the Gordon Ramsay project on the horizon, the build-up to Christmas should have been perfect, but, sadly, things don't always work out that way, and my relationship with Lydia took a turn for the worse. The damage caused by my cheating along with the friction between us over my closeness to Mark had never really gone away. Ironically, it was in the immediate aftermath of Mark's leaving that things came to a head. Lydia had hated the amount of time I spent with him and it became a source of irritation to her. For my part, I couldn't see why I shouldn't have both a best friend and a loving partner, but I never seemed to get the balance right.

At the end of every series the producers would always hold a big wrap party, which all the cast and crew would attend. This time around, they decided to put up a huge screen at the party in order to play some clips from the show. One of the sequences they planned to showcase was the scene in Mark's apartment during which we'd sat on the sofa and I'd cried while we said our goodbyes. Lydia and I were naturally going to the wrap party together and I was expecting to have a great time.

It turned out to be the party from hell.

My feelings about Mark's departure were still very raw and while the clip of our final scene was playing at the party I began to get a bit choked up. Mark was in Australia by now, but I was still very scared about how the next series of *TOWIE* would unfold without him. People at the party could sense my unease and many of them came up to me to reassure me.

'Don't worry. It'll be all right, Arg – everything'll be fine,' they said.

Unfortunately, it was a sentiment that Lydia didn't share.

In fact, I got the distinct impression that she felt I was being pathetic. She couldn't understand why I'd got so emotional. As the scene unfolded on the big screen, I looked over at Lydia and saw her pulling funny faces that made it clear she thought the whole thing was cringeworthy.

What the hell were you doing? her face seemed to say.

Her reaction made me feel dreadful and, as the night wore on, Lydia was increasingly offish towards me. When I went up to her she would ignore me and walk off to talk to somebody else. After a few drinks I was feeling very upset and hurt. As I watched Lydia on the dance floor at the party something snapped inside me and I marched over to confront her.

'Lydia, what the f*** is the matter with you?' I demanded.

A terrible row followed during which Lydia screamed back at me. We both vented our frustrations and it caused a major scene at the party, so much so that Debbie had to come running over to try to defuse the situation. At one point Lydia tried to throw a drink over me, and the glass slipped out of her hand and smashed on the floor. After that, Lydia and I steered clear of each other for the rest of the party. We were both fuming and we didn't talk for days.

There were still a few weeks to go before Christmas and our big day with Gordon Ramsay, so, in the meantime, Lydia decided to go off for a brief holiday in LA with Lauren. I wanted to buy Lydia something special for Christmas to show I cared. She had never owned an expensive watch before, so I thought I'd push the boat out. I chose a Cartier Ballon Bleu watch, which had a classic face and a brushed-steel bracelet. I bought it from my former employer at the jeweller's, Jimmy Kane. It cost just over £3,000. When I gave it to Lydia during the *TOWIE* Christmas Special she was thrilled to bits.

On Christmas Eve, Lydia and I went out to Nu Bar together for a few drinks. We didn't have a particularly great night and we were quite drunk when we got into the back of a cab to go home. I was staying at her place but, as we walked into the house, something just didn't feel right between us. I was tired of putting on a false front when I suspected that deep down Lydia's heart wasn't in it any more. For the first time in our relationship, I decided to opt for the sofa rather than share a bedroom with Lydia.

'I feel a bit drunk and I don't want to keep you up all night by snoring. I'm going to lay down here on the sofa,' I said.

Lydia didn't object. It was quite a sad moment. I just didn't feel happy. We had tried and tried to make things work but we were so weary of arguing by now that I felt exhausted by it all.

Sleeping on the sofa turned out to be a bad idea. We'd arrived home at about two in the morning and everyone else in the house woke up at around six o'clock to open their presents. I had a terrible hangover and on top of that a camera crew were about to arrive to film our special link-up with Gordon Ramsay. It was the start of a day that turned out to be massively stressful because everything was a rush.

Lydia came downstairs and gave me my Christmas card. I had been expecting her to give me my present on Christmas morning, although I could see that she had nothing in her hands apart from the card.

'I'm so sorry, but I just had no time to get you a Christmas present. I've ordered you something but it didn't arrive in time,' she said.

I opened up the card. Inside she'd drawn a little picture of a Mulberry travel bag, the gift that she had ordered. Up until now, Lydia had always spoiled me with nice gifts at Christmas and on birthdays, so I'd been expecting something nice, especially after buying her a Cartier watch. All I'd got was a card with a drawing inside. After all the trouble I'd gone to in order buy her something special, I felt hurt.

I didn't have much time to dwell on it, because the Channel 4 camera crew soon arrived and the house turned into chaos. They parked a gigantic satellite-broadcast unit outside and there seemed to be wires and power cables everywhere. The crew then set up a huge screen in Debbie's kitchen so that we could watch Gordon Ramsay while we followed his instructions.

It was exciting, but at the same time it took the edge off of the fact that it was Christmas, because all of the children had to stay out of the way. My hangover was thumping and I was feeling terribly hot under all the television lights. When the filming started it was a bit confusing, because there were a lot of time delays, but Gordon was a true professional and he talked us through everything. It was an amazing show, but I must confess that there were parts of it that felt like hell. Lydia and I were grating on each other's nerves, although we were careful to adopt cheesy smiles for the cameras. I am useless at cooking and I kept making mistakes. I remember that I dropped the parsnips and nearly burned the stuffing!

Gordon kept coming on screen to have a little bit of banter with us and ask how we were getting on.

'Arg is useless!' Debbie quipped.

By the time we finished filming I was feeling shattered and I still had my headache. The best part of the day was gone by now and the kids had long since opened their presents. The magic of the occasion seemed to have vanished. I had sensed that something had been building up between Lydia and me since Christmas Eve and things finally came to head on Boxing Day evening. Lydia had her serious face on and part of me guessed what was coming next.

'I just don't think it's working any more,' she said. 'I don't think we should be together.'

'But Lydia ...'

'No, James. We've tried and tried and we're just not happy. It's not the same any more. It's just not working.'

'I just don't think it's working any more'

I was heartbroken but I knew she had a point. I agreed with everything Lydia said but I still loved her and didn't want to lose her. She was the woman I'd imagined I would marry and have kids with. I shed some tears during our conversation, but I think we'd been through so many arguments by now that it didn't really sink in. We'd already made plans that we would be together on New Year's Eve, when I was due to sing at Nu Bar. For the sake of appearances, we agreed that we'd still go ahead with it, but after that we would go our separate ways. In fact, we ended up sleeping together on New Year's Eve and, when we awoke on New Year's Day, we agreed we'd go for one more final dinner together to say goodbye.

'I don't want to end on bad terms,' said Lydia. 'Let's end it in an amicable way.'

It was a weird feeling while I got ready for our last dinner. Part of me felt sick inside at the thought of saying farewell, but I also hoped that it was an opportunity for me to change Lydia's mind. I got dressed up in my best suit and gelled my hair. I wanted to look good to give myself the best chance of winning her over. I arranged to pick Lydia up in a cab and we went to a restaurant in Loughton. She looked beautiful in a blue dress and I took a picture of her on my phone camera, which I still keep a copy of on my mobile today. Over dinner Lydia explained her position to me.

'James, I'll always love you,' she said. 'I'm not saying that in the future we can't get back together because one day we might,' she continued. 'But at this moment in time it's not working. I think you need to be single and I need to be single. We need to do other things in our life. We're both still young.'

I could feel the tears welling up within me.

'Please, Lydia,' I begged. 'Are you sure we need to break up? Are you sure we can't work this out? I love you and I don't want to lose you.'

'No, James. It has to be this way. We promised we'd finish things on a good note, so let's not go over old ground.'

I was on the verge of breaking down but I was aware that I was in a busy restaurant and didn't want everybody to see me cry. I got up and left the table in order to go to the bathroom to compose myself. When I returned we spent the rest of the meal chatting about old times. As we spoke about all the close moments we'd shared over the years I could sense that Lydia was warming to me as the drink started to relax us both. We paid for the meal and, as we slipped into the back of the taxi, something unexpected happened.

We began to kiss.

At first it was just a delicate touch on the lips but within a few seconds we were snogging passionately. My head was all over the place.

Much as I love this girl, what's going through her mind? I thought.

Lydia was sending me mixed signals and I was totally confused. That night Lydia and I made love in her bedroom. The next morning I awoke assuming that because we'd made love we'd be able to patch things up, but Lydia still had other ideas.

'It doesn't change anything,' she told me.

I was devastated by the fact that Lydia didn't want to be with me any more after four years. I spent the next few days at home in a state of shock. I had no idea what the future would hold and my emotions were in turmoil. Lydia and I decided to keep our break-up a secret from the media. We knew that if the press found out it would create a lot of interest and neither of us wanted to go through all the fuss. We faced a challenge keeping a lid on it because the press office at *TOWIE* had started to arrange interviews to publicise the new series. They had organised a big cover shoot with *Fabulous* magazine, which is distributed free with the *Sun*. Joey, Mario and I were all due to attend with several of the girls from the cast, including Lydia. I knew it would be a difficult assignment, but Lydia and I agreed to put a brave face on it and we decided to go along without informing anybody that we had split.

Looking back, I think it was a mistake for me to have gone on the *Fabulous* shoot, because I ended up making a total fool of myself. The shoot took place out in the countryside and we all had to travel there by coach. I hardly spoke to anybody on the way, but when we arrived Lydia and I did a quick photo together. It felt horrible and awkward because we had to smile for the cameras and pretend that everything was OK. Deep down inside I was hurting a lot and, as the day wore on, I became angry and frustrated at having to put on a façade. When it came to shooting the cover image, I assumed that I would be part of the group, but the photographer had other ideas.

'We're going to try a line-up of the girls on their own,' one the magazine staff explained.

'What? You mean I'm not on the cover,' I protested.

'No, Arg, we don't need you for the cover. We're just going to use the girls and maybe try one or two with the other boys.'

Call it ego if you like, but I had automatically assumed that the magazine would give me star billing. Now that Mark was no longer there, I'd convinced myself that I was the biggest star. It had never crossed my mind that I'd be used only on the inside pages. I sat there fuming. Then, to my horror, the photographer invited Mario to step in to join the line-up. Soon afterwards, Joey was asked to give it a go as

I'd convinced myself that I was the biggest star

well. I'm embarrassed to admit it now, but I was extremely offended and I started to act like a diva, waltzing around the studio in a huff. I assumed they wanted Mario and Joey because they both have very sculpted bodies, whereas I was looking very overweight.

How *dare* they? I thought.

When I asked them why they didn't want me, they relented and asked me to do a cover shot, but just as I was about to pose they changed their minds and told me I wasn't needed after all.

When the magazine staff confirmed I wasn't wanted for the cover I was furious and I reacted by throwing my toys out of the pram. I stormed off to my dressing room to collect my things. Then, without telling anybody, I walked out of the studios. I'd had enough and I decided to go home, even though I knew we still had more interviews to do. When I got outside I found myself in a field in the middle of nowhere and I had no idea how I was going to get home. I simply walked up the road until a car drove by. I stuck out my thumb like a hitchhiker. Fortunately, the car stopped and the woman driver recognised me.

'Could you give me a lift to the nearest station, please?' I asked.

The woman agreed and I later caught a train. By now my mobile phone was in meltdown. The *TOWIE* press office rang me and demanded to know where I'd gone, but I refused to return to the shoot. I was in a blinkered fury. When I look back now and think about how I behaved, I feel very ashamed. It was extremely unprofessional and it still makes me cringe. I would never normally dream of walking out in a strop like that over something so trivial, but at the time I was hurting like hell over Lydia dumping me, and my emotions were all over the place.

The powers that be at *TOWIE* were furious with me for embarrassing the show in front of the magazine. Afterwards, I received a phone call from my manager informing me that *TOWIE* had decided to ban me from attending the National Television Awards as a punishment. After the BAFTAs, the NTAs were the social highlight of the year, so I was gutted, especially as most of the cast would be attending via the red carpet.

Mark could see I was hurting and, as usual, he had the perfect suggestion to lift my spirits.

'It's a mess and you need to get away from it all,' he said. 'Why don't you come to Dubai with me? I've got to go there to do some filming, so all the accommodation's already paid for up front. Everything's sorted. All you need to do is pay for your flights.'

Mark said he had a suite booked at the Atlantis, which is situated right at the heart of the manmade Palm area of Dubai. We were joined by our friend James Kenzie, from the pop-rap group Blazin' Squad.

'It's exactly what you need right now,' said Mark.

The only complication was that Lydia's twenty-first birthday was approaching on the following weekend. Even though we were no longer together, I still wanted to be around to wish her happy birthday, so I arranged my flights so that I would be back in the country by the weekend for her big day.

Dubai turned out to be fantastic. It's like a cross between Las Vegas and a paradise island. We spent the evenings going out to all the best nightclubs and it took my mind off my troubles back home. There were plenty of Brits out there, including lots of girls who recognised us from the TV. We attracted a fair bit of female attention and I admit that I chatted to several women during our nights out. I was on the rebound and I flirted with several girls because it felt good to have some female company. I'd been there a couple of nights when I received a text from Lydia. She'd brought her birthday party forward to midweek and was upset that I wasn't going to be there.

Maybe I should change my flights and go back early, I thought.

Mark and Kenzie were aghast when I mentioned the idea.

'Arg, you're doing it again,' warned Mark. 'You're still thinking with your heart, not your head, and you're being weak. Don't go rushing back.'

Despite their warnings I couldn't get the thought of Lydia's party off my mind. In the end I caved in and rang my airline. I worked out a schedule that would get me back in the nick of time for the party, which I discovered from one of Lydia's friends on Twitter was being held at a restaurant in Camden. I didn't breathe a word to Lydia. I wanted it to be a surprise. When I finally made it to the restaurant the party was in full swing.

Lydia was in shock.

'Happy birthday, Lydia!' I said.

'James – what are you doing here!' she exclaimed, as I gave her a big bouquet of flowers.

225

At first she tried to play it cool but I could see that deep down it meant everything to her that I'd made the effort. There were so many friends and family present that it was a while before we had a chance to speak together alone.

'I hate being single,' she confided. 'Did you see anyone else while you were in Dubai?'

'No, Lydia,' I answered. I failed to mention that I'd chatted up several women while I was out there.

That evening we went to a club called Gilgamesh before sharing a taxi back to Lydia's home and on the way she began to open up about her true feelings. She started to cry and she told me that she still loved me. I hugged her and held her close, and briefly it was as if all my dreams had come true. Lydia and I spent the night at her house, where we made love in her bedroom. It was the perfect end to my mad dash back to the UK and I fell asleep with her in my arms. I had my darling Lydia back.

Or so I thought.

I had my darling Lydia back. Or so I thought

Life can sometimes deal you some terribly harsh blows, and what happened next was almost beyond belief. As I look back, it still makes me feel sick inside. Lydia and I awoke the next morning and we were cuddled up together in bed when her phone rang. It was her manager, Kirsty, who explained that the press had contacted her regarding a negative story that they intended to publish about me. The *Sunday Mirror* was planning to run a piece that would allege that I'd behaved badly towards Lydia by flirting with girls while I'd been on holiday in Dubai. Lydia erupted into a boiling fury and threw me out of the house.

'Get out!' she screamed at me. 'No more, that's it.'

The new series of *TOWIE* was due to start a few days after Lydia's birthday but I had no enthusiasm. I filmed a number of scenes with Joey Essex and Diags, who were both an immense support to me while I was going through this low period. They could both see how upset I was and when my parents went away for a few days they came to stay with me in order to try to keep my spirits up.

Meanwhile, somebody approached Lydia and told her that all the rumours about my being unfaithful were true. To this day, I don't know who contacted her – Lydia just said that it was a friend we have in common. I think it only confirmed what she already knew in her heart to be true. I was still trying to deny it, but nobody believed me (it wasn't until a long time afterwards that l finally admitted it on camera).

When you have been with somebody in a relationship for so long it's hard to make a clean break, so, even though we'd split up, we did spend one final night together, during which we slept with one another.

It was on the day before Valentine's Day and afterwards Lydia swore me to secrecy.

I'd been planning to give Lydia a Valentine's gift for some time and I'd already bought her a pair of Manolo Blahnik shoes just like the ones that Mr Big had bought for Carrie Bradshaw in *Sex in the City*. Lydia always said she saw herself as being like Carrie, and I was her Mr Big. The shoes cost £700 and I had to have them flown in especially from Germany. I'd previously bought her two pairs of Christian Louboutin and a pair from Charlotte Olympia, so I had an eye for good shoes.

When I tried to give the shoes to Lydia at a *TOWIE* party she completely blanked me. I was very hurt. I couldn't understand how she could be so cold towards me when we'd slept together only two days earlier.

In the meantime, Lydia and I filmed a 'clear-the-air' scene in which we said our final goodbyes. The conversation ended with me breaking down in tears and weeping openly. I gave Lydia the shoes as a farewell gift, although that part was never shown on TV. What the viewers also weren't aware of was that Lydia and I were later involved in a furious bust-up. It happened when she discovered I'd told Joey about the secret night we had spent together prior to Valentine's Day.

Lydia was furious. She called me up while she was driving in her car and started screaming at me down the phone, calling me every name under the sun. She was in a total rage and while she was on the line I heard her car screech to a halt outside my house. Lydia jumped out with the Manolo Blahnik shoes and she threw them down into the driveway.

'You can have your f***ing shoes back now, I don't want them,' she shouted, before driving off.

That was how our relationship finally ended for good, with a tearful farewell on television, followed by a pair of shoes being chucked back at me. It took me nearly a year to come to terms with the pain of our break-up. I was broken to pieces emotionally and for a long time I was very bitter and argumentative towards the people around me. At first I found it impossible to cope with the thought of life without Lydia. The pain that I felt inside ate away at me every day in the weeks and months that followed. Everything I had wanted out of life had been based on spending my future with her. I'd always assumed that we would one day settle down and start a family together. Now all I could see ahead of me was a big black void. When I'd met Lydia I had been an overweight twenty-year-old who'd never had a girlfriend and had very few prospects. She'd been there for me at every step of the way while my early singing career had developed and she had figured in all of my plans for the future. Despite all our ups and downs, it felt as if I'd shared every part of my life with her. Now it was all over and it had a huge impact on me. I hated getting up in the mornings and I couldn't even see the point in putting on a clean shirt without being able to see Lydia. I was heartbroken.

Slowly, with the love and support of my family and good friends such as Mark, Joey, Diags and Tom Pearce, I learned to live without her. I can talk about it now without getting angry or upset, although I am still full of sadness. I did cheat on Lydia and I was therefore the one in the wrong. I let my ego get the better of me and I will always regret that. I like to think I'm slightly more mature now and if I could wind the clock back and do things differently I would. At the time of writing this book, Lydia and I no longer talk to each other, which is a shame, although I regularly keep in touch with Debbie. I had been welcomed into Lydia's family with open arms, so when we broke up I didn't just lose my partner: it felt as if I'd lost part of my family as well. I sometimes read interviews with Lydia in magazines in which she is quoted as saying horrible things about me. It makes me think that she is still bitter and hurt – and they say there is a fine line between love and hate. I have never met anyone I loved like Lydia and part of me will always love her. I don't think we'll ever get back together, because so much has been said and done that things are irreparable – although anything can happen in Essex.

15

MY YO-YO DIETING AND SURVIVING THE LONDON MARATHON

It's no secret that my weight sometimes goes up and down like a yo-yo. The reason is that I just love food. I eat to celebrate when I am happy and I eat to comfort myself when I am feeling down. I never need an excuse to tuck into a hearty meal, and I admit that I'm very partial to junk food. I get a lot of stick about it on social networks such as Twitter and Facebook. I've had to get used to it over the years and I try to take it like water off a duck's back. Twitter is a brilliant way of keeping in touch with *TOWIE* fans and for connecting with people (I was flattered when the R 'n' B star Chris Brown followed me after I sent out a tweet about him), but the flipside

I get a lot of stick about my weight on social networks

is that it is a cruel platform for cyber-bullies. It's become a bit of a pantomime because, whatever you tweet, you can always expect tons of abuse back. Some people seem to find it funny to let rip at anyone they've seen on the telly, but some of the comments can be hurtful. The abuse I get is nearly always about my weight. People tweet messages like, 'You fat bastard', or 'You fat piece of shit, what have you eaten today?'

Charming!

I do my best to laugh it off because I know that it goes with the territory, but it's not exactly great for your self-esteem. Mostly it doesn't bother me because I am naturally an upbeat person with a bubbly outlook. If people want to call me a fat bastard it's up to them (I suppose it's just their way of having a joke). My weight also attracts a lot of attention from the media and the papers have been known to write headlines such as IT'S LARGE ARG! or THE TUBBY CROONER.

Most of it is good natured and I am happy to play along, but there have been times when it has hit my confidence. It can make me feel a little low at times. The heaviest I have been is around 19½ stone, which sounds a hell of a lot. However, because I'm 6 foot 2 inches tall, I carry it better than I would if I were shorter. I am also lucky because the last place that I tend to gain weight is around my face. In photos I can get away with it because my facial features stay relatively slim. It's my thighs, my legs, my love handles and my man boobs that I struggle with!

My biggest issue when it comes to my weight is that I have a huge appetite. I follow in the footsteps of my Granddad Seamus in that respect, because he was a big man who enjoyed eating large meals. Seamus was a wonderful man who could demolish a mountain of food and come back for more – and I am the same.

My ideal breakfast would be a sizzling hot bacon sandwich or a fry-up consisting of eggs, bacon, sausages, baked beans – you name it. A few hours later I will happily follow up by eating a pizza or a burger for lunch, or even with a trip to Chicken Cottage (my favourite local takeaway). Dinner could be an Indian or a Chinese meal or pie and mash. I have been known to binge on food and I can keep eating pizza even when it feels like I am completely full.

You get the picture.

My mum likes to encourage me to eat healthily and occasionally she will take me to task about it.

'You've got to look after yourself, James,' she said to me recently. 'All that junk food's not good for you.'

'I know, Mum. You're right, but it's not easy.'

'Well I'm going to hide all the chocolate and crisps if you don't cut down,' she warned.

Unfortunately, most of the foods that I like cause me to pile on the pounds. I tend to find myself in a constant cycle of putting on weight, followed by periods when I eat healthily in an attempt to get slim.

During the times when I am dieting I can be very meticulous about what I eat. Breakfast might be smoked salmon and scrambled eggs with no toast or bread; lunch could be grilled chicken and salad followed by an evening meal of chicken, spinach and broccoli with no potatoes. The result is that my weight is constantly going up and down. There are times when I've managed to get down to around 15 stone and I feel great and people tell me that I look good.

The strange thing is that, as I have said previously, I wasn't a fat child. My mum has got albums of photos of me that show a happy-looking boy with a normal frame.

'James, you were actually quite a wiry child,' my mum tells me.

It was towards the end of secondary school that I started to get chubby. I think that was partly due to the fact that I was not very fit. I put all my efforts into amateur dramatics and did very little sport. My asthma initially stopped me from being great at football, so, apart from the odd game of tennis, I didn't get much exercise. To this day I still hate going to the gym and I will use any excuse to get out of it.

Part of my problem is that I eat when I am bored and it makes me feel good. I can be very greedy with sweets and crisps and I am a regular visitor to petrol stations, where I stock up on snacks. I have a little regime where I pick out the following:

- one packet of crisps (usually Walker's salt-and-vinegar Squares);
- one chocolate bar (either a Snickers or a Kinder Bueno);
- one packet of chewy sweets (either Haribo or fruit pastilles); and
- one soft drink (such as a Mars milkshake).

I'll happily purchase all four at once and I'm capable of scoffing the lot in a single session! When I left secondary school I wasn't much of a hit with the ladies before I met Lydia, and I think I began to comfort-eat. Perhaps I couldn't see any reason to watch my weight because I didn't have a girlfriend. I grew to about 18½ stone. While some of my mates were out dating girls, my way of treating myself was with food. I've always had lots of friends, so it wasn't that I was lonely. It was just that I fell into the habit of overeating because it was one of my main sources of pleasure. I love food. If I am feeling low I might cheer myself up with a curry. Unfortunately, if it makes me put on more weight, I'm more likely to feel low again, in which case I eat. It's a bit of a vicious circle.

My lifestyle after I joined *TOWIE* has also led to my gaining weight. When I'm out filming at different times it tends to make me eat badly. I find myself snacking in the gaps between filming, and, of course, there are so many scenes filmed in restaurants and bars. It means I consume a fair bit of alcohol, which is packed with calories. The large number of personal appearances that I make in nightclubs also means that I am around booze. All those late nights are when I'm tempted to round off the evening with either a kebab, McDonald's or a bagel from Brick Lane.

When I manage to slim down, I feel full of energy and enthusiasm. Being a lighter weight is good for my self-confidence. When I am at my heaviest I feel lethargic and lazy and I seem to generally just have far less energy. I'm tempted to just lie in bed longer than I should do and I get tired more easily. It can get sometimes me down, although normally I bounce back pretty quickly and vow to lose some weight.

Being a large size also makes going shopping for clothes a

real drag, especially in high street stores. There are times when I simply can't find anything to buy. I love clothes from shops such as Reiss, Zara and Topman, but I often go into stores and nothing will fit. Many shops go up to only a size 36 waist, whereas, when I am at my heaviest, I am size 40.

Even the XL sizes occasionally won't fit, which pisses me off. There are so many nice clothes that I would like to wear but they're just not available in my size. Even when I can squeeze into them they often don't suit me. I normally have a clear idea of what I would like to wear and which outfits match, but when I try them on they just don't look right and that makes me feel pretty bad at times. I hate going shopping with friends because they always get all the nice bits and pieces while I am left scraping around!

There have been times when my weight has led to some very funny situations. Apart from the constant banter on *TOWIE* (where everyone always takes great delight in the fact that I can twitch my man boobs), I also get a lot of requests from magazines to take part in diet features. On one occasion my manager, Neil, received a phone call from a newspaper supplement.

'We'd like to invite Arg to lose some weight with our help. It's for a big feature in the magazine,' they explained.

The plan was for me to be weighed and photographed for an article that would record my vital statistics and explain to readers that I was going on a carefully controlled diet. The magazine meticulously planned everything so that over the next few months I would have a menu and fitness regime that was designed to help me lose weight in a healthy way. I would then be weighed and photographed again so that they could compare the difference. When I went in for the first picture shoot they were eager to explain how committed I would need to be.

'You must follow our advice very closely, Arg. It's important that you stick to the regime,' they urged.

I was assigned a dietician and a personal trainer to help me and I went away full of good intentions. As the weeks went by I did my best to do everything they told me, but I slipped on many occasions and I probably had the odd sneaky trip to McDonald's. At the end of an agreed period of time, the magazine was planning to do a 'big reveal' article in which I would show off my new slimmed-down body to the cameras.

'We can't wait to see how much you've lost,' they told me.

I knew I had struggled, so I wasn't looking forward to the big reveal. When I went along to the studio and stood on the scales it was a disaster.

'Er, Arg, you've actually *gained* weight!' they told me.

I was horribly embarrassed and full of apologies. My manager now says I am the only person in the history of weight-loss articles who has managed to put several pounds *on*! The magazine quietly dropped the feature. (I later took part in a similar feature for a different magazine, *Men's Health*, and on that occasion I did manage to lose two stone, so at least I learned my lesson.)

I'm often approached to endorse special diets

I am also often approached by companies asking me to endorse special diets and slimming products. I'm sometimes willing to give them a try, although that, too, can lead to some funny situations. There was one occasion when I'd been trying out a new type of diet. Things were coming along OK, so I'd arranged to meet a couple of executives from the company to discuss things further. They agreed to travel to Woodford near where I live and I planned to meet them after lunch. I was feeling very hungry that morning, so before the meeting I slipped out to my local carvery restaurant. My appetite was ferocious, so I piled onto my plate a huge mound of roast potatoes and Yorkshire puddings. I was greedily tucking into my banquet when another disaster struck.

'Er, hello, Arg – I think we're due to meet you later,' I heard somebody say as they approached my table.

I looked up to discover that it was the diet people. They'd arrived early and had popped into the restaurant to kill some time. I'd been caught stuffing my face while I was supposed to be on a diet!

When I split from Lydia it was one of those occasions when I piled on a lot of weight. I was in bad shape both emotionally and physically. I went through a period when I just couldn't be motivated to get out of bed. I'd spend time locked away in my room with the curtains drawn. I literally did not want to leave the house. If ever there was a time when I ate for comfort, this was it. I gorged myself on fast food and I would make constant trips to the fridge for snacks. My mum and dad were worried about me and they did all they could to help by showing me love and support. My friends in *TOWIE*, especially Joey, Diags and Tom, were also there for me when I needed them, and I slowly began to get over the heartache of losing Lydia. I needed a new challenge.

What I want is something to motivate me and take my mind off Lydia, I thought.

It was around this time that my manager received a call from the charity Cancer Research to enquire if I would be willing to run in the London Marathon on their behalf.

'James obviously makes a lot of press coverage because of his weight, so it would be amazing publicity for us,' they explained.

Despite my aversion to most sports, running is one of the few physical activities that I quite enjoy. My dad had run a half-marathon when he was younger, so it's probably a bit of a family trait. The more I thought about doing the London Marathon, the more I thought it was a fantastic idea.

Cancer Research is a cause that had been close to my heart ever since Granddad Seamus died from cancer. It would mean a lot to me to be able to raise some money in his memory. Cancer is a terrible condition that affects millions of families, including my own. If I could run the Marathon, not only would I be achieving something truly amazing, but I'd also be helping others. It also seemed like the perfect project to take my mind off Lydia, while also motivating me to lose some weight. In fact, I imagined that I would lose a *lot* of weight through all the training that it would involve. I agreed to meet with Cancer Research.

'We have to be sure that you're serious about doing the Marathon. This is a big responsibility,' they explained.

Despite my previous poor track record with diet-and-exercise projects, I was determined to make a go of things. I wouldn't be running just for me: there was a charity at stake – and I knew that hopefully, somewhere, Granddad Seamus would be watching over me. To complete the London Marathon in his memory would mean a great deal to my family. I reassured the people from Cancer Research that I was fully committed.

I knew that the challenge I faced was enormous. I'd left it very late to sign up and there were only six weeks in which to train before the race (ideally, training lasts six months). I tipped the scales at 18½ stone, so I had a lot of lost time to make up for. It was at the back of my mind that my asthma might be a factor, but as I've grown older I've become better at learning to control it. I was hopeful that, if I could run at my own pace, the asthma wouldn't be a problem.

Joey Essex was one of the first people I told, and he promised to support me, although at first he couldn't quite believe it and he reacted with his usual good banter.

'Are you serious, Arg? That's a long way to run, man. Don't you have to do special training and stuff like that?' he said.

'Well, I'll need to train, but anyone can enter,' I replied.

'Yeah, but a chubby boy like you – how are you going to get around the course?' he said.

'It's all official. I'm doing it for Cancer Research.'

'Yeah, but what if you collapse like a blob?' he smiled.

I laughed. 'I won't collapse. Will you come along and support me on the day?'

'Yeah, of course I will. I'll be there to cheer you on and give you a bit of first aid if you need it,' he joked.

When it was announced in public that I would be taking part in the London Marathon it caused a bit of a firestorm on Twitter. A lot of people were angry because there is so much competition for places and they saw me as somebody who was jumping the queue because I am on TV.

'You are taking the piss. You don't deserve a place and you won't even make an effort,' they ranted at me.

Some of the messages I received were very irate. Some members of the public thought I was an overweight bloke who had no chance of reaching the finishing line. People were saying that I would end up like Jade Goody, who had been forced to pull out of the race after collapsing in 2006. Quite a few people were of the view that I wouldn't even turn up on the day.

Things went from bad to worse when some photos of me eating junk food appeared on a newspaper website. It sent out the wrong message and one of the race directors from Virgin, who sponsor the Marathon, called my manager to ask if I was putting in the proper effort. They were worried that, if I failed to show up or collapsed on the day, it would be a PR disaster. I also made the mistake of sending out a tweet during the early days of training in which I hinted that I'd not been doing enough exercise.

'Arg, if there is any more bad publicity like this then the organisers are going to ask you to give up your place,' my manager Neil told me.

241

All the fuss only made me all the more determined to prove everyone wrong. I think the only people who really believed that I would complete it were the representatives from Cancer Research, because they'd seen how serious I had been.

During my six weeks I really threw myself into the training. Two other members of the *TOWIE* cast, Cara Kilbey and Billi Mucklow, were taking part. They are both naturally slim and athletic. Cara is a good runner and Billi is a yoga teacher, so they were in a very different position from mine. I went on a training run with them and I could see that they were much fitter than I was, but I didn't let it worry me.

I would run at least five miles a day and sometimes all the way from my home in Woodford Greed to the outskirts of Epping and back, which is a round trip of close to ten miles. I eventually managed to knuckle down to a healthy diet.

I also went off to a fitness camp in Norfolk called No1 Boot Camp. It was run by a company that a lot of the *TOWIE* cast use when they want to get in shape. All your meals are provided in a healthy fashion and their fitness facilities are excellent. The company that owns the centre also operates a boot camp in Marbella. I was between filming at the time, so, in addition to going to Norfolk, I thought it would be a great idea to also go out to Spain to do a bit of training. I didn't fancy going alone, so I asked Joey if he'd agree to come along.

'Come on, Joey, we'll have a great time,' I said.

We flew out to Spain together and checked into the boot camp, which consisted of an amazing complex in Marbella. The accommodation was made up of basic wooden chalets

242

with two sets of bunk beds per room. They were clean and comfy. There was a fully equipped boxing gym, plus a normal gym with weights and all the latest apparatus. Outside, there was a swimming pool and a huge assault course. It was the perfect setting to train for a marathon.

While I was out in Spain something very strange and unexpected happened, and it concerned Gemma Collins. When I checked into the boot camp I asked the owner if anybody else was due to stay there that week. It was a regular haunt for *TOWIE* cast members so the chances are that you often bump into people who you know.

'Gemma Collins is due to arrive tomorrow,' the women at the front desk told me.

Joey and I had a good giggle. We obviously both knew Gemma from *TOWIE* and we were aware that she's quite a character. She'd previously said on the show that she'd fancied me during a game of truth or dare. I'd laughed it off because I had been dating Lydia at the time and I just didn't see Gemma in that way. In fact, I thought she could be quite annoying. She can be very loud and forthright with her opinions, so I was fully expecting her to shatter the peace and quiet we were looking forward to. However, there are two sides to Gemma's personality. She is big and bubbly and socially she can be great company. We'd often have a good bit of banter whenever we appeared on screen together.

During boot camp we were awoken at 6.30 a.m. for a training session at 7 a.m. Breakfast was at 8 a.m. and consisted of something wholesome and energetic such as porridge (just what you need when you are training for a marathon). The rest of the day was spent doing various fitness regimes designed to get you in tiptop condition. The food was delicious. It was always very healthy and well prepared by the chefs, but it left me wanting more because the portions were deliberately controlled. During the evenings there was a cinema room where you could relax after a hard day.

Gemma arrived the day after Joey and I had, and we said our hellos. She was in good spirits and was out there to enjoy a bit of a break and to get into shape before the next series of *TOWIE*. One of the activities that we all took part in together was climbing La Concha, a mountain peak that overlooks Marbella. It was a hard physical slog that involved walking up some very steep slopes and at times having to use your hands and feet to clamber over rocks. Joey and I both got to the summit and we were very proud of ourselves. Gemma didn't quite make it to the top, so she missed out on some breathtaking scenery: you could see all the way across the Mediterranean and catch a glimpse of the African coastline in the distance.

Meanwhile, it turned out that Gemma was quite pleasant company in Marbella and we got along very well. She wasn't annoying at all. On our last night something happened between Gemma and me that came completely out of the blue.

I was about to get a complete shock.

We'd all decided to go down to Puerto Banús on our last evening at boot camp. Gemma and some of the other girls from the centre came along and we had a few drinks down by the port. Joey and I then got separated from the rest of the group and we went off for a drink at Linekers Bar, where we met an old acquaintance who was the part-owner of a lap-dancing establishment. We got chatting and he invited us into his club.

'Shall we go along, Joey?' I asked.

'Yeah, come on, then. It'll be sick,' Joey replied.

By now we were both a bit drunk and were shown into the lap-dancing bar. It was dark and there was a main stage area with a pole for women to dance around. We were like a pair of giggly schoolboys. I'd never been inside a place where the women were all walking around half naked. I'm pretty sure Joey felt the same way, but we both behaved ourselves. There was a strict rule that you could look but not touch, and we both adhered to it like gentlemen. The owner of the bar treated us to a lap dance on the house and we sat there as a pair of gorgeous women waggled their boobs and their bums in front of us. It was harmless fun, but God only knows what the paparazzi would have made of it if they could have got a glimpse.

By the time we arrived back at boot camp that evening I'd forgotten all about Gemma. Joey and I were both slightly the worse for wear and he went off to look for someone in one of the other chalets, where I assumed he'd crashed out asleep. When I entered our chalet three of the bunk beds were empty but in my bed there was an uninvited guest.

It was Gemma.

Alone.

In my bed.

It struck me as a little strange, but in my boozy state I didn't question it too much. I just assumed she'd either gone into the wrong room or maybe she had just popped in for a late-night chat and fallen asleep. I was in a merry mood so I climbed into the bunk next to her and gave her a little cuddle.

'What the hell are you doing here?' I asked her playfully.

'Oh, hello, Arg. Did you have a good night out?' she asked sleepily.

I don't remember her giving me any explanation as to why she was in my bed, but I do recall a bit of laughing and giggling. Then I felt **Then I felt Gemma's hand start to wander** Gemma's hand start to wander down below the sheets.

What the hell's happening now? I thought.

As I lay there, Gemma began to touch me intimately. It was unexpected to say the least, but it felt strangely nice and I allowed her to carry on. I don't know what made her do it, but in my boozy state I was happy to go along. Perhaps it was her way of giving me a bit of a treat. It felt a bit weird, because we didn't kiss or do anything else sexually. Afterwards, Gemma fell asleep and I moved to another bunk, where I crashed out.

When we awoke in the morning we were both quite embarrassed. Gemma swore me to secrecy.

'Please don't tell anyone, Arg. I don't want them to get the wrong idea,' she said.

I agreed to keep it quiet – and luckily nobody else at boot

camp had cottoned on. I was slightly bemused by the whole incident, but Gemma is a nice girl and I just put it down to a bit of drunken fun between two people who were both single. I certainly didn't think it would lead to a relationship, but, then, I didn't have too much time to think about it.

I had a marathon to run.

When the day of the London Marathon arrived I was confident that I was in pretty good shape. I had lost 2 stone in the space of six weeks and I was feeling fit and healthy. I had raised several thousand pounds in pledges of sponsorship for Cancer Research and I was looking forward to the race. I still had a few minor doubts because I'd had such a short time to train, but I did my best to put my reservations behind me. During the final stages of preparation I'd been told it's a good idea to increase your intake of carbohydrates. I didn't need to be told twice. After all the austerity at boot camp, I jumped at the chance to load up. The day before the event I went to a pizza restaurant in Loughton, where I tucked into a huge bowl of pasta with lots of garlic bread and mozzarella cheese. On the morning of the race I stopped at a McDonald's, where I ordered a double-sausage-and-egg McMuffin. I thought it would give me more energy, but when I got to the starting line-up everybody laughed when I told them that I'd pigged out. Joey, Diags and Tom Pearce all came along to wish me luck, so I had plenty of support. Joey presented me with a big comedy hat that he'd made for me to wear during the race. It consisted of a big yellow arrow pointing to my head with 'ARG' written on it.

'It'll bring you luck and everyone'll cheer you on when they see your name,' Joey said with a grin.

It was nice sunny day and everywhere I looked there were huge crowds of runners milling around. You could feel the excitement as everybody finally got ready for the big moment, and I could feel myself getting psyched up. Oddly, my preparations involved smearing myself in lots of Vaseline. One of the things the boys take the piss out of me for is that I have very large nipples (they call them burger nipples). I was worried that they would chafe during the race, hence the Vaseline. I was taking no chances.

As I moved towards the starting line I bumped into Gordon Ramsay, who was also taking part. It was the first time we'd spoken since the Christmas show and we said a brief hello and spoke for a few moments. Will Young, whom I'd met through ITV, was also taking part and when we saw each other we shook hands and wished each other well.

I could feel my heart pounding as the final moments ticked by to the beginning of the race. I was proud to be wearing a Cancer Research vest and I was determined to prove wrong all the people who'd doubted that I would finish. I took my place in the line and suddenly ... *Go!*

We were finally off. I started at a fairly good pace and I soon settled into a rhythm that was comfortable. My legs and arms felt good and my breathing was nice and steady. As I made my way around the first few miles of the route I could see that the crowds were out in force. The atmosphere was amazing. It felt like a Cup final, with people on both sides of the road cheering at the tops of their voices while we ran past.

I will never forget the support that I got from the crowd. It was fantastic, from the start to the very end. I could hear people shouting things like, 'Come on, Arg!' and 'We love you, Arg. Do it for Essex!'

The Marathon is so special because you share such a warm camaraderie with the crowd and your fellow runners. It is like a huge team event with everybody roaring you on to achieve the amazing feat of running the gruelling distance of 26.2 miles. As I sailed along I could feel other runners patting me on the back or smacking my bum in encouragement as they went past me. All the publicity about me meant that a lot of people knew I was taking part. There were people at the roadside holding up signs with my name on and wishing me well. It gave me a real boost.

It felt as if I were flying around the course and each time I passed a new mile marker my confidence continued to grow. Every few hundred yards there were people in the crowd holding out chewy sweets or chocolates for the runners so that we could stock up on our energy. I was happy to accept my fair share and at one point I think I may have eaten a few too many, because I briefly started to feel a bit sick, but it soon passed.

The *TOWIE* camera crew had planned to be at certain points early on the course in order to film me going by, but my initial pace was much quicker than anybody expected, so they kept missing me. During my training, I'd been warned by people who'd previously done the Marathon that some runners experience something known as 'hitting the wall'. It's a phrase for when you suddenly get overwhelmed by exhaustion and it's supposed to feel as though you'd run full pelt into a brick wall. But as I cruised around the course nothing seemed further from my mind. I think the atmosphere generated by the excitement of the crowds carried me around the first half of the race. I couldn't believe I was doing so well. Even my burger nipples seemed to be pain-free!

So far, so good.

I was confident I was going to make it. Every now and then I used my asthma inhaler to keep my breathing nice and smooth and there was no sign of any problems. My mum and dad and other members of my family were moving between various points along the route to cheer me on and I got a big boost when I saw them all at Canary Wharf.

It was only from about Mile 12 onwards that I began to notice that, from time to time, somebody would drop out of the race and collapse at the roadside. At first it was just one or two, but as the race wore on it seemed that every few hundred yards there would be somebody laid out with exhaustion and surrounded by paramedics. I was still feeling OK in myself, but I must admit that it gave me a twinge of apprehension to see all the ambulances and I began to doubt myself. That could easily be me, I thought. Those people at the roadside were probably fighting fit, but I've only trained for six weeks.

Despite my fears, I continued to do my best and the mile markers just kept on coming. Eventually, the *TOWIE* crew caught up with me and I paused to film a couple of interviews for them at the roadside. I was also interviewed for TV by Olympic gold medalist Denise Lewis. Soon I was running past a sign that read MILE 14, then MILE 15. It felt crazy, because I was doing so well as Mile 16 approached. Or so I thought.

Suddenly out of nowhere I hit the wall. *Bang!*

It seemed to happen in an instant. One minute I was fine and the next I could not physically move my legs. They seemed to be frozen still and they felt like huge lead weights beneath me. I was completely overwhelmed by a horrible feeling that I couldn't run any further. It felt as if my whole body was out of fuel and it was a strange sensation. I hadn't felt exhausted until Mile 16, but now I simply just couldn't move. This was the dreaded wall that everybody had warned me about. I limped over to the roadside and tried to stretch the tiredness out of my legs, but it didn't seem to make any difference.

Suddenly out of nowhere I hit the wall

From that point on every step was agony.

I can only describe it as ten miles of sheer hell. Slowly, my muscles began to respond and I was able to jog for a while before taking a rest. That was how I carried on for the remainder of the course, repeating that sequence over and over again, stopping whenever I needed to. During the final few miles, I was in a bad way, but I'd come so far that I was determined to finish. I was running on sheer willpower. My body felt as if it was empty.

At around Mile 19, I saw Joey and my family at the roadside cheering me on. The sight of them and the noise of the crowds cheering overwhelmed me and I got a bit choked up. It's very easy to become emotional while running the

Marathon because you are stretching yourself to the limits of your endurance. I was totally exhausted, but Joey gave me a little hug and offered to take my hat from me.

'No, Joey, I'm going to carry it across the line,' I said tearfully. (It all seems a bit cheesy to me now, but it meant a lot to me at the time.)

I amazed myself by carrying on, even though I was in complete agony. I was so close now to achieving something special that I knew I would never forgive myself if I gave up after coming so far. I gritted my teeth and slowly made my way towards the end of the race, step by painful step.

By now I was probably staggering and limping like an injured man, but I didn't care. All that mattered was reaching that finishing line. When I finally got there the relief was overwhelming.

I've done it!

It had taken me six hours, which included stopping to give a couple of interviews to the *TOWIE* crew. I was well and truly knackered, but I have never felt more proud of myself. The crowd got me through, and I now plan to go back every year to support others. When I put on my finisher's medal I felt like a champion athlete. It was a fitting tribute to the memory of Granddad Seamus. It was one of the most rewarding things I have ever done and I am truly grateful to Cancer Research for believing in me when others didn't.

16

BACK TO MARBS AND PASSION WITH GEMMA

The summer of 2012 was fast approaching – and I was about to enjoy a roller-coaster romance with Gemma Collins. Despite the cheeky surprise that Gemma had given me under the sheets at boot camp I never envisaged that we would end up as an item. Nothing had developed between us since our brief tryst in Marbella, but we'd remained good friends and we shared a healthy chemistry whenever we appeared together on *TOWIE*. Neither of us had breathed a word to anybody about what happened in that wooden bunk bed, so it stayed our little secret throughout most of Series 5 of *The Only Way Is Essex*. I'd laughed off the incident and put it down to nothing more than a bit of drunken banter.

I liked Gemma for her warmth and bubbly personality, but at this stage I just didn't think of her as somebody I might end up dating. I could see that she was a very pretty girl and I liked her company, but I loved her as a pal rather than as a prospective partner. We had a nice rapport with one another but I always thought that would be as far as it went.

What I hadn't bargained for was just how perceptive the producers of *TOWIE* can be. They are extremely hard to keep a secret from and they obviously need to have their finger on the pulse when it comes to knowing who has done what with whom. If you have a secret you can be sure that they'll eventually find out about it. They are amazing at getting stuff out of you and it's very hard not to be totally honest with them. I was chatting with one of the producers one day when the subject of Gemma came up. Normally, I am the biggest blabbermouth in Essex, but our bunk-bed liaison was one secret that I'd managed to keep intact.

Our bunkbed liaison was a secret I'd managed to keep intact

Until now.

When the producers pressed me about whether I was holding anything back, I'm afraid I caved in and told them what happened. It might seem a bit ungentlemanly of me, but you have to remember that *TOWIE* is a big goldfish bowl, and nothing stays quiet for ever. Besides, I had a sneaking suspicion that, despite her early fears about what people would think, Gemma wouldn't really mind. She had been playing up to me in front of the cameras at every opportunity and it was obvious that she fancied me. Nevertheless, I was still very nervous about having it mentioned on air, but the producers were keen to use it in a storyline. In fact, they thought the whole thing was hilarious, because it was so unexpected.

Soon, the whole production crew seemed to be talking about it. It was quite funny, I realise now, because I'd occasionally see a small group of them having a hushed conversation and, when I asked what they were discussing, they would give me a curt reply.

'Oh, nothing, Arg, just what happened at boot camp.' Then they'd wink.

The producers convinced me that if the storyline were done in a humorous way it would make harmless fun. As the finale to Series 5 approached, I decided to share my secret with Joey and Diags at a big party while the cameras were rolling. The boys thought it was hilarious and it soon went around the party like wildfire. Joey told Sam Faiers and eventually word got back to Gemma. I didn't think that she'd be too angry and I decided that I would give her a big kiss for the cameras to show her it was just a bit of fun. I had a sneaking suspicion that if I kissed her it would steal the show and make a great end to the series; plus, I knew that Gemma would probably love all the attention.

I felt slightly awkward at the party that night because Lydia was there and she flirted on the dance floor with a new bloke she had started to see. It made me feel uncomfortable and, as the party wore on, there seemed to be no opportunity to have a conversation with Gemma. After a while, I abandoned my plan to kiss her and I decided to leave. As I was walking out of the building I heard Gemma come running up behind me. It came as a bit of a shock, because the producers hadn't given me any warning that she was about to confront me.

'Arg, where are you going?' she yelled.

I was nervous about how she would react, but I needn't have worried, because Gemma had a big smile on her face.

'Why have you been going around telling everyone?' she asked, referring to our tryst in Marbella.

At first Gemma tried to deny what had happened at boot camp, but when I protested that it was true she laughed and admitted it on camera. My heart was beating quite fast by now because it was an unusual situation to find yourself in on television. We had a bit of a giggle and Gemma made it clear that she thought it was obvious there was something special going on between us.

In fact she told me that she loved me.

I wasn't sure that I felt the same way, but I went along for the ride. That was the moment I chose to give her a big kiss. I leaned forward and we snogged in front of the cameras. It was the first time I had kissed Gemma and it felt nice. Our embrace made the final scene of the series, and when it was broadcast it caused an enormous amount of excitement on Twitter. Everyone seemed to be talking about it, although at the time I still didn't think it would lead to anything between us. It had been a nice gesture for the cameras, but I took Gemma's comment about being in love with me with a pinch of salt.

The next day I was due to fly to Las Vegas. Mark was out filming a new TV project in LA and the plan was that he would drive to Vegas to meet me and a few of the boys so that we could spend some time soaking up the sunshine and clubbing together. When I was on the way to the airport I sent Gemma a quick text to wish her well, and I was concentrating on the thought of being reunited with Mark for a boys' holiday. While I was in the taxi my mobile rang.

It was Lydia.

'I really need to speak to you, James. Can we talk?' she said.

I was surprised that she had called. Lydia had been with her new man, Tom, at the party and I was slowly starting to get over our split, so I wasn't sure that there was anything to discuss.

'Lydia, I'm on the way to Las Vegas for a holiday with the boys. I just want to enjoy myself and get away. I can't speak to you now,' I said.

Lydia insisted that it was important, so I agreed I'd call her back. I still had feelings for Lydia, but I'd given up all hope of trying to repair things. I saw the fact that she had started seeing somebody else as being the point of no return, and I wanted to move on with my life.

I'd even finally confessed to cheating on Lydia during a conversation with Debbie, which was shown during the last episode of the series. It was a big admission, but I couldn't see the point in trying to hide it any more. I told Debbie that the rumours that I had slept with girls behind Lydia's back were true. There was no need for me to label myself a love rat like that in front of cameras, but I felt so guilty about it that when it came up in conversation I didn't want to lie any more. It was like the final act of closure on the relationship.

It was like the final act of closure

As I reached the airport I received a text from Lydia, which contained a link to a long and very moving email that she'd written to me. The gist of it was that Lydia thanked me for finally being honest about the fact that I had cheated on her. She said that deep down she had always known I had been unfaithful, but that she put up with it in the hope that I would stop. She signed off by saying that I would always have a place in her heart and that it was a shame that things hadn't worked out between us. I got a bit choked up when I read her words but I knew that I had to be strong, so I didn't write back. I just wanted closure and to enjoy my holiday.

When I arrived in Las Vegas I got my first real taste of what a big stir my kiss with Gemma had caused. There were photographers waiting for me at the airport and, as I walked through the arrivals lounge, they started to shout questions at me.

'Arg, what's happening between you and Gemma?' they barked.

They seemed to want to know every detail. Back home, all the papers and the magazines were going crazy for a new angle. I did my best to laugh off their questions and I hot-footed it into a taxi.

Vegas itself was a real laugh. Mark and I stayed in a suite at the Encore Hotel and we had a fantastic time, being joined by several friends during our nights out on the town. We were followed by paparazzi everywhere we went, which seemed strange in a land where nobody had heard of me.

While I was in Vegas I received one more text from Lydia. It read along the lines of, 'Just one last thing, can you please tell me did anything happen between you and Amy?'

Mark was with me at the time.

'Arg, don't bother writing back,' he said. 'What's the point?'

He was right. I couldn't see the need to get into a conversation about the secret Christmas kiss that I had shared with Amy, not while Lydia's emotions were running so high. I didn't reply to her text.

I had a fantastic time in Vegas and by the time I returned to the UK my batteries had fully recharged. Gemma and I had not been in contact while I was away. We'd both just gone our separate ways. Despite all the press speculation, we were not boyfriend and girlfriend at this point, so I wasn't due to meet Gemma again until all the cast got together to film a *TOWIE* special in Marbella. We were all asked to meet at Southend Airport and while I was in the departure lounge I spotted Lydia. I was standing next to Sam, who urged me to go over and say hello.

Lydia and I exchanged a few polite words. She asked me if I had enjoyed myself in Las Vegas and I told her it was a great place and that she should try to visit it one day. I didn't think much more of it, although during the flight Lydia and I kept catching each other's eye.

When we arrived at Málaga Airport, by pure chance I found myself standing next to Lydia at the baggage carousel. She had a strange look on her face and I sensed she was in the mood for trouble.

'Oh, how's Gemma, then?' she asked me. 'I bet your sex life's good.'

I was staggered.

259

'What are you talking about, Lydia?' I replied.

Lydia then made a nasty comment that took me by surprise. It was along the lines of, 'I bet you two'll need a reinforced bed, so you don't break it when you're together.'

'What the hell are you talking about? Gemma and I haven't slept together, but what's it go to do with you?' I asked.

'Oh, I'm so glad that I've got Tom,' she replied. 'He's so good to me. He takes me to nice places and we stay in nice hotels.'

I'd been trying to remain calm but the idea of Lydia and Tom sleeping together in a hotel made me see red. My emotions were still very raw and I am sorry to say that I hit back with a spiteful comment that I now regret.

'Well, listen here, Lydia,' I said. 'Hopefully, Gemma will satisfy me and I won't need to go elsewhere like I did with you.'

It was nasty and wrong of me to say such a cruel thing, but I was fuming about her mentioning Tom. As soon as I said it I could see that my words had cut Lydia like a knife. At first she lunged towards me as if she were going to strike me, but as I darted away her face crumpled into tears. I felt guilty about it, but it showed how sore I was still feeling inside.

Later she sent me a text saying I had broken her heart

Lydia then put on her sunglasses and I could see the teardrops streaming down her face. I was angry and ashamed that it had come to this. Later on she sent me a text saying that I had broken her heart.

*

Marbella was as glitzy as ever. I checked into the luxurious Sisu Boutique Hotel, where I had reserved the famous Scarface Suite, which is themed on the Al Pacino movie of the same name. It was decorated entirely in black and gold with Versace fittings, and there was a huge mural of Tony Montana (the Pacino character) on the wall. It cost me a few quid extra, but I was earning quite well by now and I loved splashing out on nice hotel rooms. The decor was very gangster chic and it made me feel like the governor.

I wanted to put my row with Lydia behind me and just get on with having a good time, but I found myself drinking quite heavily. Gemma flew to Marbella on a later flight. She was her normal bubbly self, and the night before we were due to start filming I joined her and some of the other members of the cast. I bought her a few drinks and we seemed to be getting on fine. There was a sort of flirty chemistry between us and it seemed as if everyone present was egging us on because they wanted us to become an item.

The next day I got a shock, because, as soon as the cameras started to roll, Gemma's attitude seemed to change. She came marching up to me in her sarong by the pool and let rip with a real broadside. She claimed that I'd been disrespectful towards her during my conversations with the boys and it was clear to me that she thought I had a problem with her weight. Then she hitched up her sarong to show me her body.

'You ain't ever gonna get this candy,' she boomed.

I was flabbergasted. For one thing, I never had any issues regarding Gemma's weight. Of course, she was a big girl and occasionally it would be mentioned during my conversations with the boys. But I've been on the receiving end of plenty of banter about my own weight, so I was hardly likely to criticise Gemma for the same thing. I was a bit miffed by her outburst because the night before we'd been getting along really well. It felt as if she'd just set me up for a fall in front of the cameras. I suspected that Gemma liked to play the weight card as a way of making herself out to be a victim, because she knew it would win her sympathy. The next day I was slightly frosty when she texted me to invite me out for dinner at a restaurant called La Sala. It crossed my mind to refuse to go along, but I relented because, after all, she wasn't the first person to put on a bit of a show for the cameras.

When I arrived at La Sala, Gemma welcomed me with a big smile, and she had saved a seat for me next to her. There was a brandy and Coke waiting for me, which she knew was my favourite drink. She seemed to be going out of her way to be charming towards me and I felt myself warming to her. During the meal she was so sweet and nice that I soon forgot all about her 'candy' outburst by the pool. We ordered some bread with garlic aioli, which she knew I liked.

Gemma's conversation that night was funny and witty and I found myself laughing with her more and more as the night wore on. She was being really caring and loving towards me and I thought how nice it felt to have someone to comfort me like that. It was such a contrast with all the commotion I'd been through with Lydia, and I began to see Gemma in a new light. I could sense that she really cared for me, and I found it all very sweet.

Sam and Billie were both at the meal with us, along with Joey and Billie's boyfriend Greg, and everyone seemed to be delighted by the fact that Gemma and I were getting along so well. I felt very at ease in her company and later that evening I decided to invite her back to the Sisu for a drink.

Looking back, I suppose there was a good chance that we were going to end up in bed together that night, but at this stage that wasn't something I'd planned. I could feel a spark of attraction and I just wanted to enjoy a bit of company alone with Gemma. I was slightly confused, because I couldn't quite believe that I was falling for Gemma's charms, but I was caught up in the moment. It felt so nice to have some female company, and with somebody I knew and liked. When we arrived at the Sisu I thought it would be nice to have some time in private.

'Look, Gemma, I've got the Scarface Suite up there and it has a great big balcony and a massive bedroom,' I told her. 'Come on, let's go up there and have a little chill-out and a drink.'

I ordered a couple of brandies to be sent up from the bar and we sat together on the bed sipping them. The whole thing felt a bit unreal and I got the giggles.

'Why are you laughing?' asked Gemma.

'I can't believe I'm sitting in bed with Gemma Collins.'

'Shut up, Arg!' she laughed.

I looked at Gemma and thought about how nice she had been to me all evening. It was obvious how much she loved me and, after all I had been through with Lydia, I felt I needed a bit of comfort.

We kissed and it felt pleasant.

One thing led to another and soon we were making love together on the bed. I must admit that I was really impressed and the sex was very good. Gemma was thirty years old and I was twenty-four, so she was fairly experienced and she knew what she was doing. It would be ungentlemanly of me to go into too much detail, but let's just say that I enjoyed myself and I think Gemma did, too. We made love just the once but I got the impression Gemma would happily have wanted more.

Afterwards I was still quite giggly. I found the idea of sleeping with Gemma slightly amusing because we'd always been friends rather than lovers, and it feels strange when you suddenly make that awkward transition to having a physical relationship with someone you've known for a while. We'd obviously shared an intimate moment together at boot camp, but in reality that had been nothing more than a boozy fumble. This was the real deal and afterwards my head was spinning because it had all happened so quickly. The first thing I did was go out onto the balcony and phone Mark.

'Mark, you're not going to believe this, but I've just slept with Gemma.'

'What are you like?' he replied. 'I've heard it all now.'

I think Gemma overheard my call but she didn't care. In fact, I got the impression that she wanted the whole world to know. We'd been plastered across enough magazines and newspapers together, so telling Mark about us hardly made any difference.

The next evening, Gemma and I enjoyed a repeat perform-ance. I had to leave the Scarface Suite because somebody else had reserved it, so I moved into the Sisu's Las Vegas suite. It was just as luxurious and it came with its own stripper's pole for dancing; plus, it had an enormous *en suite* Jacuzzi. When I went out onto the balcony and gazed down, I spotted Gemma on a balcony below. She was dressed in a silky nightie and looked very alluring. I had been drinking and I was feel-ing in the mood, so I thought, Why not have some more of what we enjoyed last night? I pictured us together in the posh Jacuzzi and I thought about the possibilities that it held.

'Come on, Gemma! Come up to the Vegas suite,' I yelled down to her.

Gemma didn't need to be asked twice.

Soon we were stripping off and she joined me in the hot tub. We had sex right there in the Jacuzzi, and once again I found it very enjoyable. Having fun like that in a Jacuzzi was a new experience.

Having fun in that Jacuzzi was a new experience

After we made love, we were visited by Jessica Wright and Ricky Rayment and the four of us went out onto the balcony together to look at the stars. It had been a very good trip and I began to put all thoughts of Lydia behind me.

After *TOWIE* finished filming the Marbs special we had a few days to spare and it seemed a shame to go straight back to the UK. Mark's parents, Big Mark and Carol, were in Marbella and they invited Gemma and me to join them, along with some of the others, on a road trip up to Alicante to see

Mark's cousin Elliott, the one who owns a restaurant there. It was a five-hour drive, but when we got there we had an amazing time. We went on a number of boat trips together and Gemma and I shared a bed during the evenings. It was like a whirlwind holiday romance and Gemma made me feel very happy.

'It's great being with you,' I told her. 'You put a smile on my face. I'm really enjoying your company.'

'Oh, James,' she said, blushing. 'I can't believe this is happening.'

I think at this point in my life, after going through such a long and difficult break-up with Lydia, I just needed someone to spoil me with some love and warmth, and that was exactly what Gemma did. I won't pretend that I was deeply in love, but she is a beautiful girl and it's fair to say that I'd grown to love Gemma as a friend.

When I came home to the UK, I was feeling confused. It didn't know whether our relationship would turn out to be nothing more than a fling in the sunshine, or would amount to more than that. I still couldn't really picture us together as a couple, because I didn't have the same depth of feeling for her as I had previously felt with Lydia. However, I did adore Gemma.

You know what? I thought. I do like her.

I wasn't just sleeping with her for the sake of it: I was enjoying it, so maybe we could make a go of things. Maybe Gemma was right for me? I was thinking, Here's this beautiful girl who likes me, so why not give it a go?

I think part of the attraction for both of us was also the

huge amount of attention we were getting from the media. A whole circus seemed to have grown up around our relationship. Everyone was writing about us and it sent our profiles sky high. It was a big story for the audience to see two of *TOWIE*'s most popular characters getting together. Gemma had always struggled with love throughout her life and I had been up and down with Lydia, so I think the viewers wanted us to find a bit of happiness. It was all very flattering, although not all of the attention was nice. There were plenty of people who made nasty comments about us on Twitter, mainly in the form of weight jibes because we both have big frames. There were also a few mates who took the piss out of me, not just because of Gemma's weight but also because of her age. I didn't care. I just went along with the excitement of it all. It was like a pleasant dream and I was caught up in it.

After we returned to the UK, Gemma was due to go off on a holiday to Turkey and I was due to travel to Barcelona on business to make a personal appearance, so our romance was briefly interrupted. While I was back in Spain I found myself missing her immensely. I'd enjoyed her company a great deal in Marbella, because it had been like a breath of fresh air to have someone I could share some romantic time with. When I got back to the UK from Barcelona I had some time to spare.

What the hell! I thought. I like being with this girl, so why don't I go and join her in Turkey?

It was a crazy idea but when I rang Gemma she was flattered by my offer to go out there and she readily agreed. I think we were both caught up in the whirlwind of having a holiday romance and neither of us wanted it to end. Gemma was staying at a place called Kalkan on the Turkish Mediterranean coast. I booked a flight and arrived within a couple of days.

I checked into a local hotel close to a villa where Gemma was staying with a group of her friends. We had a wonderful time together. It felt fresh and exciting to be with someone who cared so much for me. During the day we'd go diving on boat trips and our evenings were spent eating and dancing in some fabulous restaurants. Our holiday coincided with the UEFA European Championship, which was being held in Poland and the Ukraine, and Gemma and I spent a bit of time watching some of the games on TV in local bars. I was very at ease with Gemma and the time we spent in Turkey was romantic and magical.

Gemma and I found that we had a lot in common and when we returned to the UK we began to date. We share a love of performing and I discovered that when Gemma was younger she'd attended a dance school that had staged productions at the Kenneth More Theatre (the venue at which I'd done most of my amateur dramatics while I was growing up). Even though Gemma is slightly older than I am, it's possible that our paths had crossed as youngsters without our ever knowing it. Gemma took a great interest in my singing career and she came along to several gigs to support me, which was nice.

Gemma came along to several gigs to support me

We were also happy to indulge in our shared passion for

food and we were regular visitors to the deli close to where Gemma lived. We'd stock up on fishcakes along with salmon-and-cream-cheese bagels, which we'd then enjoy together in her flat. If I stayed overnight she would cook me the most enormous breakfasts, with bacon and sausages piled high on the plate. The portions were so huge that they were more than enough to satisfy my enormous appetite. I almost got the impression that she was trying to fatten me up! Gemma always promised me that one day she would cook me a big steak in peppercorn sauce, although she never quite got round to it.

The magazines all seemed delighted that we were now officially boyfriend and girlfriend and we had lots of requests to do interviews and photoshoots. A new series of *TOWIE* was about to launch and our relationship was soon displayed on TV for all the viewers to see.

Unfortunately, we didn't stand the test of time.

I was happy to take things step by step, but, to be honest, I never quite felt that we recaptured the special feelings that we had shared in Turkey. We continued to enjoy a strong attraction, but I didn't feel the deep love for Gemma that I'd previously felt for Lydia. I thought Gemma could be adorable, but after we arrived back in Essex the reality of daily life began to set in and things very quickly became rocky between us. There were times when Gemma seemed very insecure about whether or not I had true feelings for her, and I think she was worried that I was going to leave her for someone else. On one occasion we had a blazing row after I went to Faces for a night out with a mate called Davy. At the end of the evening I had jumped into a car with him along with some girls who were accompanying his cousin. All we did was drop them home before going on to another party, but the paparazzi took some photos and Gemma was furious.

'You've cheated on me!' she screamed.

Gemma was in a right strop and she turned the air blue.

'I haven't done anything wrong. I don't even know them,' I protested.

I suspected that, because she knew that I had cheated on Lydia, Gemma had a lack of trust in me as well – but the photographs outside Faces were entirely innocent.

We also had arguments because Gemma felt that I spent too much time hanging around with Mark.

Here we go again, I thought. This is just like it was with Lydia!

Things came to a head one day after we'd been filming together. Gemma wanted to go out with me for the evening afterwards, but I had already arranged to see Mark. She got angry when I told her that I couldn't be with her and she stormed off. I was out in the street a bit later when I saw Gemma drive by in her car. As she raced past, she leaned forward and gave me the middle finger.

It was typical Gemma: brash, ballsy and full of bravado.

A few weeks later I discovered that, while she was driving by, she had a secret passenger in the car at the time. He was a bloke called Rami and he'd ducked down out of sight so that I couldn't see him as they whizzed by. Rami was an ex-boyfriend whom Gemma had dated prior to our getting together in Marbella. When I asked Gemma about it she denied cheating on me. That was the funny thing about Gemma: she would declare her undying love for me, but she'd happily go off and see her ex when she didn't get her own way.

Our relationship was very up and down. One minute Gemma would be telling me that I was the world's greatest boyfriend, only for me to be labelled the world's worst partner a short time later.

When Gemma was in the mood she could still be extremely kind and charming. On one occasion she booked tickets for me to go and see a stage production of *Jersey Boys* in the West End. Gemma knew how much I loved musicals and she secretly arranged for me to meet all the cast backstage afterwards. It was a very thoughtful gesture and I had a fantastic time because I'd love to perform in the West End one day. Prior to the show we checked into the Dorchester. I'm very old fashioned in that I don't like letting girls pick up the bill, so I paid the tab for the hotel. Gemma was so grateful that the day after we'd seen *Jersey Boys* she took me shopping in Harrods and bought me a pair of smart black Dolce & Gabbana shoes, which I wear when I am singing. It was an example of how kind and generous she could be when she put her mind to it.

We could also have a very good laugh with one another and I felt very confident when I was around her. There was one time when Mark had caused a bit of a stir because a semi-naked photo of him had emerged on Twitter. I took a similar shot of myself for a joke, with my private parts showing. I texted it to Gemma and she thought it was a great laugh. It

271

was a childish thing to do but it shows the level of harmless banter that we used to get up to.

The problem was that as time wore on we found ourselves arguing more and more. There were times when Gemma still seemed convinced that I disliked her for being overweight. I didn't mind Gemma's size because I saw it as a natural part of who she is. She's big, fun and bubbly. But if I made any reference to her size it felt as if she would jump down my throat. I put my foot in it over dinner one night when I compared her to a cross between Vanessa Feltz and Diana Dors. I didn't mean it as a criticism, but as soon as I opened my mouth I realised that I had said the wrong thing. She was furious.

'I can't believe you were so cruel,' she told me after we stopped filming. 'I wish you would shut up about my weight.'

Gemma also accused me of being controlling towards her and she claimed that I tried to prevent her from wearing makeup. In fact, all I had done was pay her a compliment by saying that she was naturally pretty and that I thought she didn't need to wear a lot of it. I prefer girls who wear minimal makeup and I think Gemma looked better when she wore less. I thought I was being nice, but at the end of the day it was up to her.

It got to the point where Gemma was frequently seen crying on TV about one thing or another that I was supposed to have said or done to her. I think some of the things she said about me were a little unfair because generally I treated her very well, even if she took the odd humorous remark I made the wrong way.

At one point I tried to patch things up by buying her a pair of kissing fish in a bright-pink tank, which I delivered to her doorstep while wearing a dicky bow and very little else. It raised a bit of a laugh and I hoped that it showed that I cared for her. I got the idea from watching Frank Butcher doing a similar scene with Pat on *EastEnders* many years earlier.

In the end our relationship just seemed to run out of steam and I knew from fairly early on that it wasn't going to last. If we weren't arguing about something that I'd said about her weight, it would be a row over my spending time with Mark. We struggled along for a month and a half, during which time I began to hear more rumours that Gemma still had a soft spot for Rami. I had a conversation with Mario, who told me Gemma was still seeing him behind my back, which she denied. I was worried that if I ended things Gemma would say it was because of her weight, but the truth was that I just couldn't see a long-term future for us.

I decided that what I needed was a break to get away from it all. I was chatting with Diags, and I asked him if he'd like to come with me. He suggested we go to Ibiza, and I offered to treat him. I jumped at the chance, because I thought it would give me some space. While I was out there I bumped into some lads from the Essex crowd who told me they'd recently spotted Gemma with a bloke in a pub in Brentwood. I decided to call Gemma for a heart-to-heart.

'I just don't think our relationship's going anywhere,' I told her. 'I keep hearing rumours about you and Rami and now I'm told you've been seen out with a man in Brentwood.'

Gemma denied cheating on me, but we'd reached the end of the line. We decided to part, although we agreed that we would remain good friends. The roller-coaster ride was over.

When all is said and done, I'm pleased to say that we are still great mates today. I still think of Gemma as a very kind and loving person, even though she has another side to her that is fiery and feisty. She showed me a great deal of compassion at a time when I was still very raw over my break-up with Lydia, and for that I will always be grateful to her.

Gemma and I are still great mates today

Gemma is also an incredibly sexy person. We've kept in touch with one another and it is no secret that we've occasionally spent time together since we broke up. In fact, we still enjoy a lot of fun together and I'll always have a soft spot for her. Viewers of *TOWIE* will no doubt have heard about the time we made love in the bushes during a game of tennis. All I will say is that it was very enjoyable. We were playing in a game together while filming when I congratulated her on a fine shot. Gemma responded by giving me a little squeeze in an intimate place. One thing led to another and we went for a walk in some woods next to the tennis court. We found a secluded and private spot and nature took its course. We made love right there and then.

It brought a whole new meaning to the question, 'Anyone for tennis?'

17

HANGING OUT WITH ONE DIRECTION AND A GIG AT THE ROYAL ALBERT HALL

I was snuggled under my duvet with a fuzzy head. It was a peaceful Sunday morning and the sunshine was breaking through the curtains in my bedroom. I'd been out drinking with the boys the night before and we'd sunk plenty of Jägerbombs together at Faces. I yawned and slowly rolled over while I relished the opportunity to enjoy a good rest. What with singing and making so many personal appearances I rarely get a day off, so I was looking forward to a sleepy morning in bed whilst nursing my mild hangover.

A nice little lie-in – just what I need to chill out, I thought.

I was gently dozing off again when the quiet was shattered by the sound of a call coming in on my mobile phone. I considered ignoring it, but I could see from the caller display that it was Mark Wright.

'Hello Arg,' he barked, his voice sounding alert and wide-awake. 'I've just been told you're not doing anything today. I'm down at the ITV studios doing some presenting, why don't you come and support me? I'd love you to be here.'

I groaned. My bed was nice and warm and my head felt like it needed more time to recover before I could even think about getting up, but I felt slightly guilty because I knew that Mark was hosting *Take Me Out: The Gossip*, the sister-show to *Take Me Out* on ITV, and that it was a big deal for him.

'Oh, I dunno, mate,' I replied. 'I'll try and get up there but I will see how it goes. I'll give you a call.'

I hung up, feeling slightly sheepish. The truth was that I was too tired and I had no intention of going, I just didn't want to hurt Mark's feelings. We try to be there to support each other, but my duvet was too comfortable to abandon. I went back into a dreamy sleep, but half an hour later the phone rang again.

It was Neil, my manager.

'You alright, Arg?' he trilled. 'Mark wants to know if you're gonna come down then?'

I was fast running out of excuses, so I decided to tell the truth.

'You know what, mate – I'm a bit too tired, I don't get many days off and I am just going to chill out today.'

'Oh, no worries,' replied Neil. 'It's just that One Direction are filming for *Surprise Surprise* today and they're in the dressing room downstairs.'

One Direction? Neil knew full well that they're one of my favourite bands.

'You're telling me that One Direction are in the ITV building right now?'

'That's right, and they're about to perform.'

'Really?' I asked.

'Yes, really.'

This was too good an opportunity to miss.

'Alright, Neil. I'll call you back!'

With that, I hung up, jumped into the shower and threw on some clothes. I've been a huge fan of One Direction ever since they burst onto the scene on *The X Factor*. Within about half an hour I was in a minicab on the way to the ITV building in Central London. Once we'd pulled up, I paid my driver and went into the foyer.

Suddenly, I saw Zayn Malik and Niall Horan from the band. They caught my eye and I was chuffed because they must have recognised me from being on *TOWIE*.

'Arg, what are you up to? Why don't you come and meet the lads?' said Niall.

I didn't need to be asked twice. I went with them to their dressing room where Liam Payne invited me to take a seat. The band were all munching on chicken from Nando's and they were happy to share their food and drink with me. The boys were really warm and friendly, and I had a little chat with Harry Styles and we posed for some photos together. Later Harry sent me a tweet, saying 'Nice to finally meet you, mate'. It was a reference to the fact we'd previously spoken on the phone, because we'd briefly shared the same tour manager. I had a great time, and in fact spending some quality time with the boys turned out to be great preparation for the next twist in the show, which saw me taking part in a One Direction tribute act!

The producers called me in to explain there was a great new project underway that would hopefully grip the nation and send our ratings soaring through the roof. I learned that some of the cast members were hoping to perform a charity show – and the producers were keen to film it.

'We're going to do a special episode of *The Only Way Is Essex* that'll be broadcast fully live – and it will cover everything that happens,' they explained.

Having done lots of theatre work in the past I was very excited. I imagined a fun-packed variety show that the cast could perform at a theatre. I was to be the compere of the show, which would be like a fun version of *Britain's Got Talent*, with members of the *TOWIE* team performing various acts in front of an audience. The cameras would be there to capture every moment, including all the real-life drama backstage – and it would all be broadcast exactly as it happened. It was an ambitious project and it had the potential to make great television. Not only would the fans be entertained by the stage show, but they'd also get to see everything that happened behind the scenes. The fact that it was live would add an element of danger and excitement: anything could happen on the night.

Part of the reason that *TOWIE* is such a huge success is that the producers try to make it bigger and better with every series, so they are always keen to keep up to speed with anything new that the cast are doing. One minute you can be staying in a boot camp on starvation rations. The next thing you know you could be enjoying a huge banquet in five-star luxury. The producers are always coming up with new ideas and we'd filmed special episodes in Marbella and also for Christmas, which had been huge hits. A live episode would add a whole new dimension. Both *EastEnders* and *Coronation Street* had previously broadcast live specials that had been a big success. At *TOWIE* we are the UK's real-life soap, so why not do a live episode, too?

'You've got lots of experience of being on stage so why don't we turn the evening into Arg's charity night,' one of the boys suggested. 'We could mime a number by One Direction.' I also thought it would be a laugh to do some tap dancing.

I was delighted to have such a big role. As well as being the compere, I would get to join in with plenty of the fun on stage. Lots of other cast members were due to perform: Kirk Norcross was planning to sing a big-band number; Debbie and Carol Wright planned to do a comedy ventriloquist act; Jess Wright was going to sing; and Diags and Chloe Sims were to do a Barbie Girl routine together.

The first thing that I wanted to do was throw myself into learning how to tap-dance, which I found really hard. I wanted to perform the routine for 'Singin' in the Rain' that was made famous by Gene Kelly, so I knew I'd need to be on top form to pull it off. I had five or six private lessons with Lorraine Porter of the Kenneth More Theatre, but I soon discovered that tap-dancing isn't something that you can just learn to do overnight. You have to be able to time every step in perfect arrangement to the beat, and you need to be light-footed and very fit. I didn't really measure up because I'd recently put on weight again and I was back up to around

18 stone. Nor did I look the part, having just had my hair cropped very short. My haircut reminded me of the skinhead I had when I first met Lydia.

One of my main problems was fitness. Despite running the London Marathon earlier in the year I was huffing and puffing and exhausted at the end of every lesson. Trying to sing, dance and tap all at once proved to be quite a feat, but I did my best and I managed to put together the routine even though it was a bit of a nightmare.

'You've taken to it pretty well,' the instructor told me, despite everything.

I also got together to rehearse with the boys from the cast who were joining me to dance and mime to the One Direction number, 'Live While We're Young'. Joey was taking on the role of Harry Styles, Mario was Zayn Malik, Diags was Niall Horan and Tom Pearce was playing Louis Tomlinson. I was taking on the role of Liam Payne. We all met up at a dance studio out in the sticks somewhere and we went through our routine with a professional choreographer. We were joined by a load of female dancers who were all really fit, which gave us a bit of a buzz.

Back on *TOWIE*, we felt confident that our One Direction impersonation would go down well during the charity show, which was to raise funds for Breast Cancer Care. It was a very energetic dance routine that left us quite out of breath at the end of it. Meanwhile, there was a huge amount of hype about the live episode because the press decided to take a large interest in it.

The broadcast began with a comic routine in which I was looking for my trousers before going on stage. Nanny Pat had them and in true *TOWIE* spirit she gave them to me in the nick of time, but from that moment onwards not much went right for us. That's the thing about *TOWIE* – it's reality TV, we're about real life with real people. We're not actors, and the point is to avoid situations that are fake or set-up. But that means that, no matter how hard the cast and the production team work, things go wrong sometimes, and when it's live, there's nothing you can do about it but your best!

We're about real life, with real people – we're not actors

I opened the show on stage with a main speech, after which I was due to perform 'Fly Me to the Moon' by Frank Sinatra. My speech overran, so my performance of the song had to be cut short from the live feed. I then dashed off to join a scene with Joey and Mario during which we were supposed to be shown getting ready for our One Direction performance, but when I turned up the cameras weren't there.

'You've missed it, Arg,' I was told.

My tap-dancing routine had to be cut to a tiny sequence of me walking around a chair, which must have left people wondering what on earth I was doing, and whether I had just lost the plot entirely.

The public soon started to unleash a hail of criticism on Twitter. Looking back, I suppose it was quite funny, but at the time I took all the criticism to heart. People were saying things on Twitter like, 'You are all shit. You can't perform.' I was particularly gutted because I felt I was to blame in some way. I was the main man in the charity show and I felt responsible.

F***ing hell! I thought. We're really in the shit here. Of course, it all turned out to be OK though. People love *TOWIE* and one unlucky night wasn't going to change that. Thankfully, we were able to follow up with a great Christmas Special in which Mark Wright came back to make a one-off guest appearance. It gave me a real boost to be back on screen with him and we filmed loads of scenes together. The viewers loved it too and the show quickly regained its magic.

I'm very proud of *TOWIE* and I think everyone who works on it deserved the BAFTA that we won. We learn new things with each series we film, we give each show our full commitment, and when we are at our finest we are one of the best things on television.

TOWIE has always been a great way of opening doors in my singing career – and opportunities don't come much bigger than a chance to perform at the Royal Albert Hall. One of my proudest moments came in spring 2013, when I was invited to make a solo performance there. It's a wonderful, historic venue that I first fell in love with as a child. I was in the school choir and we used to get invited to the Royal Albert Hall once a year with all the other schools from my area to take part in a big concert. I can remember packing up my recorder and going up to London, where I was one of thousands of children who were all taking part in the event. The atmosphere would always be amazing. It's a truly iconic building that is steeped in grandeur. As well as playing the recorder, I also sang with my schoolmates, but I was really just one voice among many hundreds. There was one child, however, who was selected to sing on stage on his own, and I can remember watching him in awe.

Oh, my God! I thought. How lucky is he to be singing solo at the Royal Albert Hall! I'd love to be able to do that one day.

So you can imagine how excited I was when, years later, I was invited to do the same. I received a phone call from a theatrical production company called Mardi Gras, which is owned by the father of a friend of mine called Jayde Jeffries. They explained that they were hosting an event there for drama schools from all over the country.

'The children have seen you singing on television and we would love you to come and perform for them at the Royal Albert Hall,' they said.

It was like a dream come true. I was over the moon, but I must admit that my nerves soon began to set in. Would I be good enough to do it? I'd obviously had plenty of experience as a singer, but this would be the first time I'd taken centre stage at such a huge venue. Could I pull it off? In my adult life up until now I'd mostly sung big-band songs by the likes of Frank Sinatra and Dean Martin, but this was a chance to get my teeth into a theatrical number. Ever since childhood, I'd cherished a DVD that had been recorded to celebrate the tenth anniversary of *Les Misérables*. One of the people on the DVD was Michael Ball, who I'd met at an ITV summer party. I used to play it all the time, so decided that I'd use this opportunity to perform a song from the show called 'Stars', because I knew it so well. I got hold of a backing track and I spent hours practising it until I felt confident enough to do the song proper justice.

When the big event arrived I was still quite nervous, because it was to be the first time I had performed a musical theatre number since my amateur days. It was a bit of a rush to get to the venue on the day itself, because I was making a personal appearance in Spain the night before. My flight back allowed me just enough time. When I arrived at the Royal Albert Hall, I stood outside and spent a moment looking at the fantastic architecture of the building. I still couldn't quite believe that in a few hours I'd be inside and singing on stage. I went inside and made my way to my dressing room. As I walked through the corridors I noticed that there were framed photographs on the walls of all the great artists who had performed there over the years, such as Frank Sinatra, Elton John and the Rolling Stones.

I felt privileged to be there.

After that I took part in a dress rehearsal, but it felt slightly strange because when I sang there was a bit of an echo around the hall because it's such a huge auditorium, and it was of course empty. It took a bit of getting used to, but the rehearsal went well and I was able to relax and get ready for the show. My mum and dad were coming along to support me, along with Nanny Colette, Nanny Brighton, Uncle Gerry and my two cousins Saffron and Shea. They would be sharing a queen-sized box together and I felt very honoured that they were all able to come along and root for me.

When the show started there were lots of fantastic acts

performed by children from all over Britain. One of them involved a dance routine in which a young girl was projected into the air in order to do a flip before being caught by her fellow performers on the way down. It was a brave move, but, as I watched from the wings, disaster struck.

The little girl took a tumble on the way down and landed on her head!

There were gasps of horror from the audience as she hit the deck with a thud. Luckily, she wasn't injured, but I could see that she was badly shaken up and my heart went out to her. The girl then showed incredible bravery by getting up and carrying on with the act.

When it was my turn to take the stage I couldn't believe the reception that I got. The venue was packed and all the youngsters in the audience were cheering and screaming. As I took the microphone, I was still feeling very touched by the bravery of the little girl who had taken a tumble. I know how hard it is to carry on when you make a mistake, because it can make you very scared to go back on stage again.

'I just want to say congratulations and well done to that girl, who carried on even though she fell. She should be proud of herself,' I told the audience.

The crowd cheered and my big moment to sing had finally arrived. I threw everything into my performance of 'Stars'. Thankfully, all my preshow fears and nerves seemed to fade away and I thoroughly enjoyed it. At the end I was greeted with huge applause. As live performances go, it was definitely one of the highlights of my career, because I'd fulfilled a childhood dream. It made me realise that, if you

If you put your mind to it, you can achieve anything

put your mind to something, you can achieve anything regardless of your background.

Another highlight for me was being asked to support Olly Murs from *The X Factor* at a warm-up show in the West Country. I hadn't been in *TOWIE* for very long at the time and Olly didn't really know me (I was asked to perform by the show's promoter, rather than Olly's management). Nonetheless, it was still a huge honour to meet him. Olly is an Essex boy himself, although at this point he hadn't seen much of *TOWIE* because he'd been touring so heavily. The next time I met him was at a Channel 4 event and he greeted me like an old friend. He's a lovely guy and a very good singer.

I'm also very lucky to have been invited onto several TV shows to sing as a result of people seeing me crooning on *The Only Way Is Essex*. One of my favourite times was when *This Morning* asked me to dress up as Santa and sing lots of Christmas songs during their last show before they broke up for the festive season.

In addition to TV work, I get asked to do my stuff at lots of corporate events, which are generally a pleasure to attend. In addition, I have my own touring show called *A Night with James Argent*, which I performed with a good friend of mine called Tony Roberts. You may have seen Tony previously on *The X Factor* or *Britain's Got Talent* (he's been on both). He's a winner of Heart FM's Next Big Thing competition and he is very accomplished as a singer. Tony does my support act (even though he's technically a better singer than I am, I get to headline the show thanks to being known from *TOWIE*!). We also perform duets.

Of course, not every gig that I've done has gone according to plan. There was one occasion when I had a booking at a holiday resort in Skegness that went horribly wrong. It's funny when I look back on it now, but at the time it made me cringe.

Before attending the booking I'd been partying with Elliott and Diags in Spain, and I'd arranged for my manager Neil to pick me up from the airport and take me straight to the gig. On the day I was due to fly I awoke to discover with horror that I'd lost my voice. I don't know if it was because the air conditioning in my hotel had dried out my throat, but all I could manage to do was croak the odd word. When I called Neil to explain, he could barely hear my voice rasping down the phone.

'That's terrible news, Arg,' he replied. 'It's a great big gig. Two thousand people have paid to hear you sing.'

'What are we going to do?' I whispered.

'Well, we can't cancel it at this short notice. You'll just have to hope that your voice recovers in time.'

I tried sipping lots of water on the plane home but by the time I arrived back in the UK my voice was worse. Flying seemed to have dehydrated me even more. When Neil greeted me at the airport I knew there was only one thing I could do.

'I'll have to mime,' I croaked.

It was a crazy plan because people don't expect you to fake it when they've paid to see a live performance, but I had no choice. I hated the thought, but it was either that or let down two thousand people. I could manage to say the odd sentence on stage but that was about it.

287

I had some backing tracks that I always take to a gig and I knew that among them were some recordings of me singing 'Fly Me to the Moon' and one or two other numbers.

'I'll just have to pretend to sing along to those and hope that nobody notices,' I told Neil.

When I went on stage at first everything went well. Neil oversaw my sound arrangements and he made sure that the recording kicked in at the right moment.

I glided around on stage and did my best to lip-synch to all the words. To my amazement it seemed to work and I got the impression everybody thought that I really was singing. When the song ended I got a great round of applause.

I then tried to manage a few brief words of welcome to the audience before going into the next number.

And then disaster struck.

I'd just started talking to the audience when the recording of 'Fly Me to the Moon' suddenly kicked in again and began to play for the second time. My mouth dropped open in shock as everybody heard my singing repeated through the speakers. It was obvious to the audience that I'd been miming. Backstage, Neil was in a panic as he frantically tried to pull the plug.

There was worse to come.

The track got stuck on my opening few lines of the song, which kept repeating over and over again. I was so embarrassed that I wanted the ground to open and swallow me. I stood there cringing. After a few moments of agony, I did the only thing that I could in the circumstances: I apologised with all my heart.

'I'm so sorry. I don't normally mime, but I've lost my voice.

I didn't want to disappoint everyone by not turning up,' I croaked, after Neil finally managed to kill the recording.

Luckily the audience warmed to me for being honest and I'll be for ever grateful to those people for being so understanding. I made sure that I stayed behind to greet everyone who wanted to meet me in person, so that I could say sorry to their face.

Thankfully, the holiday camp's management were impressed by the way I handled it – and I was very honoured when they later invited me back.

I'd had a lucky escape!

I'm still just an ordinary bloke at heart, despite being frequently on TV, so it's always exciting when I get to meet celebrities through my work. One of the nicest people I've ever had the pleasure to bump into was David Beckham, whom I met at the *Sun*'s Military Awards. I was in the loos when he walked in with two of his sons. David had a big smile on his face and he nodded a greeting to me. I

I'm still just an ordinary bloke at heart

don't mind admitting that I was starstruck, but later on during the night I plucked up the courage to go and properly say hello to him.

'Hello, Arg,' he replied (I was chuffed that he knew my name).

'Have you heard of *The Only Way Is Essex*?' I asked him. 'You were bought up in Essex, weren't you? Aren't you originally from Chingford?'

'Yeah, of course, I've heard about the show, mate. I know what you are all doing,' he replied.

The pair of us then got chatting about a great pie-and-mash shop that I know in Waltham Abbey, where we'd recently done some filming for *TOWIE*. David was living abroad at the time, but he said the same pie-and-mash shop was the first place he always took his kids whenever they got off the plane! He was very down to earth. I was impressed by how he made time to talk everybody, fans included. He was always happy to look them in the eye and pose for photos.

One of my childhood heroes, whom I got to meet through my work, was Will Young. I'd followed Will's progress on *Pop Idol* while I was a teenager and as a special treat my mum took me up to Oxford Street to go to one of his book signings. When we arrived the store was swamped with people and I was so far back in the queue that I never got to meet him. I was really upset at missing him. I finally go to meet Will years later when I appeared in *Daybreak* and Will was next door about to go on *This Morning*. One of the staff at ITV was kind enough to show me to Will's dressing room and I said hello. The funny thing was that I felt like a starstruck teenager all over again and went bright red! I told Will all about the story of when I tried to see him at Oxford Street and we had a good laugh.

I also met Alan Carr when I appeared on *Chatty Man* with some of the other *TOWIE* cast members. The actor Tom Hardy was also on the show, and so was Ellie Goulding, who performed a song.

Another celebrity who was a delight to meet was Kelly Brook, whom I am happy to say I got drunk with. I've always thought that Kelly is gorgeous and I can confirm that she's every bit as nice in the flesh as she is in her photographs. I was introduced to her in a guest box at the 02 Arena when Mark and I were invited to watch a Rihanna concert by a corporate sponsor. Kelly was charming and we chatted together while we tucked into a giant buffet of fabulous food. Kelly said she was a fan of *TOWIE* and she also told us how excited she was to be appearing in a new film with Keith Lemon.

As the drink began to flow I found myself getting slightly tipsy. I was eyeing up a delicious-looking piece of carrot cake on the buffet when Kelly suddenly grabbed a spoon and began to feed it to me! It was a right laugh and I can remember thinking that not many blokes can say they've had Kelly Brook spoon-feed them cake!

By the time Rihanna was in full flow on stage, the booze had well and truly gone to my head. I sidled up behind Kelly and began to do some dirty dancing. When I think about it now it makes me blush, because I was bumping and grinding like there was no tomorrow. I must have made a bit of a spectacle of myself, because Mark had to thump me on the arm a couple of times to remind me to behave myself.

'You can't do that – it's Kelly Brook!' he exclaimed.

Thankfully, Kelly didn't seem to mind. I suppose it just goes to prove the old saying: 'You can take the boy out of Essex, but you can't take Essex out of the boy!'

18

SURPRISE SURPRISE AND WORKING IN A CELEBRITY SPA

One of my fondest memories is from when I was invited to sing on the new version of *Surprise Surprise*, the popular ITV programme that makes people's dreams come true. I'd grown up watching the show when it was presented by Cilla Black, so I was intrigued when I received a phone call about it from ITV.

'It's a bit of a secret, Arg, but *Surprise Surprise* is coming back and it's going to be hosted by Holly Willoughby,' one of the producers told me.

ITV said the new series was launching in the autumn and that they were secretly planning to surprise a woman who was a fan of *The Only Way Is Essex*. The woman's family had a very moving story. It concerned two sisters, one of whom had been planning to get married when their mother had tragically died of cancer. Due to her bereavement, the bride felt too distraught to go ahead with the wedding, but her sister had been a real pillar and helped the family to pull together. Thanks to her support, the wedding eventually went ahead. The *Surprise Surprise* team were planning to make the sister's dreams come true by giving her the full *TOWIE* treatment. They wanted me to perform 'Fly Me to the Moon' before springing the surprise on the bride's sister at the end of the song. The plan was that she would be sitting in the audience unaware that anything was about to happen. I would then walk over and present her with a red rose and invite her up on stage. Sam and Billie Faiers would then join us and the lady would be given a well-deserved Essex makeover at Minnies (the boutique that Sam and Billie run in Brentwood). It sounded like a lovely show to be involved with.

'You can count me in,' I told ITV.

I loved the idea of being able to make a *TOWIE* fan happy and I was also impressed by ITV's grand plans for the show.

'The sister always watches *The Only Way Is Essex* and you're her favourite,' they told me. 'We know that you love singing so we want to give you the opportunity to give the best performance of your life.'

ITV said I would be supported on stage by an eleven-piece band, which would include a brass section, drums and keys. Normally when I perform it's to a backing track, so this would be the first time I'd sung alongside a proper big band. There seemed to be no expense spared and the producers arranged for a top musical

It would be the first time I'd sung alongside a proper big band

director called Mike Dixon to oversee everything. I was very honoured because Mike is a huge name in the West End, having been musical supervisor for *We Will Rock You* alongside Brian May. Mike is also musical supervisor on the West End show *The Bodyguard*. Not only was I going to have my own band, but I was going to be working with one of the best directors in the country – so the show was a bit of a dream come true for me as well as for the lady we were surprising.

I got on really well with Mike during rehearsals and he gave me some great help and advice. I told him that I'd love to sing on a West End stage one day and he was kind enough to introduce me to some of his contacts.

The episode of *Surprise Surprise* was great fun. I've met Holly Willoughby many times on *This Morning* and it was good to be working with her again. We share a connection, because her husband Dan Baldwin is an Essex boy who went to the same secondary school as I did, although we were a few years apart and didn't know each other. Dan is an executive on Keith Lemon's *Celebrity Juice*, which I've also appeared on. Keith Lemon always makes me laugh and he's just as funny in real life as he is when you seen him on the telly.

The band *Surprise Surprise* laid on were amazing and with Mike's help I managed to pull off a performance that I was very happy with. More importantly, the woman we surprised had a fantastic time. When I ducked into the audience as my song came to end she had no idea we were about to single her out. I moved from person to person with the rose that I was holding before finally pausing to stop alongside her.

'I luuurve . . . *you*!' I crooned, as I handed the rose to her.

I then led her on stage to meet Holly along with Sam and Billie. It was a very emotional show and I felt privileged to be able to play a part in making someone feel so happy. I know it also made my mum feel very proud to see me involved in something so nice. As for my singing, it must have gone well, because Holly Willoughby gave me a little smile afterwards and said, 'Well done!'

One fun show that I have appeared on a couple of times is *Family Fortunes* with Vernon Kay. The first occasion was when *TOWIE* took on the cast of *Benidorm* in a celebrity episode. Later, I got invited back with my own family. I was joined by my dad, my sister, Nanny Brighton and my cousin, Aaron. We did well, because we ended up winning a family cruise! Vernon Kay is a real joker and he's always one for springing things on you. Midway through the show it was mentioned that I'm a bit of a singer, so he put me on the spot and we ended up singing a little duet of 'That's Life' together.

Vernon also gave me a shock when I went on his Saturday show on Radio 1. I'd been doing a bit of hospital radio on *TOWIE* at the time, so he invited me up to the BBC studios in London to join in with the big boys. I enjoy doing radio because it gives you a chance to have a bit of banter on air, which is something I feel natural doing. When I arrived at Radio 1, Vernon greeted me with a smile and when the show began we had a quick chat about *TOWIE* and played a few songs together. I was in the studio live on air and surrounded by hundreds of switches and buttons, when Vernon suddenly decided to get up and leave me on my own.

'Right, this is your big chance to prove yourself on the radio. I'm just popping out,' he said.

I was terrified!

I think it was Vernon's way of playing a little joke on me. All I had to do was play a number by Lady Gaga, but there were millions of buttons and I felt like I didn't have a clue.

'Erm ... this is "Bad Romance" by Lady Gaga,' I stuttered on air.

I pressed the button to bring up the music but to my horror nothing happened.

Oh hell! I thought. The whole nation's listening and I've messed it up.

Luckily, the next button I hit was the right one and there was only a brief pause before the music kicked in, but it gave Vernon a good laugh!

They have a funny nickname for me at Lime Pictures and ITV. They call me the Ian Beale of *TOWIE* because I've been there since the beginning, just as the character Ian Beale has in *EastEnders*. I've always made it clear that I don't want to go anywhere else and I've pretty much been in every episode (in fact, at the time of writing there is only one show that I've missed, which, in case you are wondering, was Episode 3 of Series 1). People joke that if *TOWIE* lasts twenty years I'll probably still be there sweeping up at Sugar Hut.

I've obviously made lots of one-off appearances on other TV shows, but, because of my commitment to *TOWIE*, up until quite recently I'd never been a regular on any other reality show. All that changed when I was approached in the summer of 2013 and invited to take part in a new telly programme called *Celebrity Super Spa*. In case you didn't catch it on air, it was a nutty show that involved me and several other TV personalities in running our own beauty spa in Liverpool. I didn't know the first thing about the beauty industry, but the idea of having to wax people's bodies and give them massages sounded like a right laugh. I'm always up for a new challenge, so I decided to give it a go.

The idea of having to wax people's bodies sounded like a right laugh

The show was due to be broadcast on Channel 5, but was made by ITV Studios (ITV's production company, whom I've obviously worked with in the past). The series was due to be filmed while *TOWIE* was off air, so it was a rare occasion when I could join another reality show without coming into conflict with my commitments in Essex. It meant going to live in Liverpool for six weeks, which appealed to me because I thought it would be nice to enjoy a change of scene for a while.

Former *Coronation Street* star Helen Flanagan was among the other personalities who were confirmed to take part in *Celebrity Super Spa*. I'd enjoyed watching Helen in the jungle on *I'm a Celebrity ... Get Me Out of Here!* and I imagined that she'd be a lot of fun to work with. The other personalities on the show were Jody Latham from *Shameless*, Yvette Fielding from *Most Haunted* and celebrity chefs Rustie Lee and John Burton-Race (who'd also previously starred on *I'm a Celebrity ...*). It sounded like a good mix of people and I was looking forward to meeting everyone.

My hunch that Helen would turn out to be a riot of fun proved to be correct and we hit it off straightaway. She seemed to me to be like a northern version of an Essex girl, which I meant as a compliment. She has a big bubbly personality and can be very mouthy at times, because she puts her emotions out there, but she is also very homely and down to earth. She's got a ditzy-blonde side to her, although she is actually very clever and did well in her A-levels. I think because we were both a bit younger than the other people on the show we clicked immediately. Within a few days of meeting Helen I felt as if I'd known her for years and we became best mates on the show. I quickly realised that she can be a bit of a diva.

Helen wound up all the other personalities by keeping us waiting for two hours when she arrived late for filming during the first episode. They were furious but I secretly found it quite funny. I've got a lot of patience and I don't take myself too seriously, so I tend not to get wound up by diva behaviour! When the other personalities rounded on Helen for being late she got quite tearful and I became her shoulder to cry on. I told her not to worry too much and to just get on and enjoy the show.

'I'm going to nickname you Diva Tits!' I joked.

Helen thought it was hilarious and we became good friends. We became like two naughty kids and we probably pissed off a few of the people on the set by larking around together. I was staying in Liverpool on my own, so most nights Helen would join me after filming and we'd go out drinking. The press started to hint that there was a bit of a romance between us, but it was really just a case of enjoying each other's company. Helen had just split up with her boyfriend, the footballer Scott Sinclair, but their relationship was still very off and on and there seemed to be a chance that they might get back together. I didn't want to get caught up in any of that, but we were both happy to spend a bit of time together. We weren't dating – we were just workmates having fun.

Helen loved to take the piss out of me for my weight, which I didn't mind in the least because she always did it with good humour.

'You never stop eating! You eat far too much food,' she'd say, laughing.

On one occasion when I arrived at the set in the morning I was still eating my breakfast, which amused Helen no end. She took a photo of herself holding up three bags of food that I'd bought from Greggs. She posted the snap on Instagram later for a laugh, with a note teasing me. I got my own back later in the series when I sent a saucy tweet about her boobs. I spotted the shape of her nipples showing through beneath her top and I took a quick photo on my phone.

'Somebody's got a NIPPLE ERECTION!!! Haha @helen-flanagan1 #Payback,' I tweeted.

I suppose it all sounds quite flirty but it was just a bit of harmless banter and, despite the speculation, we didn't become an item. However, we did spend a lot of time together during the evenings and, if the circumstances had been different, who knows what might have developed between us?

The weather was mainly nice and sunny while we were filming, and during the warm evenings Helen and I would stay outside for hours together in a little nook outside my hotel. We'd sit there with a bottle of wine and two glasses, getting tipsy while we shared anecdotes about our lives. Helen would chain-smoke while she told me about her relationship with Scott and also what it was like going into the jungle. We had a lot of deep conversations and I told her all about my past experiences of breaking up with Lydia. While we were talking, we'd play YouTube music videos by the likes of David Gray and Passenger on our mobile phones. At one point I felt as if we were starting to like each other more than as just good friends, but nothing happened between us, which was probably out of respect for Scott.

Being in Liverpool was like a breath of fresh air, because it was nice to meet different people in new surroundings. The city reminded me of Essex in a lot of respects because all the girls were glammed up and the people there love a party. Liverpool has some fantastic Georgian buildings and the locals were always very warm and friendly towards me whenever I complimented them on their architecture. I visited the Cavern, where the Beatles started out, which was fascinating. When it was time to return to Essex, I bade Helen farewell but we swapped phone numbers and we've stayed in touch. We'd had a fun time of *Celebrity Super*

Being in Liverpool was like a breath of fresh air

Spa and the show itself was a success. It had been a summer to remember.

I was very honoured when *TOWIE* asked me to fly down to Cannes to represent the show at a TV festival. While I was there, I bumped into Matt Lucas from *Little Britain*, and we had a good chat. I loved Cannes, and I later went back there to do some boxing training with British hopeful Tyson Fury and my pal Pat Waites.

It was around this time that the producers of *TOWIE* had a surprise in store. We were being sent to Las Vegas to film a double episode that would launch the new series. I'd put on a few pounds over the summer, so I went back onto my healthy-eating regime. I wanted to look my best in Vegas, where Joey, Tom and I were all determined to have a great time. The three of us tend to stick together on *TOWIE* and we love doing things as a group. We got up to some crazy stuff in Vegas, such as the time Joey and I went to an outdoor centre where you can play basketball in JCB diggers. The idea was to use the giant arm to move a 'ball' around and plunk it into a 'net' made out of a giant tyre. It was hilarious fun.

I was staying at the Palms Casino and on the first night I had an unexpected encounter with Gemma. It began when I was in my room and I received a weird phone call.

'Hello, Mr Argent. It's the front desk here. The escort girls that you booked are down in reception,' cooed a strange voice in an American drawl, while somebody else giggled in the background.

It didn't take me long to realise that the phone call was

actually from Gemma and Bobby Norris, who were trying to wind me up.

'Yeah, very funny,' I said. 'Where are you?'

They were downstairs, and I invited them up to my room. When they arrived I was struck by how nice Gemma looked. I'd had a few drinks and I was in the mood for love – and I could see a twinkle in Gemma's eye. It had been a long time since we'd been an item, but I was still very fond of her.

Would we get it together tonight? I wondered. I asked Bobby if he'd mind leaving us. 'I need to talk to Gemma in private.'

Unfortunately, Bobby got quite offended and he went off in a huff back to the room that he was sharing with Gemma.

'That was rude. You can't talk to him like that,' said Gemma, who promptly went off to console Bobby, leaving me on my own.

I felt a bit bad about being abrupt to Bobby, so I called reception and I asked to be put through to their room.

'I'm coming down to see you,' I said.

I went and apologised to Bobby and the three of us had a drink. That night one thing led to another and Gemma ended up coming back to my room. We made love, although afterwards Gemma swore me to secrecy. I guess she had her own reasons for wanting to keep it private, but, as I have said before, nothing remains a secret on *TOWIE* for very long. When the new series started I let slip to the boys about what had happened between Gemma and me. She was furious and vigorously denied on air that anything had happened between us in Vegas. I didn't think it was a big deal and I couldn't see what all the fuss was about. After all, we'd slept together plenty of times before. I was a bit upset, however, that Gemma had made me out to be a liar. Having said that, I realise I was in the wrong to betray a confidence.

One of the highlights of the Vegas trip was that I got to train at Floyd Mayweather's famous boxing gym. It was an awesome place and was kitted out with every piece of equipment that you could possibly imagine. I was lucky enough to go back there in January 2014, when I trained with Floyd Mayweather Senior, Roger Mayweather and future world champ J'Leon Love. Joey Essex and I were also lucky enough to meet Mike Tyson when he called into the Palms Casino. I was in my room at the Palms when one of the producers, Jenna, called me to explain that Mike was in the house. I rang Joey and the pair of us went downstairs, but by the time we got there Mike was surrounded by a huge crowd and his security team were preventing people from meeting him.

'No, guys, no pictures! No pictures!' repeated the security men as we approached.

'Don't worry, I'm an expert at blagging my way into things like this,' I explained to Joey. Tyson is one of my all-time favourite boxers and I wasn't going to miss a chance like this.

'Mike, listen, we're big fans of yours and we're from Essex,' I called out.

Amazingly, I'd managed to get his attention.

'Essex? Essex? Is that where the gangsters come from?' replied Mike.

I realised that he was referring to the film *Essex Boys*, which is all about drugs wars. The movie had been a hit in the States and Mike had obviously seen it.

'I know Essex. I once did a show in Loughton,' continued Mike.

We soon got chatting about life in the UK and Mike agreed to pose for a photo with Joey and me. We were chuffed to bits.

Later that night Joey and I shared a beer and agreed that being in Vegas was like a dream come true. I couldn't believe how far I'd come in the space of three years. We were in one of the most glamorous cities in the world and we were living it large, or should that be living it Arg . . .

EPILOGUE

AND FINALLY ...

So that's the story of my life so far. Thanks for sticking with me. It's been a journey that has taken me from being an ordinary boy in Essex to rubbing shoulders with the stars. I've been lucky enough to travel around the world and I have met many wonderful people. I like to think that, despite everything, I am still the same old Arg underneath it all. I still enjoy a good drink with my mates and I love slobbing out in front of the telly. I've learned that the really important things in life are your friends and family, so you should always treasure them the most.

As for the future, I'd like to have a big family of my own one day. Ever since I was a child I've always been surrounded by kids. I enjoy being around children and I love taking them out, so I'd definitely like to have kids of my own. Ideally, I'd want to have at least a girl and a boy, but the bigger the family the better. I hope that one day I'll meet a nice woman who will agree to be my wife. Who knows who that will be?

But I'd like it to be somebody who will be a soulmate whom I can share my hopes and fears with. I've made a few mistakes along the way when it comes to relationships, but I hope that I am now a better person for it.

I'm a true Essex boy at heart, so I think I'll stay here for all of my life. I just can't see myself ever leaving this part of the world. I'm pleased to say that I've just bought myself my first flat in the heart of Chigwell. It's a comfy bachelor pad and I'm very proud of it. I'd like a big house of my own here one day with a nice garden for the children to play in. It would also be great to have a place on the Costa del Sol to spend some time in over the summer. I would love to have a place abroad as a home from home. I'm lucky enough to work in an industry where it's possible to afford things like that, but, if I can do it, anybody can.

I think that singing will always be a big part of my life and my dream is that I'll one day be able to perform in the West End. But who knows what doors might open in the future? There's no rush. I'm happy to stick with *TOWIE* and see how things go. In many ways I feel as if my life is just beginning.

If you're reading this and you've got dreams of your own, my advice is to stick with it. If you think positive then positive things will happen.

ACKNOWLEDGEMENTS

I'd like to thank my family and friends for all their support – my mum, my dad, my sister and my two nans; the Wrights, the Kanes, the Brights and the Brooks; The Famous Eleven; my Faces family – Tony H, Tony B and John Clark; my Marbella family – Peter and Melissa Black; Neil at Sisu; my Manchester family – the Kumanis (boohoo.com); Jim's Kitchen; my friends at Chicken Cottage and Wood Oven, South Woodford. I've also got to thank Jim McDonald, my boxing tainer, and No1 Boot Camp.

At Lime and ITV, I'd like to thank: Tony Wood; Ruth Wrigley; Sarah Dillistone; Claire Farragher; Nicky Hegarty; Shirley Jones; Phil Harris; Sean Murphy; Suzanne Readwin; Tamsin Dodgson; Daniella Berendsen; Derek McLean; Kate Maddigan; Claire Zolkwar; Angela Jaine; Genna Gibson; Federico Ruiz; Mike Spencer; Laura Woolfe; Tayo Yusuff; Danny Ellis; Peter Fincham. Special thanks to Gyles Neville for pushing me, helping me progress and getting me through the tough times; and most importantly Rachel Hardy PR!!!

Thanks to Lewis Simmons, for my singing opportunities; my family at the Kenneth More Theatre; and, of course, to all my *TOWIE* cast mates past and present.

And finally a massive thank you to Gary Thompson and my manager, Neil Dobias.